Errol Flynn

GENTLEMAN HELLRAISER

Errol Flynn

GENTLEMAN HELLRAISER

DAVID BRET

JR
BOOKS

First published in Great Britain in 2004. This edition published in 2009 by JR Books, 10 Greenland Street, London NW1 0ND
www.jrbooks.com

A catalogue record for this book is available from the British Library.

ISBN 978-1-906779-53-5

1 3 5 7 9 10 8 6 4 2

Printed by CPI Bookmarque, Croydon CR0 4TD

This book is dedicated to
Eden (1985–99)
Amália Rodrigues (1920–99)
and Les Enfants de Novembre

N'oublie pas...
La vie sans amis c'est comme
un jardin sans fleurs

Contents

Acknowledgements

Writing this book would not have been possible had it not been for the inspiration, criticisms and love of that select group of individuals whom I still regard as my true family and *autre coeur*: Barbara, Irene Bevan, Marlene Dietrich, Dorothy Squires *que vous dormez en paix*; Montserrat Caballé, René and Lucette Chevalier, Jacqueline Danno, Hélène Delavault, Tony Griffin, Roger Normand, Betty Paillard, Annick Roux, Monica Solash, Terry Sanderson, John and Anne Taylor, Francois and Madeleine Vals, Caroline Clerc and Charley Marouani.

Very special thanks to Eric Lilley and Ken MacDonald, all at Robson Books, and the British Film Institute.

Especial thanks to my agent, David Bolt...and to my wife, Jeanne, still the keeper of my soul!

Introduction

In *The Intimate Sex Lives of Famous People*, perhaps the definitive study of the topic, Errol Flynn is listed in no fewer than *thirteen* categories:

Men Who Enjoyed Girls 16 Years or Younger; Polygamists; Open Marriages; Sex Trials; Great Lovers & Satyrs; Caught In The Act; Busy Entertainers; Macho Chauvinists; They Paid For What They Got: Clients; Endurance & Staying Power; Voyeurs; Peeping Toms; Practitioners Of Oriental Techniques; Aphrodisiac Users.

To this may be added Brawler, Narcotics Expert, Mother Hater, War Correspondent, Yachtsman, Raconteur, Drunkard...but above all, Star. For who could possibly forget those Saturday morning matinees when we all flocked to see *The Adventures of Robin Hood, Captain Blood, The Charge Of The Light Brigade, Don Juan*...epics which have never been surpassed?

Errol, quite frankly, did not *care* what the world thought of his carousing, long before dictating his tell-all autobiography, *My Wicked, Wicked Ways*. Yet there was considerably more to this complex man than even he let on. Errol packed more into his 50 years than most of his hard-living contemporaries could have fitted into a dozen lifetimes, yet confessed to having just the one regret – an inability to play the piano!

The quintessential hedonist, Errol nurtured a quite staggering appetite for young men and under-aged girls, the latter referred to by him as 'San Quentin Quail'. To help him in his quest for these he gathered about him a group of loyal 'fuck-buddies' – David Niven, Bruce Cabot, William Lundigan and others – who, when they were not sharing the easy pickings, were partaking of the star himself or watching the sex-shows at his Hollywood mansion through the two-way mirror which he had incorporated into the floor of his 'jerk-off' room.

Errol loved to brawl, a taste he acquired as a young man working as a gold prospector and slave-trader in the uncharted regions of New Guinea – a country he was forced to flee from when accused of murdering one of the natives. He would always go out of his way to start a fight – initially because he enjoyed the experience of winning, and latterly because his box-office power was on the wane and money was in short supply, and he saw fighting as a way to sue people. He never drank and experimented with drugs because he was trying to blot out his problems – but for the sheer hell of it – and he was convinced that as such he would never become addicted to either, which he of course did, managing to survive their ravages long after doctors had given him up for dead...transforming his once beautiful face and body into that of a washed-out wreck, though still possessed of that innate charisma which had made him the idol of millions.

Errol loathed his mother because this domineering, high-principled woman had drilled into him whilst a child that sex and genitalia were dirty...As a result of which he often went out of his way to publicly humiliate her, almost always referring to her and introducing her as 'The Cunt'. And above all, he hated his particular brand of stardom – the fact that he was regarded the world over as a swashbuckler, a type-casting which he claimed had prevented him from exhibiting his true colours as a dramatic actor, something he was only allowed to do in his latter films.

Marlene Dietrich called him 'Satan's Angel'. Rebel, pervert, lecher and charmer, Errol Flynn was, contrary to his own biased opinion, a star without equal and one of the genuinely great icons of the twentieth century.

This is his story.

1

In The Wake of the Human Tornado

'The Good Lord gave you a fist so that you could keep it clenched.'

Errol Flynn's father, Theodore, was an eminent marine biologist, the son of Irish emigrants who had settled in Australia in 1883, the year before his birth. His mother was Lily Marelle Young, a 21-year-old descendant of Midshipman Richmond Young, one of the mutineers on the *Bounty*, and for many years she kept a sword in her home said to have belonged to Captain Bligh himself, which Young had brought back from that fateful voyage.

For several months after their marriage, the Flynns lived in Sydney, until Theodore was invited to join a scientific expedition to the South Pole. His wife sailed with him on the *Aurora*, a cramped, uncomfortable steam-powered boat, and it was as the vessel reached the Tasmanian coast that Lily Marelle discovered she was pregnant. A few days later, while Theodore continued his journey, she was put ashore at Hobart, and it was here on 20 June 1909 that she gave birth to a son.

Upon his return to Tasmania, several months later, Theodore decided to settle there, and accepted a position of some importance at Hobart University. By this time his wife had dropped the name Lily, declaring it to be common: henceforth she would only ever answer to Marelle, the French word for 'hopscotch'. However, the son whom Marelle so despised, on account of the fact that his conception had shattered her dream of seeing the Antarctic, had not even been given a name. Theodore saw to this at once: the child was baptised Errol Leslie Thomson Flynn.

As a youngster, Errol was ever the fearless rebel, one aspect of his character which would never change. Because he essentially was a father's boy, he would go out of his way to displease Marelle, and take frequent but deserved thrashings which she doled out with almost sardonic relish. And if a beating came from Theodore – more often than not with his big black umbrella – then so much the better. At three, already a strong swimmer, he was punished for venturing too far from the shore; at five, for playing 'doctors and nurses' with a local girl at a church tea party. At six, he stole a rowing boat and ran away from home to become a pirate. Most of the time, Theodore – perhaps regarding the boy as no more than a chip off the old block – saw the funny side of Errol's adventures. Marelle, on the other hand, screamed at and insulted him as if he were some degenerate with psychopathic leanings, and very soon she began telling him how she wished he had never been born at all.

The first time Marelle expressed such feelings, Errol left home for three days and Marelle, truly believing that this time she had gone *too* far, took to her bed with what appears to have been a nervous breakdown. This didn't prevent her from thrashing him even harder, however, once she had recovered and Errol erred again, this time with a neighbour's ducks. While watching half a dozen or so of the birds being fed scraps, he observed how one would swallow a piece of fatty belly-pork then, two minutes later, expel it – undigested – from its rectum. This gave him a brainwave: tying a piece of the meat to a length of string, he fed it to one duck, waited for it to come out of the other end, then fed it to another, and so on, until all the ducks were joined by the string. 'I was the inventor of the world's first living bracelet,' he later recalled. 'At once I commercialised. I sold tickets to my friends. The ducks dragged themselves around in all directions.'

To a certain extent, Errol's waywardness was tempered by his being allowed to accompany his father on his expeditions. Now Professor of Biology and Zoology at Hobart, Theodore was widely acknowledged as Australia's leading authority on marsupials and sealife: he spent several years tracking down the

Tasmanian devil or 'tiger', a nocturnal, badger-sized marsupial then thought to have been extinct. Theodore caught several of these ferocious creatures, and even kept one in a cage at home.

This 'bonding' with his father ended abruptly, however, when Errol was around ten, and his 'wanted' sister, Rosemary, arrived on the scene. For two years, he was virtually ignored by both his parents. Then came puberty. According to Errol, he lost his virginity at the age of twelve by means of collecting an outstanding debt from the Flynns' maid, a plump woman named Carrie. 'Not handsome, but available,' was how he later described her. Apparently, over a period of time Errol had been dipping into his piggy-bank to help Carrie out, and one evening when his parents were out and she was babysitting, his curiosity got the better of him and he began exploring under Carrie's dress. Beginning at her calf and moving tremulously upward, she then suggested a pleasurable way of settling her one shilling and ninepence debt. However the fumbled sex with Carrie was strictly a one-off deal: when Marelle found out what had happened, Errol was given the hiding of his life, and the maid was dismissed.

Soon after this incident, Theodore Flynn was invited to supply London Zoo with what would be Great Britain's first consignment of duck-billed platypuses, and as he was to deliver these personally, he decided that Errol should accompany him. Errol's schoolteachers were constantly complaining about his behaviour, and in any case the boy was easier to control when his mother was not around. This trip proved to be an exception. Errol was left in charge of the six animals, which had to be fed exclusively on a special kind of water-worm. In his wisdom, however, he decided to spice up their diet. During a brief stopover in Durban, he collected a bucket of tadpoles, to which they were allergic, and when two of them died, he found himself confined to his cabin until the ship reached Southampton.

A few weeks later, Marelle arrived in London, and because it now looked as though the Flynns would be staying in the city for some time, Theodore enrolled him at the South London College, in Barnes. This was not a wise move: Errol later dismissed the two years he spent there as the most dismal of his life.

The principal problem, of course, was discipline. Errol loathed being told what to do and especially hated having to sleep with a dozen other boys in a crowded dormitory, while one of the junior masters, a lame man named Coombs, prowled the building in search of willing young bodies to satisfy his lust. 'My dreams at night and my waking thoughts were terrorised by the man's presence,' Errol remembered, adding how Coombs would place his hand on his knee in the hope of seducing him – a practice which continued for several months, until the teacher was caught sodomising the twelve-year-old wicket keeper from the school's cricket team and dismissed.

Neither did Errol see much of his parents, even during the school holidays. The Flynns were experiencing a matrimonial crisis, albeit a temporary one. Marelle had stormed off to Paris, and as Theodore was too busy to bother with his son, Errol found himself almost totally alone while the other boys went off to join their parents. Sometimes, he would take the bus into London, though more often than not he would walk to save on the fare. But as his allowance was low, even such local excursions were rare, so he spent much of his time reading in his dormitory.

Shortly before his fifteenth birthday, Errol was expelled from the South London College for truancy and fighting: since arriving at the establishment he had been the butt of the other boys' jokes on account of his broad Australian accent, and he had very quickly learnt how to stick up for himself. He was strong, and tall for his age, and he would often scrap with the older boys just for the sheer hell of it. From Barnes, he moved to Colet Court, a smaller school which kicked him out after just one month, this time for shouldering up to one of his teachers. 'I had an insatiable desire to run through the world and not be hemmed in by anybody,' he said later. 'I hated institutions like schools, with walls and fences.'

Errol's expulsion coincided with the recently reunited Flynns' decision to return to Australia, where he was enrolled at Sydney's Northshore Grammar. Here, on 'home' territory, he became even more of a problem. In England, he had been mocked because of his accent Here, for some bizarre reason, it was because he was a professor's son who had seen more of the world than they had – and because some of them had heard 'rumours' of what transpired within British public schools. These taunts about his masculinity were of course soon put to rights by a few well-aimed punches, and this time there was no outside interference: teachers at the Northshore, in those days, were notorious for allowing rebellious pupils to fight the aggression out of their system. 'I fought dirty,' he remembered. 'I was out to win, not negotiate.' His tactics won him respect and popularity, though this did not make school any more bearable.

With the exception of literature, Errol abhorred every subject on the school curriculum, and devoted himself to sport: he won innumerable trophies for swimming, diving, boxing and athletics, but the activity at which he *truly* excelled was tennis. Within weeks of moving to Sydney he had beaten everyone in the school's tennis team. His teachers and coaches were no match for him, and he began competing nationally. Northshore entered him for the Davis Cup, and at sixteen he was Australian Junior Champion and well on his way towards competing at Wimbledon.

Errol's love life was equally competitive. He had become involved with two females: the school's thirty-something, rough-edged maid, Elsie, and a young debutante named Naomi Dibbs, the daughter of a Sydney businessman to whom he actually became engaged. To Errol's below-the-belt way of thinking, it was the perfect arrangement: Elsie would provide him with the sexual favours which would come from Naomi *only* after they were married. Their trysts, too, he found more exciting because they took place after lights out and away from the school. Once the masters had retired to their quarters, Errol would sneak out of the dormitory window and drop the fifteen feet to the soft earth below. Unfortunately, he learnt to his chagrin that Elsie was not interested in having sex with him when she already had an older, experienced lover from the same school. This other young man did not know this, though, for he decided to teach this 'brash little upstart' a lesson by strategically placing a corrugated iron sheet under the window, which of course awakened half the neighbourhood when Errol landed on it. Not only did he lose Elsie, after fighting with and very nearly drowning his rival, but he was also expelled from the school. And the next day, blaming Naomi for his dilemma – on the pretext that, had she let him have his way with her, he would not have gone looking for it elsewhere, he broke off their engagement and demanded his ring back!

For the first time in his life, Errol did not have his father to support him financially: Theodore had recently discovered the fossilised remains of a prehistoric whale in a remote Tasmanian cliff, an important find that he had personally accompanied on its journey to London, where it had been put on display in the British Museum. Errol therefore decided to get a regular job as a clerk at a wool-dealing company run by Sir Edward Gibbon, a friend of his father's. Here he became pally with a man called Thomson, a member of the infamous Razor Gang – so named because of the trademark slashes which they left across the faces of their victims – then the scourge of Sydney's run-down Dirty Half-Mile district. Both Errol and Thomson were fired from Gibbon's for riffling the petty-cash box, and though it is not known if Errol actually joined the Razor Gang, his association with Thomson ended in July 1926 when the young man was found in a gutter with his throat cut.

For several weeks, sought by the police, Errol roughed it in a cave which was home to a group of tramps, and it was while there – in a newspaper which he was about to wrap himself in to keep warm – that he read of the gold strike taking place in New Guinea. He at once got in touch with the authorities, and was told that the fare to this land of opportunity – and untold danger – was £18. Errol came up with half of this amount by selling Naomi Dibbs' engagement ring, and he borrowed the rest, plus enough to tide him over until he had found his feet, from an uncle who, he claimed, was only too happy to help him out so that the family might see the back of him.

'From then on I began the wanderings that have never ceased,' Errol wrote in his memoirs over 30 years later, though much of what happened in New Guinea is enshrouded in mystery, and the truth may now never be known. All we have to rely on is Errol's account of his adventures, and the somewhat dubious reminiscences of several American and Australian soldiers who served on the island during World War II, a decade after he had left (by this time, of course, his actor's status added considerably more interest to the subject). It would therefore appear more sensible to dismiss most of these handed down 'tales' and rely upon Flynn himself, whose honesty throughout his autobiography – written towards the end of his life when he no longer cared what others might have thought about him – has never been doubted by his critics, friends and colleagues.

Errol landed at Rabaul, the capital of New Britain, some 400 miles off the New Guinea mainland, and immediately found himself a room – and a bedmate – in a tawdry bordello. One of his fellow passengers on the ship had also supplied him with a letter of introduction for the District Commissioner – it was essential that he get a job so as to raise the collateral for his stake in the goldfield. This meeting took place the next morning, and when the older man told him that he was looking for a sanitation officer, Errol replied that he was an expert in such matters: not specifically a lie, for he had picked up the basics of sanitation while assisting his father. He was given the job, at £4 a week, and a room in a tiny bungalow shared by other government cadets.

To 'colonialise' himself, and no doubt to impress the natives, Errol lost no time in purchasing a commissioner's white uniform, complete with pith helmet and walking cane, in which he cut a very imposing figure as he toured the island in a government car, accompanied by two native policemen, teaching the local populace how to keep themselves and their properties clean and reduce the spread of the innumerable diseases which were then rife.

Neither did Errol waste much time getting to know the island's females. 'Whilst I was in New Guinea, I allowed my cock to rule my head,' he told one reporter during the fifties. 'And, just as you sometimes end up with a sore head through thinking too much, so I ended up with a sore dick on account of my other pursuits.' One day, during his travels, he came across a tiny pool favoured by natives, where he decided to take a dip – with the wife of a senior government official, a beautiful young Polynesian woman named Maura. One thing led to another, and the two had a brief but turbulent affair which ended when Maura's husband found them in bed together. A violent fight erupted during which both men were badly hurt, and Maura accidentally caught a punch in the face which resulted in her spending several days in hospital. Errol did not, however, lose his job. Maura's husband was by all accounts an unpopular man, and because he had put *him* in hospital, Errol was promoted...and assigned to a team of officials which was sent to Mandang to investigate the murders of four gold prospectors. Of this mission, nothing is known save that it lasted two months, and that during it Errol was informed of Maura's death: she had been among the passengers on a pleasure flight on a German Junker aircraft, the first the New Guineans had ever seen, which had crashed into a cliff shortly after take-off.

Upon his return to Rabaul, Errol decided that he had had enough of working for the government, or anyone else for that matter. He had sailed to New Guinea to dig for gold, and so far he had raised nothing towards the price of his stake. He came a little closer towards achieving his goal, however, when during a 'fucking and whisky' session in one of the port's sleaziest saloons, he met a man named Al Tavisher, a disreputable copra tycoon who offered him £40 a month to run one of his plantations at Kavieng, in New Ireland on the Bismark Archipelago. Errol accepted the position, despite not knowing what copra was – and he only discovered, once he had committed himself by gentleman's agreement and there was no turning back, that the hundred-strong workforce under his control comprised two rival tribes of mostly 'reformed' cannibals!

It was an inordinately tough job for a lad of barely eighteen, though Errol was able to delegate most of his instructions through a native-speaking 'boss boy', who flogged shirkers and on the odd occasion had the worst troublemakers jailed or even shot. Soon after his arrival, too, Errol had to cope with a full-scale tribal war; and survey the subsequent damage: pregnant women had been impaled on stakes, and children decapitated and their brains – a local delicacy – ceremoniously removed. Errol and his boss-boy had no option but to bring the perpetrators of these atrocities to heel, and after a perfunctory trial twelve natives were publicly hanged.

This harrowing incident inadvertently supplied Errol with a new love interest – a pretty young Melanesian girl named Maihiati, whom he found shivering from fear in the jungle, having fled the carnage which had wiped out most of her family. Typically, the first feature Errol observed were the girl's breasts – 'The classic ski-jump type, a lovely little hollow, and then the line goes way up into the air and doesn't dip,' he remembered, explaining how, if anything, *he* had been initially frightened of *her*.

According to Errol, once the two had convinced each other that there was nothing to be afraid of – and made love, there and then – he took Maihiati back to his little plantation bungalow, where she was given a job helping the cook. 'There was no love in this relationship,' he said afterwards. 'It was strictly biophysical. But the little girl helped much to make a man of me.' He refers too in his memoirs to his father's dictum: 'Any man who has anything to do with a native woman stinks in the nostrils of a decent white man.' To which he had replied, 'Dad, I stink!'

There was also an incident when Errol was arrested for hitting one of his Chinese servants who had 'insulted' him by addressing him by his surname and omitting the 'Mr'. Brought before the same District Commissioner who had given him his first job in New Guinea and, astonishingly, asked to choose his own punishment – a £30 fine or two weeks in jail – Errol plumped for the latter, well aware that there was then no prison in Kavieng for white men, and he served his 'sentence' at the home of Tom Price, an Englishman who was in charge of the native prisoners. The pair spent much of these two weeks drinking and playing cards, and Errol got over the pain of being separated from Maihiati by bedding a different girl every night... and contracting what he called 'the pearl of great price', gonorrhoea.

For several weeks Errol was laid low, not with the actual malady, but suffering from the after-effects of a potion prescribed by a quack doctor. Hoping to be cured twice as quickly, Errol doubled up on the dosage and almost died. Then, upon his recovery – starting to tire of the copra trade, but not giving up on it entirely and still no nearer to his gold-prospecting goal – he opted for the fishing industry, and formed a partnership with a shady character named Dusty Miller. On the pretext that many of his labourers were suffering from beriberi on account of vitamin deficiency, he and Miller acquired six two-man canoes and a licence from the government permitting them to dynamite for fish off the New Ireland coast. It was a highly dangerous employment, and one which the young entrepreneur soon abandoned when he saw some of the casualties from mistimed or mismanaged explosions or from the sharks. There was scarcely one fisherman in the region not missing at least one limb.

Errol and Miller's next move was to borrow money from the Burns-Philips Shipping Company for the purchase of a schooner which they baptised the *Maski*, a local name for the jungle, which according to Errol was also Papuan slang for 'screw you'. The boat was used initially to convey copra from Errol's plantation to the New England mainland, until the pair realised that they could

make more money ferrying passengers between Kavieng and
Rabaul, a ten-day voyage which, because neither of them knew
how to navigate, took twenty. Even so, once this 'teething problem'
had been overcome, the Flynn-Miller Ferry Service was a successful
enterprise, and made them and Burns-Philips a modest profit and
enough of a name for them to attract a joint commission from the
Australian and British governments to conduct an expedition along
the then largely unexplored 600-mile Sepik River. The operation
was to be headed by a Dr Herman F. Erben, himself an explorer,
adventurer and specialist in the treatment of tropical diseases.

Had Errol and his partner *known* that the trip was being paid
for from governmental coffers, they almost certainly would not
have been party to it. What they *were* told, initially, by the
director of the shipping company, was that the purpose of the
venture was to acquire footage for a Hollywood movie.

Errol found the idea of being filmed glamorous, but even so he
hedged: the Sepik was one of the world's most perilous locations,
the territory of several tribes of rival headhunters. It was also
festooned with snakes, mosquitoes, crocodiles, leeches and blood-
sucking bats, and was a haven for deadly diseases. He was
eventually persuaded by money – £25 a day, a massive sum in
those days – and all the food he and his native crew could eat. The
mission meant, ostensibly, that he would have to say goodbye to
Maihiati, though he did not feel too guilty about this because,
before leaving, he plied her with gifts. 'I had begun a practice that
I was to bring to a fine art later in Hollywood,' he wrote in his
memoirs, referring to the huge alimony payments which he would
eventually pay to his wives and mistresses.

The Sepik expedition lasted two months, and as anticipated, the
Maski and her crew faced every conceivable danger: showers of
poisoned arrows from the savages, malaria, leeches, stomach
upsets, and of course the crocodiles, which attacked the boat
every time it hit a sand-bank, when everyone had to get out and
push. Warren Reeve of *Photoplay* actually saw a complete print of
the film early in 1936, and was impressed by one scene in
particular:

Only the light crash of feet tearing through the matted ground
growth ruffled the deathly silence of the jungle. Heading a column

of black native bearers, a tall arrow-straight youth with keen eyes and a blond silken stubble of whiskers parted the thick green leaves with his elbows. A holstered revolver rubbed his right thigh. The tall youth was the guide. Already [the expedition] was three days from the last government outpost, entering the head hunter country. Anything could happen now, and suddenly it did. Black, bushy heads mushroomed magically out of the tropic thicket. The blacks squealed, dropped their packs and scattered in panicked confusion. The trees rained whistling darts. The young man dropped to his shins, tore a stinging arrow from his ankle. He pulled himself behind a tree trunk. His pistol spat at the quivering leaves where savages had been. It was silent again. He turned with an odd Irish grin to the white man with the camera. Its lens was levelled at his good-looking face. A crank was still turning.

When the party were just two days up river – the furthest anyone had ever been – Errol learnt the real reason for the mission: fearful of a possible attack on the area by Japan, the governments of Britain and Australia needed to know the geographical features of this mysterious British territory, the second largest island in the world, so that they would know how best to defend it. For a while, Errol did consider turning back, but as difficulties only usually stimulated him, he decided to press on. He also liked being filmed: there was an irrepressible streak of bravado within him, and even at just nineteen he was extremely photogenic. Handsome, muscular and tanned, and already 6 feet 2 inches, he spent the entire two months stripped to the waist. In the surviving footage he looks, as indeed he was, supremely fit.

Most important of all, though, Errol was able to earn more than enough money to buy his stake in the goldfields at Edey Creek. He began prospecting in February 1929, having sold his share in the *Maski* back to Dusty Miller in order to acquire the necessary digging equipment and a small team of Kanaka native labourers. The patch of land he had purchased was in wild country – 8,000 feet up a mountainside, several days trek inland from Salamaua, again in headhunter country. When Errol's party arrived there, however, there was virtually no gold to be found in his patch, and as soon as he began running out of money and provisions, he had no option but to return to Salamaua. Here he was hired to co-navigate a ship, the *Matupi*, by its elderly captain,

Ed Bowen. The idea was that the pair would sail up the coast as far as the port of Aitape, then decide how to make their fortune – either by prospecting for gold again, or by a combination of slave-trading and hunting birds of paradise in nearby Dutch New Guinea. They opted for the latter, pressganging a dozen or so natives into sailing with them, whom they would eventually sell to the copra plantations. This resulted in them being trailed by the Dutch police, who fired on them, killing one of the native helpers and forcing another to hide in the reeds, where he was eaten by crocodiles. Errol himself escaped, but as he could not stay in Altape without being arrested, he made his way back to Salamaua, where for several weeks he hired himself out to tourists as a jungle guide. During one of these forays, his party was ambushed by headhunters: one of his guides was killed, and Errol shot dead one of his attackers. Errol himself was hit in the heel by an arrow, and carried the scar for the rest of his life. Upon his return to base, however, he was arrested, charged with murder, and flung into a temporary jail – a rough, bamboo cage. And as if he did not feel wretched enough, while incarcerated he fell victim to another attack of gonorrhoea.

In his subsequent trial, having no money to appoint a lawyer, Errol defended himself – not just against the murder charge, but against being made an example of in that, as a 'terroriser of savages', by invading the territory around the Sepik, he had only antagonised these people, *and* undone all the work being conducted by missionaries, who were trying to civilise them. Errol pleaded self-defence, quite rightly, on the first count, and added – lying under oath – that his position of recruitment officer for a copra plantation was exactly that, and that he was no slave-trader. The natives, he concluded, needed to work, and he had only been there to help them out, and that in his own way he too was a missionary! Errol also produced a 'witness' named Jack Ryan, a prospector pal who had been miles away at the time of the ambush, but who spoke out for Errol's 'impeccable' character and asked the judge, point-blank, how *he* would have reacted, had he been accosted by a tribe of hostile, spear-wielding savages in the middle of the jungle! Errol and Ryan then both asked where the body of the murdered man was, and the trial had to be adjourned until an expedition was sent out to comb the area where the attack had taken place. No body was found, save that of Errol's native guide, who by tradition had to be left where he had fallen, and both the charges against Errol were dropped.

The next day, having decided *not* to sell his stake in the Edey Creek goldfields for the time being, Errol returned to Kavieng, where he received hospital treatment for his venereal disease. Because this had gone untreated for so long, he had to have permanganate of potash injected directly into the urethra, a primitive and horrendously painful procedure which left him with a serious bladder infection. The necessary treatment could only be obtained in Australia, so he left for Sydney without delay. Dusty Miller, his former partner, paid for the trip.

Errol stayed in Sydney only long enough to be cured of his affliction, to resume his non-sexual relationship with Naomi Dibbs and become engaged and unengaged, and to fleece several restaurants by wolfing down meals and rushing off without paying. He also managed to sell his stake in the goldfields for a staggering £2,000, but did not, however, hold on to his newly found riches for very long. Wandering down to the harbour one afternoon in a drunken stupor after an all-night binge, he observed a 'FOR SALE' sign on a beautiful 44-foot yacht named the *Arop*, and on impulse forked out the £1,500 asking price. Then, once he had sobered up – having rechristened his boat the *Sirocco* – he and a trio of redoubtable sailors he had met in a dockside dive set off on the 3,000-mile voyage to New Guinea to dig for gold!

Errol's aim, this time, was to make enough money to travel to England and study literature and history at Cambridge. Again acting on impulse, however, he suddenly opted to settle in the lush countryside next to the Laloki River, 30 miles from Port Moresby in the Gulf of Papua. Selling the *Sirocco* and dismissing his crew, he engaged a team of natives to build him a small wooden house, and set up the region's first tobacco plantation, using the 'expertise' he had gleaned from textbooks supplied by his father. Of course, he also hired an experienced boss-boy to supervise the proceedings.

This boss-boy's name was Allaman, and he made the mistake of introducing his 'white-man gaffer' to Tuperselai, his pretty but fiery fourteen-year-old daughter. Errol at once fell in love with the girl, and bought her from her father for two pigs and a handful of shillings. For several months, once Errol had convinced her that she was not a slave and that he would never harm her, he and Tuperselai lived in the shoreside house as husband and wife. Then, quite unexpectedly, Errol received a telegram from Sydney which would change the course of his life.

Charles Chauvel was an Australian film producer chum of Herman F. Erben, the man whose party Errol had escorted up the Sepik. He and the Australian actor John Warwick had watched footage of the young man in action – most notably a clip of Errol fighting off an irate crocodile with a bamboo pole – and they had been further impressed by the fact that he was a descendant of the Midshipman Young of *Bounty* fame. Chauvel was about to make a feature entitled *In the Wake of the Bounty* and had already contracted Warwick to play Young. Errol was now offered £50, plus expenses, to play Fletcher Christian!

Until now, Errol had not been remotely interested in acting: his only brushes with the profession had been listening to his mother rehearsing for an amateur dramatics production and a one-off visit to the theatre to see the dancer, Anna Pavlova.

In his memoirs, Errol claimed that the man who had engaged him for the film, the *same* man who had commissioned him for the Sepik expedition, had been one 'Joel Swartz'. This was pure invention. Such a name does not appear in the film's credits or in contemporary documents, whereas Erben's does. In 1959, however, he had a sound reason for not wishing the public to know that he had been linked with Herman F. Erben, as will be seen. Errol also claimed that the film had been shot in Maatvai Bay, Tahiti. In fact, though most of the locations *were* filmed there, all of Errol's scenes were shot on a Sydney backlot, where the deck of the *Bounty* had been reconstructed. 'For three weeks I worked with Swartz in the picture without the least idea of what I was doing,' he recalled. 'I had touched on something that the world called an art form and it had affected me deeply.'

Errol – listed in the credits of the film as Leslie Flynn – was only saying this in retrospect: as an acknowledged jack-of-all-trades, making the film was just another way of earning a quick buck, and as soon as shooting was completed he returned to Tuperselai and his tobacco plantation to pick up where he had left off.

In the Wake of the Bounty was an exceedingly poor film. Little more than a documentary, it was narrated by actor Arthur Greenaway, whose raucous pronunciation is only marginally less infuriating than the ghastly Hawaiian music soundtrack. Errol's voice, with an exaggerated, nasal Queen's English accent, is equally annoying, particularly when he pronounces plum lines such as, 'The die has been tossed, Edward Young, and there is no turning back. The future holds the most *awesful* adventure of all!' Indeed, the film would never have been remembered at all had it not been for Errol's subsequent fame.

Although turned down for distribution in the United States, the rights were purchased by MGM four years later when they began shooting their definitive *Mutiny on the Bounty* with Clark Gable and Charles Laughton – but only so that fragments of the Tahiti location shots could be incorporated into the pre-publicity shorts. No one took any notice of the muscular young actor playing Fletcher Christian, even though by this time Errol was well on the way towards becoming a household name.

Back at the Laloki River, Errol's tobacco plantation was not proving as successful as he had anticipated, because the Australian government had recently introduced measures curbing the importation of tobacco, arguing that this was having a debilitating effect on the country's own tobacco industry. Peeved because Papua was a dependency of Australia, Errol voiced his opinions in an acerbic letter to the editor of the *Sydney Bulletin*. It was published, and Errol set off at once for Sydney, hoping to persuade local businessmen to support his enterprise. He was accompanied by eight Melanesian natives who until then had never been out of the jungle. Throughout the voyage they wore full tribal costumes and tusks through their noses...but upon arrival in Sydney Harbour there were so many gasps from onlookers – whose eyes were fixed on their calico penis-sheaths – that Errol was ordered to buy them all trousers before they were allowed ashore.

The visit caused enough of a stir to make the front page of the *Sydney Bulletin*, and for the editor to invite Errol to submit a regular column – detailing his adventures and jungle forages – for which he was paid £5 a month. The businessmen, however, were not impressed by his patter. Errol put his natives on the next boat to New Guinea but decided to stay on for a while in the city. *In*

the Wake of the Bounty was about to be given its première and he
wanted to milk the occasion for all it was worth, even though the
low-key event was at a small cinema and the manager took some
convincing that he was in the film. He turned up in a nineteenth-
century naval officer's uniform, wearing a Fletcher Christian wig
which he later said reminded him of 'an elderly keeper of a
whorehouse in King William Street, a little place of some integrity
which I was prone to frequent'.

For a few weeks Errol lived, loved and spent recklessly – and for
the *third* time he took up with Naomi Dibbs who, he lamented,
was *still* a virgin and clearly intent on remaining so. His nights,
therefore, after he had escorted Naomi home, were spent cruising
the brothels and dives of Sydney's red-light district. Soon broke,
he was forced to seek refuge in a hostel for down-and-outs. Even
so, he maintained his 'colonial' dignity, and resorted to his old
tactic of strolling into society eateries as if he owned them, and
absconding before the waiter brought the bill. It was outside one
of these establishments – Ushers – that Errol met Madge Parks, a
sophisticated, married woman some twenty years his senior.

According to Errol, Madge sauntered up to him and asked a
simple street direction, only to suggest, moments later, that maybe
they should have dinner together. Their affair, which appears to
have consisted of little more than a series of extended sex sessions,
lasted one week – long enough for Errol to come to the conclusion
that she was a nymphomaniac, and to run off with her jewellery.
'I knew it was the most dastardly thing I had ever done,' he said
later, confessing that at the time he had only regarded the theft as
a loan. Indeed, some years later he did attempt to locate Madge
Parks to make up for what he had done.

Correctly guessing that his lover would report him to the police,
Errol removed the stones, mostly diamonds, from their settings, and
concealed them in the hollow handle of his shaving brush. He was
apprehended on a ship, minutes before it was due to leave Sydney,
and meticulously searched. His camera was smashed to bits, but he
threatened the two 'shit-heels' – a favourite Flynn euphemism for
policemen – with a good hiding should they carry out their threat of
an internal examination after he had cracked, 'Why don't you take a
leg apiece and shake me? I might have them up my arse!'

The ship conveyed Errol as far as Brisbane, where he tried –

unsuccessfully – to sell the jewels. Then, broke again, he set off across Queensland for New Guinea, taking whatever work came his way. His first job was digging wells at Diamond Downs. Then he was taken on by a sheep farmer who was hiring men to herd a huge flock the 800 miles to Townsville, in Cleveland Bay. First of all, however, he had to serve his apprenticeship on the ranch, as a 'hogget-dagger', a task he would years later delight in describing to friends across the dinner·table. Errol was the second of four men in a sheep-shearing assembly line. The first man's duty was the removal of the excreta and bluebottles from the young male sheep's, or hogget's, rear end. 'All I had to do was stick my face into this gruesome mess and bite off the young sheep's testicles,' he would explain with relish, adding, 'I had good teeth. I bit and spat out the product into a pile of what they called prairie oysters...delicious to eat, but not delicious to remove. I was getting big money, but my jaws started to freeze up!'

Errol may have made the grade as a 'dagger', but he never got an opportunity to drive the sheep to the coast: the sheep farmer had two attractive daughters, and caught Errol in bed with one of them, forcing him to make a hasty exit. He eventually did reach Townsville, after hitching rides on a succession of freight trains. From there, he wired his old pal, Jack Ryan, and asked him for a loan. With this came good news: back at the Edey Creek, his name had been entered into a draw with other prospectors and he had won half a stake in the goldfields!

Errol sailed without delay for Salamaua, feeling as he put it, 'a little like Diamond Jim Brady'. Because he had no money to buy so-called 'indentured' or forced labour, he lured a tribal chief into believing that he could turn halfpennies into silver shillings – by dipping them into a kettle of mercury – and in exchange for his 'magic bowl' he set off with a team of twenty helpers. His stake, however, yielded but 50 ounces of gold, by which time the chief, realising that he had been duped, had gone on the warpath. This, and the fact that indentured labour was against the law, forced Errol to move quickly. Selling his natives to a copra plantation, he bought a passport and a few days later boarded a ship and set off for the Philippines on what would be the first stage of a lengthy, arduous but adventurous journey to England.

Several years later, when Errol would be safely settled on the other side of the world, his questionable activities during his last months in New Guinea would be proven by the discovery of a journal which he had left behind in a Salamaua hotel. The contents of this – entries mostly for January 1933 – would be published in 1960 by the *Pacific Islands Monthly* to counteract what the publication's correspondent, Stuart Inder, denounced as the 'gross exaggerations' of Errol's posthumous autobiography, *My Wicked, Wicked Ways*.

Much of Errol's prosaic diatribe in these entries concerns the Sattelberg Mission, near Finschafen, where he and his 'boys' apparently stayed. Errol was especially perturbed with the chauvinistic behaviour of the missionaries towards their womenfolk – and the fact that they looked down their noses at him when he stood up as a lady entered the room. He then speaks of his interest in a pretty little Dutch girl, for whom he plans his first shave in three days. His descriptions of the countryside are meticulously detailed, and his account of his devious methods employed to acquire his workforce are, if nothing else, honest:

> January 17th. First boy this morning, good stamp of native. He'll look well leading an ox about, though he doesn't suspect it yet. He thinks he's going to be my cook. This is a very good omen. To get a boy from the Chief's village means that I'll almost certainly get as many as I want from other villages...

The Philippines, it would appear, were not Errol's original destination upon leaving New Guinea. His plan was to go to China, as he observes in his journal in a surprisingly portentous statement for one so young:

> I'm leaving economic security and I'm leaving it deliberately. By going off to China with a paltry few pounds and no knowledge of what life has in store for me there, I believe that I'm going to front the essentials of life to see if I can learn what it has to teach and above all not to discover, when I come to die, that I have not lived... The best part of life is spent in earning money in order to enjoy a questionable liberty during the least valuable part of it. To hell with money! Pursuit of it is not going to mould my life for me. I am going to live life sturdily and Spartan-like, to drive life into a corner and reduce it to its lowest terms, and if I find it sublime I

shall know it by experience... Time, for example, just one hour of time is far more important than money. Whenever you waste your time over printed words that neither enlighten nor amuse you, you are in a sense committing suicide.

During this voyage, aboard the German freighter *Friderun* in April 1933, Errol again encountered Herman F. Erben. 'He wore a broad, Dutch grin, showing enormous teeth parted,' he wrote in his autobiography. 'His ears were monsters that stood out at about the angle of an enraged elephant about to charge. His face was covered with blond hair...his bare legs and thighs showed the same hirsuteness, so that he looked like a blond, amiable orang-utan in a mink coat.'

Errol was not being devious in changing Erben's identity. By 1959, when he was putting together *My Wicked, Wicked Ways*, he had not heard from his friend in many years and was not even sure that he was still alive. His publishers, however, given the nature of some of the book's revelations, were terrified of naming Erben without his or his family's permission, so Errol was advised to give him another name, as he had done with some of his lovers. Herman F. Erben therefore became Dr Gerrit H. Koets.

In years to come, Errol's association with this sinister man – who was actually Austrian-born – would irrefutably help tarnish his reputation and give way to the most virulent and wholly unnecessary smear campaign. Twelve years Errol's senior, Erben served with the Austrian Field Artillery during World War I, and immediately afterwards worked as a cameraman for the Sachafilm Studios in Vienna, before finding his true vocation as a specialist in tropical diseases. A graduate of Vienna University, in 1924 he gained a scholarship to study metabolic research in New York. Two years later he qualified as a doctor, and for a time worked at the Pacific Institute. In 1930 he became a US citizen. In order to achieve this, he had to swear on the Bible that apart from the occasional visit to his family in Vienna – during one, he had been asked to leave after posing for a photograph masquerading as Hitler – he had served the required five-year unbroken residency in America. Had Erben admitted that he had been involved with the previous year's Sepik expedition, his application for citizenship would have been rejected.

Erben's first commission as an American citizen was an assignment in South America for the Pacific Institute. His next meant being posted to New Guinea, where he studied the effects of hookworm on the natives. What Errol almost certainly did not know was that his friend – a Jew who actually *shared* his anti-Semitic views – was also fiercely anti-British and a member of the Nazi Party. The latter was not regarded as unusual at the time, though: for most Austrians, carrying a Party card meant the difference between gainful employment and the dole queue.

During their stay in Manilla, Errol and Erben shared a large, beachside hut and spent a great deal of their time fleecing the locals at cock fights, a lucrative business in this part of the world. Although they knew absolutely nothing about this barbaric sport, it did not take them long to work out a scam: by sharpening their bird's beak and coating it with deadly snake venom moments before a fight, they ensured that they won every time. And because their bird was always smaller than the other contender, it was an outside bet. Most of the money they won was squandered on booze and women. Eventually, however, they were rumbled when an opponent's bird dropped dead in the ring after a cursory peck on the comb. Fleeing for their lives, with the equivalent of $4,000 in takings, the pair headed for the harbour, to stow away on the first boat scheduled to leave the port – the *Empress of Asia*, bound for Hong Kong.

Once the boat had left the harbour, the friends emerged from hiding to purchase two first-class tickets. They stayed in Hong Kong long enough to lose half of their ill-gotten gains at the race-track, then boarded a packet-boat for Macao, the Portuguese colony which Errol branded 'the cesspool of the world'. Here, he predicted, he would make his fortune by playing fantan – a then popular Chinese gambling game which Errol had mastered in New Guinea.

En route to Macao, Errol began one of his most passionate but potentially dangerous love affairs, with a woman who had the unlikely name of Ting Ling O'Connor – Errol described her as 'an Oriental Garbo, with the swagger of a Mae West'. Ting Ling was also hoping to make her fortune at the gambling tables.

For a week, the pair were inseparable. They fleeced every casino they entered before homing in on the red-light district, where they frequented the opium dens. 'My body came out of my body,' Errol recalled. 'There was Flynn, four feet over my head, floating. Here was my love of my life by my side – so now we were three. I made love to Ting Ling in ways and manners that I would never believe myself capable of.'

Unfortunately, Errol found out too late how costly this passion had been when Ting Ling disappeared with the better part of his winnings. Worse he was then informed by the manager of one casino that she was a 'shill': a professional opportunist and whore who had been working the Hong Kong-Macao route for years, under a number of aliases, duping unsuspecting men of all ages into parting with their money.

Despondently, Errol and Erben returned to Hong Kong, where Errol had deposited his 50 ounces of gold with Barclay's Bank. However, hours after disembarking, he fell ill with malaria – a malady which would trouble him for the rest of his life – and then discovered that while aboard ship a pickpocket had relieved him of Madge Parks's jewels. Once more, the pair were broke, but this time they decided to do something which was *above* board: they enlisted with the Royal Hong Kong Volunteers. China and Japan were in the grip of the Second Sino-Japanese War: the Japanese already occupied Manchuria, they had entered China, and there were rumours that they would soon capture Hong Kong.

Errol and Erben were among a 400-strong contingent which was dispatched to Shanghai, already under attack – and also under several feet of snow. Instead of augmenting the front line, however, the pair were assigned to a team whose duty was clearing the snow and digging the entrenchments. After three weeks their minds were set on desertion. Here, they hit a snag: it was not possible to leave Shanghai without a Province Permit, a document similar to a United States Green Card which was stamped with a date when the holder must legally leave the country or apply for an extension. Errol borrowed one of these from another soldier, observed that it was almost identical to a Chinese laundry slip, and got to work: covering the company logo with a large British postage stamp and a blob of sealing wax, he added an 'official' signature, along with the date he was obliged to leave Shanghai, then made a second permit for his friend.

The ruse worked and Errol and Erben boarded a packet-boat

headed for Saigon, and from there took a ship for Bengal. They did not reach their destination, on account of Errol becoming involved with a consumptive Japanese woman named Mayako. 'I decided that if she were so ill that she might die, and so young and so beautiful,' he recalled, 'then she should certainly have a fling before passing away.' He had not, however, reckoned on Mayako's jealous husband who, having caught the pair kissing in her cabin, took a pot-shot at Errol with his revolver, missing him by mere inches before being wrestled to the ground by two burly stewards. Even so, when the boat reached Colombo in Ceylon, Errol and Erben were the ones forced to leave: Mayako and her husband had bought first-class tickets, while the two friends were travelling steerage.

Never one to learn his lesson, within minutes of arriving in Colombo, Errol hired a rickshaw to convey himself and Erben to the best brothel in town. 'The heart and soul of any city is its whorehouses,' was his well-tried maxim. 'Go there first. Afterwards pay your respects to the Governor, if he will receive you, but if you want to find out what's going on, definitely the whorehouse!' What he apparently did not do on this occasion was pay sufficient respect, or money, to the tetchy rickshaw boy: when the latter demanded a tip but received only abuse and the threat of a good hiding, he pulled a knife and slit Errol's stomach open.

Errol was rushed to the nearest hospital. The blade had missed any vital organs, but still required sixteen stitches, which burst two days later when he tried to get out of bed. In future years, just as he liked to shock diners with his 'sheep-dagging' anecdote, so he loved to surprise people by suddenly dropping his trousers and showing them the nine-inches-long jagged scar which stretched from his scrotum to his navel. The incident made him paranoid about losing his most prized assets and, or so he confessed to Earl Conrad, the man who helped ghost his autobiography, also led to his promiscuity.

'I've lived for, with and by my balls,' he said. 'I learned to value my balls *so* much that possibly I decided to make continual use of them – in the event some small man might one day succeed where this one almost did.'

From Colombo – having absconded from the hospital without paying the bill – Errol and Erben took the ferry to the Indian mainland. They then caught the train to Calcutta because Errol had heard how the brothels there were among the best in the world, but they must have been disappointing because the episode scarcely warrants mention in his memoirs. One week later they embarked, steerage class, for the West African coast, crawling down one side of India and halfway up the other before crossing the Indian Ocean to French Somaliland. Here, Errol spent a night in jail after brawling with two customs officials. The pair then headed for Marseilles, where on 20 June, his 24th birthday, Errol bid a tearful farewell to Erben. Their journey, by way of Addis Ababa and the Suez Canal, had included a stopover in Marrakesh, where they had been invited to a peepshow. 'I saw a braying donkey mounting a French girl,' he recalled, adding how, though offended, he had found an obviously perverse scenario so funny that he had been rooted to the spot by 'irresistible compulsion'.

In Marrakesh, too, Errol paid his first visit to a *male* brothel, though it would be by no means his last. 'To me, *that* sight was horrible,' he wrote in his memoirs, recalling the establishment's insistence on supplying only teenage boys, 'but, as the saying goes, one man's meat is another's poison, and we must remember Ancient Greece and the epoch of Pericles, even Socrates.' Errol may have been surprised by what he saw in Marrakesh, but this would not deter him from spending the rest of his life pursuing under-aged lovers of *both* sexes.

2

The Young Buck and the Spitfire

'I only know if I touch the arm of a girl or a woman who fires me, I have got to go as far as I can or as she will let me.'

According to Errol, when he arrived in London in June 1933 he had just two shillings in his pocket – which he blew on his taxi fare from Victoria Station to the Berkeley Hotel. Here he conned the management into giving him a room by producing some of the 'spoils' from his travels, including the Shanghai permit, and by explaining that he had lost his luggage in French Somaliland. For surety, he showed them his certificate, signed by the manager of Barclay's Bank in Hong Kong, to the effect that his funds from the sale of his gold would be coming through at any time. He also sought financial help from his father. Theodore Flynn was by this time Professor of Biology at the University of Belfast, but his response was not encouraging: if his son could afford to stay at the Berkeley, how come he was short of money?

After spending two days worrying about how he would pay his bill, Errol resorted to desperate measures: doubling up 'in agony' in the hotel dining room, he caused such a commotion that a doctor was summoned. Appendicitis was diagnosed – it was either that or food poisoning, the doctor declared, adding that the young man would have to be admitted to hospital at once. Terrified that the hotel might be held responsible, the manager arranged for Errol to be taken to a private clinic, where the tests carried out on him proved negative. Again, fate came to Errol's rescue when he fell for his pretty nurse. 'An English nursing home for the rich is so arranged that the patient's door has a lock on it,' he remembered, explaining how the nurse had kept him a virtual sex slave in his room, only to spoil the idyll by suggesting that, as he had almost certainly got her pregnant, they should marry! That same day, Errol received a call from Barclay's informing him that his money had come through – over £500 – and as soon as it was dark, he climbed out of his window and disappeared.

By this time Errol had made up his mind to become an actor, despite knowing nothing about stagecraft other than what he had read in books. And yet the very first theatrical agency he tried sent him for an audition with the Queen's Theatre, on Shaftesbury Avenue. He was engaged as a non-speaking extra in their production of *Once in a Lifetime*, a parody on Hollywood musicals starring Cora Goffin. Four weeks later, the play closed in the West End and embarked on a provincial tour. First stop was the Northampton Opera House, the home of the town's repertory company. After arriving here, Errol did not continue with the tour: a chance encounter with the bandleader, Carroll Gibbons, led to him being offered a part in a 'quota quickie' film entitled *I Adore You*.

Little is known of Errol Flynn's first film as a legitimate actor, other than that it was a musical featuring Harold French and Margot Grahame, and that Errol appeared in a dance sequence choreographed by Ralph Reader, of Gang Show fame, which was shot at London's Savoy Hotel. 'Quota quickie' was the term applied to cheap movies which the British studios churned out almost like factory products in the decade following the transition from silents to sound. By order of the 1927 Cinematographic Act, 30 per cent of all films shown in Britain had to be home-produced (though not necessarily home-financed), but as the British Film Industry then as now could not compete with its American rivals, some of these films were rushed out so quickly that they were inevitably dire, and have subsequently been lost or destroyed. *I Adore You* was one such film, although several stills from it have survived.

Disappointed that there were no more film offers, and not even any auditions, Errol's next move was to place an advertisement in

Spotlight. Under his photograph he listed his most recent stage and screen roles, all of them big hits in Australia, he declared in his publicity blurb, and all, with the exception of *In the Wake of the Bounty*, invented titles. The ploy did not work: any producer worthy of his name would have checked out these famous 'vehicles' and discovered that they were bogus. Errol therefore contacted the Queen's Theatre again, and when they refused to have anything to do with him, he set his sights on Northampton, the only place in England he knew outside of London.

According to Errol, the director of the Northampton Rep, Robert Young, answered his advertisement in *Spotlight* but showed more interest in his cricketing skills than his acting abilities: the company were about to engage in an important match against Coventry but were one man short. Errol professed to being an expert, even though he had hardly ever played the game. Not surprisingly Northampton lost, but Young still took Errol on, at £3 a week, and put him into a pantomime.

Little of this is actually true. Errol's first part at Northampton was that of Edward Wales, in Bayard Veiller's *The Thirteenth Chair*, which opened on 18 December 1933, well out of the cricket season. Robert Young also denied having seen Errol's advertisement in *Spotlight*: some years later he claimed that the would-be actor-thespian had turned up at his house one Sunday afternoon and reeled off a list of his remarkable sporting skills. Young, on the lookout for an athletic type for the rep's next production, decided to take him on.

Errol certainly made the most of his Northampton debut: using what was left of the money from his gold stake, be bought a bright red Swallow sports car, and drove to his first press conference of local reporters, where he rattled off the spiel which Robert Young had so obviously swallowed, and more besides. 'He had played the leading parts in the last six Australian films and was brought over by a London film company,' the *Northampton and County Independent* reported in January 1934, while the *Chronicle and Echo* enthused, under the heading, 'Errol Flynn – Film Star and Sportsman':

And that is not all about this versatile personality. Mr Flynn reached the finals of the amateur boxing championship of

Australia, and he was among those chosen to compete in swimming contests at the Olympic Games. Despite his experience on the films, however, he prefers the stage to the screen, and at the moment is most interested in repertory.

Errol spent a reasonably contented if not hell-raising eighteen months in Northampton, although he later dismissed the town as 'a dowdy, dreary place where they manufactured boots'. In all, he appeared in 22 of the company's productions, in roles ranging from the wicked prince in *Jack and the Beanstalk* to Krogstad in Ibsen's *The Doll's House*. Initially, he lodged at a house on Hazelwood Road, owned by a couple named Kemp who were taken in by his ever-present smile and affable disposition. They even turned a blind eye on his carousing and the fact that he took a different girl to his room almost every night...(girl being the operative word, for most of them were in their teens, and some were still at school). 'Flynn's height, Greek god countenance, apparent affluence and fast car were all attributes of his attraction,' observed Gerry Connelly in his account of these formative acting years, *Errol Flynn in Northampton*.

What the Kemps would not put up with, however, were the visits from the police. The first came after the owner of a shoe factory opposite his lodgings reported him for gross indecency. Each morning, while the mostly female workforce were waiting for the gates to open, Errol would 'hambone' in front of his bedroom window, stripping off his clothes, and executing a hula-hula dance while masturbating and belting out his favourite song:

It was in Baghdad that my mother met my dad,
He sang, 'Nelly, put your belly next to mine!'

'It paid to advertise, believe me,' Errol boasted of his exhibitionism. He was never apprehended by the police, though they did get him on another charge when his car was discovered outside his local with several broken lights and no insurance and tax discs. A court appearance on 7 March saw him plead guilty on five counts, and his fines totalled £3 10 shillings, more than a week's wages. He did, however, keep his licence on account of a yarn which was swallowed by the magistrate – that he needed his car to visit his family in Ireland, from which he was 'reluctantly separated' by his career. As for the Kemps, they told him that he would have to leave. He did, owing them several weeks rent.

As would happen with most of the dilemmas in his life, Errol landed on his feet. Very much the conman, he soon sweet-talked another couple, the Starmers, into letting him move into the top floor flat in one of their two properties just along the street from the Opera House. The move coincided with what Errol called his 'debut as a Shakespearean actor' – in effect, his *only* brush with the Bard, and an inauspicious one. In his memoirs he boasted that he had played the lead in *Othello* opposite Freda Jackson's Desdemona, and he even criticised the woman who would become one of Britain's most distinguished actresses by describing how their love scenes had been marred by her 'beer and onions' breath. Jackson took exception to this remark, declaring some years later that not only did she *dislike* beer and onions but the part of Othello had not been played by Errol. Indeed, Peter Rosser's name appears in the programme, while Errol is listed as having played Lodovico and the First Senator. Similarly, his claims that he played the hero in Sapper McNeile's *Bulldog Drummond* were untrue: he had actually been given the much smaller role of Marcovitch.

Errol *did* take the lead in Frederick Lonsdale's murder-mystery, *The Fake*, which opened on 19 March 1934. Following so soon after the critically panned *Othello* – throughout which most of the cast had had to be prompted – few of the Opera House's regular patrons turned up to see him until the end of the week, after the *Chronicle and Echo* had enthused, 'That clever young actor, Errol Flynn, came into the limelight again last night. As Geoffrey Sands, he was always splendid, although such splendid acting deserved a larger audience.'

Despite the diversity of his roles with the Northampton Rep, Errol was dissatisfied with working on a provincial stage. After the dangers and delights of the Far East, he had expected a little more excitement, and he had never given up hope of working in more films. He plied studios with photographs and copies of his grossly exaggerated curriculum vitae, and at the end of May he was summoned to an audition with Irving Asher, the director of the British division of Warner Brothers First National, whose studios had been established a few years before at Teddington, just outside London.

Asher, ever on the lookout for extras and bit-part players for his quota-quickie pictures, brushed past Errol in the corridor outside his office and was at once bowled over by his size. He had no idea who he was because his secretary had arranged the appointment – one of around 50 that day. Errol mistook him for a lawyer. When Asher remarked, 'You're a big fellow. What have you *done*?' he retorted, 'Do you want my life story, sport, or a list of my previous convictions?' Already captivated by Errol's looks, Asher was so astonished by his wit – and his cheek – that he offered him a seven-year optional contract, starting off at £20 a week, without even bothering to travel up to Northampton to witness for himself if he could act or not!

The contract coincided with Errol's somewhat hasty exit from Northampton four weeks before the company's summer break. During rehearsals for an inconsequential whodunnit, Owen Davis and Sewell Collins' *9:45*, Errol had 'a slight altercation' with Robert Young's wife, the actress Doris Littell, who had recently begun a stint as stage manager. Errol had apparently taken exception to Littell's suggestion that everyone in the company – save herself, of course – should take it in turn to play a minor role and thus reduce jealousy among the cast. As a result of this, on the evening of the première, immediately after the curtain, Errol headed for the Swan Hotel, got drunk and returned to the theatre only minutes before the second performance. This resulted in a bust-up with Littell, whom he smacked across the face, knocking her down a flight of steps. Errol took his dismissal calmly, mainly because he was waiting for the studio call from Irving Asher. What is strange, however, is that Robert Young still wanted to be associated with him. Young had secured parts for several of his cast, including Errol, in three productions at that year's Malvern Festival. Not only did he still allow Errol to participate, he also announced his departure in the local press, concluding, 'But who knows? This promising young actor may return to us for the new season. We certainly hope so!'

The Malvern Festival was a disappointing experience. Although Errol appeared in all three productions – Marlowe's *Dr Faustus*, John Drinkwater's *A Man's House* and Dennis Johnston's *The*

Moon in the Yellow River – his parts were small and considered so inconsequential by him that he extracted his revenge on the Festival's organisers by deliberately mixing them up.

The management were far from pleased when he strode on to the stage during the Johnston play, in which he played an Irish policeman, wearing his Roman guard's costume from *A Man's House*. The young actor could not have cared less: that same week he received a summons from Irving Asher, who told him that from now on, bit-parts would be a thing of the past. It also seems certain that Asher, a loquacious bisexual, had developed a crush on him. It is doubtful, however, that it was reciprocated: Errol would always show the greatest of contempt for the so-called casting couch, even when the upper hand belonged to a beautiful female, and the numerous affairs he did have with men were all based on mutual attraction.

Errol was subsequently offered the lead in a whodunnit entitled *Murder at Monte Carlo*, based on the novel by Tom Van Dyke and directed by Ralph Ince. It was shot over a three-week schedule at Boreham Wood (later Elstree Studios), and represented standard fare for murder-mystery fans: a young reporter and his girlfriend (Eve Gray) from a rival newspaper are sent to Monte Carlo to cover the murder of the inventor of a revolutionary roulette wheel, but end up solving the crime themselves in an unsensational reconstruction scene.

The plot was poor, the sets wooden and the dialogue dire, yet all the critics agreed that the film's leading man – even though his acting left much to be desired – was the most handsome they had seen for some time. On the strength of this, Irving Asher cabled Jack Warner in Hollywood to say that he had found a 'Charles Farrell George Brent type with one hell of a personality'. Warner cabled back, instructing Asher to sign Errol at once. He was offered an official contract for six months, at $125 a week, then packed off to Savile Row with a £200 allowance to kit himself out for his 'future career'.

For Errol, the prospect of visiting the United States was just one more in a never-ending chain of adventures, and he had absolutely no intention, at the time, of settling there. He sailed for New York on the SS *Paris* early in November 1934, and as usual encountered his share of high-seas drama. Among the upper-crust passengers travelling first class was a trio of beautiful woman, each of which he was intent on seducing. He had already met Merle Oberon – a huge success as Anne Boleyn in *The Private Life of Henry VIII* – in London, and she was now en route for Hollywood to star in *Folies Bergère* opposite Maurice Chevalier. Errol may have got a little further with Oberon had he not marched up to her in the ship's ballroom and announced, 'G'day sport!' before telling everyone that she too was from Tasmania...and that her real name was Queenie O'Brien!

Secondly there was Lili Damita, a snobbish French actress who had also appeared on the screen with Chevalier. Again, Errol propositioned her in the ballroom, this time politely requesting a dance. Damita's response was to look down her nose at him and mutter, in French, 'Maybe some other time, sport!'

After such a snub, which he interpreted as a supreme insult on his virility, Errol decided to steer clear of the third young woman who had taken his fancy, Naomi Tiarouina. She, however, had certainly noticed *him*. Warner Brothers had booked Errol into New York's St Moritz Hotel, where he was instructed to stay until he received his studio call: the company had yet to find him a suitable film vehicle, but he was promised that this would not take long. It was in the hotel lift that he bumped into Tiarouina – apparently a fantastically wealthy Russian princess – and minutes later he was in bed with her. According to his reminiscences of the event, what should have been a pleasurable experience turned sour when, as he was on the point of orgasm, Tiarouina grabbed a steel-bristled hairbrush and began beating him on the bare buttocks until she drew blood! 'She had a strange glint in her eyes, a truly savage look,' he recalled. 'It was my first experience with sadism.'

The next morning, Errol was introduced to Warner Brothers' New York publicity agent, Blake McElroy, whose first task was to take him on a sightseeing tour of the city. Errol declared that he was much more interested in seeing Harlem than the New York McElroy had had in mind, and although a complete stranger to the area, his instinct for 'sniffing out only the lowliest bag-shanties' lured the pair to a seedy dance club. He very quickly found himself a partner – a beautiful creature whom he began fondling in a darkened corner, only to discover that 'she' was a he.

Errol later pretended that he had been shocked by the incident, though by the time he wrote about it, 25 years on, his experiences with all aspects of sexuality were legion.

Two days later, Errol set off on the week-long train journey to Hollywood, stopping off in Chicago, where he met Sam Clarke, the Warner Brothers executive whose job it was to prepare him for a hopefully successful movie career. Basically, this meant a hasty rewrite of his life story. Not many people in the United States had heard of Tasmania, Clarke told him, so henceforth – as Errol flatly refused to change his name – he would be presented to the public as an Irishman! The publicist then added that the average American's perception of Irishmen was that they were either ugly as sin or downright beautiful and that they were farmers or traffic cops! As Errol clearly was ethereal-looking, and as the studio publicist genuinely believed that there could be no such creature tilling the land, his first publicity photographs depicted him in a motorcycle cop's uniform. And if *this* notion was insufficiently ludicrous, he was then asked to pose for the press embracing his 'long-lost Irish cousin, Maureen O'Toole'... actually Suzy Goldstein, a hoofer and part-time studio date from the Bronx!

En route to Hollywood, Errol's publicist attempted to drill into him how he should or should not treat its moguls, that select handful of all-powerful, mostly Jewish émigré executives who dictated the lives of the stars they had turned into overnight sensations. Stars could easily be dismissed if they failed to submit to the grossly draconian whims of the studio system, but Errol was having none of this. Throughout his entire life he would abhor discipline, and he would retain a particular loathing for the Jewish community, which stemmed from the prejudices which had effectively been bred into him. Tasmania, in the years before the last war, was one of the most racist countries in the world. The last Aborigines had been ousted from the territory as far back as 1876, since which time the Jewish community, particularly in Hobart, had been subjected to incalculable spite and persecution. They were not allowed to join the police force or hold government posts, and those who ran shops and businesses were persistent targets for vandals. Errol, therefore, having been raised on this 'mother's milk anti-Semitism', would always resent being told what to do by the Jewish king-pins, and he would take an instant dislike to virtually anyone, including lovers, who were discovered to be of the faith. His prejudices, however, had yet to surface in public life and he simply told Sam Clarke that he was and always had been his own man, and that not even the mighty Jack Warner would order *him* around. Clarke, having heard it all before, warned colleagues that here was one upstart who would very quickly be sent back to where he had come from. He was even more convinced he was right when he watched Errol march straight past Warner's secretary and barge into the great man's office without knocking. And if this was not enough to ensure an enforced exit on the arms of security men, Errol then very politely remonstrated, 'And now, sport, about that $100 overcoat I had stolen in Chicago the other day...' All Warner could do, he later confessed, was admire the youngster's guts and reach for his cheque book. The seventeen-years-long Warner-Flynn feud had begun!

With his elder brothers – Harry, Albert and Sam – Jack Warner had established a small nickelodeon cinema in New Castle, Pennsylvania, before moving to Hollywood and setting up their own company in 1923. Four years later – mindless of the cynics, who declared that such a gamble would never pay off – they had made the first sound film, *The Jazz Singer*, and then had been feted as the most successful movie partnership in America. This cut no ice with Errol, who spent his first six weeks in Hollywood boxing, playing tennis and chasing women. The studio had provided him with a small apartment near the Los Angeles Tennis Club, and he worked out in the same gymnasium where Rudolph Valentino – himself an expert boxer – had fought the legendary Jack Dempsey. A chance remark from the brash Australian – 'Anything Valentino could do, I can do better!' – prompted Sam Clarke to add a little more to the Flynn legend: Errol had not merely boxed for fun, he had competed with the British team in the 1928 Olympics, and Errol personally consolidated the story by telling the press that he had won a bronze medal! Incredibly, no-one seemed bothered about checking the facts until some years later, by which time there had been *two* medals, both of them gold!

During these first few weeks in Hollywood, a small part in Max Reinhardt's spectacular *A Midsummer Night's Dream*, starring

James Cagney and Olivia de Havilland, was talked about. Cagney, however, dismissed Errol as an 'arrogant pup', so he was offered a bit-part in an unspecified film with Loretta Young instead. She, however, rubbed him up the wrong way in Jack Warner's office after he had politely extended his hand, demanding abruptly, 'Should I *know* you, young man?', to which he responded, 'That depends on how much you've been around, my dear!' Many years later, when he was more famous than she was, Young would turn up at one of Errol's parties and he would ask, with perfunctory charm, 'Haven't I seen you somewhere before? In a silent movie, perhaps?' Young would never speak to him again.

Eventually, Errol was put into *The Case of the Curious Bride*, the second of First National's dreary quartet of Perry Mason films within which the supersleuth was portrayed by former silent star, Warren William. It was an inauspicious start: Errol played Gregory Moxley in a 61-second, non-speaking flashback scene at the end of the film – and a corpse on a mortuary slab near the beginning. 'Some people claim it was my best role,' he later cracked.

The Case of the Curious Bride enjoyed a moderate success for its Hungarian director, Michael Curtiz, who would go on to direct many films for Errol Flynn. There was a little more for Errol to do – two scenes totalling five minutes, opposite Claire Dodd – in *Don't Bet On Blondes*, his next film, with Warren William once more playing the lead. The film was directed by Frenchman Robert Florey, who told him that his greatest regret was that he had never directed Valentino, with whom he had had a passionate affair. This was the second time the Latin lover's name had been brought up in conversation, and again Errol boasted that anything 'that Eyetie poofter' could do, he could do better. Florey retorted, 'You mean that you *also* like taking it up the ass when you're spreadeagled across the hood of your car?' For once, Errol was left speechless.

Just days after this conversation, Errol bumped into Lili Damita again, this time at the Los Angeles Tennis Club. More amenable than she had been aboard the *SS Paris*, within minutes she had invited him back to her bungalow – formerly the home of Valentino and his second wife, Natacha Rambova – at the Garden of Alla complex on Sunset Boulevard.

The Garden of Alla – a number of residences set in three and a half acres of beautifully landscaped gardens, with tropical fruit trees and a Black Sea-shaped swimming pool – had for more than a decade formed the nucleus of the legendary lesbian 'sewing circle' founded by the Crimean-born actress, Alla Nazimova, perhaps the most controversial of all the Hollywood superstars. Visiting such a place, even for an unshockable man of the world like Errol, must have been something of an eye-opener. Nazimova's 'artistic converts' included *both* of Valentino's wives, the film director Dorothy Arzner, Dolly Wilde – Oscar's niece, who one critic described as 'the only Wilde who liked sleeping with women' – and Lili Damita, who during her first year with Errol was romantically linked to two women, the actress Dolores del Rio, and the Mexican socialite Carmen Figueroa.

The difference, basically, between Nazimova and Damita was that while the Russian liked to be surrounded by intellectual females, Damita could almost always be found amidst a coterie of homosexual men. On account of this, Errol's subsequent excursions to the Garden of Alla could only cause speculation – from Damita's male friends that this strapping, devilishly handsome but vulgar young creature was one of their own and from the studio that had signed him that he was a 'twilight menace' who needed to be sorted out.

It was at one of Lili Damita's soirées at the Garden of Alla where Errol first met David Niven, who described him as 'a great athlete of immense charm and evident physical beauty, crowing lustily atop the Hollywood dung-heap', and who over the next few years would be regarded as his best 'fuck-buddy' and something of a soulmate. Not yet a big star in America, the British actor was the same age as Errol, equally lascivious, and like him had been furnished with a reinvented pedigree by studio publicists: the fact that Niven was the son of a Scots *second* lieutenant who had been killed in action during World War I was not good enough for them, so they had up-ranked Niven Snr to 'a very famous, much decorated general'. Again, no-one checked up on the facts.

Niven recalled his meeting with Errol in his memoirs, 'As [Damita's] little coterie was around her that night, for a while Flynn and I each thought the other was a "fag". After sniffing suspiciously we got this sorted out, and a tour of the dives off Hollywood Boulevard became the logical outcome of the evening.' Of his friendship with Errol, he concluded, 'You always knew precisely where you stood with him because he *always* let you down... and he thoroughly enjoyed causing turmoil for himself and his friends.'

It is almost certain that Lili Damita, as an acknowledged expert on the subject, had already worked out that Errol was interested in having sex with men – to him, another form of experimenting as opposed to him yet realising that he had genuine homosexual tendencies – though for the time being he managed to dispel rumours by telling absolutely anyone that 'Tiger Lil', as he called Damita on account of her ferocious temper, was the best 'tumble' he had had in years. Jack Warner, however, was not a man who took uncalculated risks once he had invested money in one of his 'products'. Virulently homophobic, and perhaps not without good reason, for in 1928 his fiancée, Anne Boyar, had been involved with Damita, he summoned Errol to his office, where he read him the riot act. First, he was living openly in sin with Damita. Second, Warner was concerned about the friendship with David Niven and wanted to know if this *had* actually progressed beyond the platonic. According to Marlene Dietrich, one of the regular visitors to the Garden of Alla at the time, it had. She told me, 'Carole Lombard was a very good friend of mine who spent much of her time with these twilight boys. One morning when she went over to Niven's place, she found him in bed with Errol Flynn. They maintained that they were not gay in the conventional sense, but just fooling around for fun. None of us thought it such a big deal, though. Lots of actors slept with each other if there were no women around.'

Whether Jack Warner actually *ordered* Errol to either marry or leave Hollywood is another matter, and it is unlikely that the ever-contrary Australian would have heeded such an instruction. In his memoirs, he admits that his thoughts on marriage at the time were 'gloomy', having seen what the institution had done to his parents. Damita, however, pressed him into making a commitment, and the 'deal' was clinched a few days later during a trip to Mexico, when the couple stayed at Carmen Figueroa's home in Mexico City. Here, while Lili Damita was 'catching up' on her friendship with Carmen, Errol was introduced to and spent a lot of time smoking pot and philosophising with one of Figueroa's pals, the painter Diego Rivera. The artist was best known perhaps for his 'Man At The Crossroads' mural erected in New York's Rockefeller Centre in 1933, which would later be painted over because it included a portrait of Lenin.

It was under Rivera's brief tutelage that Errol was encouraged in some of his less redeemable qualities. Rivera had married another Mexican painter, Frida Kahlo, in 1928 (they would subsequently divorce and remarry), a semi-invalid whose work, mostly torturous-looking self-portraits, reflected the suffering and mental turmoil wrought upon her by being forced to live with a man who treated her like dirt. Rivera's doctrine was as simple as it was abhorrent: while men were emotionally equipped to deal with being 'fucked and forgotten', women should be categorised with dogs and 'other lowly hysterical species'. They should never be allowed to step out of line, the law of Zarathustra should apply wherein they should permanently remain the servants and recreation of the warrior, they should be thrashed regularly, and most important of all, they should be regarded as utterly dispensable. For the rest of his life Errol would adhere to Rivera's theories, with one exception – his dogs would generally be treated with more respect than the women in his life. Many years later, Earl Conrad would ask Errol what 'intellectual accord' he had searched for in his women, bearing in mind that he was a very knowledgeable man, and Errol would respond, seriously, 'I missed the mental stimulation when I was younger. From the time I began to have women on the assembly-line basis, I discovered that the only thing you need, want or should have is the absolutely physical. No mind at all. A woman's *mind* will get in the way.'

In Mexico, Damita told Errol as much about herself as she wanted him to know. Born Liliane Madeleine Carré in Bordeaux in 1901, from an early age she had aspired towards a career in the French music hall. In 1917 she had become one of Mistinguett's chorus girls. Three years later, by which time she had changed her name to Lili Damita and become the mistress of Alfonso XIII of Spain, she had taken over from Mistinguett in the Casino de Paris revue, *On Dit Ça*, though her reviews had not been particularly good, and soon afterwards she had headed for Vienna, where she had worked the cabaret circuit. Here she had met the very same Michael Curtiz, then unknown outside Europe, whose name would become synonymous with that of Errol Flynn. Curtiz put her into *Red Heels*, a landmark in Austrian cinema, but Damita had not been in any hurry to make another film. Soon after its completion she moved to Berlin, where she appeared in a number of revues, including, for several performances, *Broadway* with Marlene Dietrich. At the beginning of 1928, she returned to Paris to appear in a revue at the Wagram with Marze Dubas – the French equivalent of Gracie Fields – where she had been 'discovered' by Sam Goldwyn, on an annual star-search of Europe, hoping to find a new Garbo or Pola Negri. Damita's first Hollywood movie was *The Rescue*, opposite Ronald Colman, but the film that really got her noticed was *Bridge of San Luis Rey*, which she made for Warner Brothers. After that, she played leading lady to Cary Grant and Gary Cooper.

Errol's 'quickie' wedding to Lili Damita took place on 20 June 1935 – his 26th birthday – in Yuma, Arizona. The couple were flown there in a plane piloted by their friend, Bud Ernst. Both signed their names in the register Errol missing out the 'Leslie' and stating his nationality as Irish, and Damita conveniently docking eight years off her age so that she could be the same age as her new husband. The next day they flew back to Hollywood and attended a honeymoon party at the Venice Amusement Park given by Carole Lombard and Marlene Dietrich. The latter was snapped by a photographer sliding down a helter-skelter with her arms around Damita's waist. 'Some people tried to make a great deal out of that picture, and another with Claudette Colbert, who was also at the party,' Marlene told me. 'And if they'd have printed the entire photograph the public would have seen some of the others sliding down after us, including Randolph Scott with his arms round Carole Lombard. Nobody suggested that *they* were more than just friends, like they did with Damita and myself. The truth is, I couldn't *stand* the woman. I thought she was bad for him, and I wasn't the only one.'

The Flynn marriage was certainly no match made in heaven. Errol was far too set in his ways to change, and Damita was as domineering and possessive as she was beautiful. The couple's rows, most of them quite ferocious and conducted in the glare of the public eye, would become legendary, so much so that some reporters actually complained if they attended a function and there was *not* a rumpus. Both swore like troopers, Errol knocked Damita around, and she had a fondness for throwing things: over the years Errol would nurse bumps on his head caused by plates, pans and other household objects, and once he suffered concussion after she hit him with a champagne bottle. Their making up was equally loud. According to any number of eye-witness reports, the noise they made while having sex at the Garden of Alla could be heard out in the street. When showering after a tennis or boxing match, Errol would show off his latest 'battle' injuries – even the long jagged scar caused by the knife-wielding Sinhalese rickshaw man was less consequential than the painful weals on his back and buttocks that had been inflicted by his wife's fingernails. One shocked reporter, asked to inspect Errol's bruised scrotum, was told, 'Lili fucks with all the glory and passion of a thousand French whores rolled into one. Come to think of it, Lili could fuck for France!'

Errol's marriage coincided with Warner Brothers' search for a suitable actor to replace Robert Donat in the swashbuckling epic, *Captain Blood*, which was about to begin shooting. Based on the novel by Rafael Sabatini, this had originally been scripted for Rudolph Valentino back in 1923, but after he had turned it down in favour of *Monsieur Beaucaire*, the part had gone to the substantially less photogenic J. Warren Kerrigan. After these two productions, however, costume dramas had taken a sudden nose-dive in popularity, but in 1934 they had been revived: *Treasure Island*, *David Copperfield* and *The Count of Monte Cristo* had broken all records at the box office, while MGM were currently shooting *Anna Karenina* and *Mutiny on the Bounty*.

Robert Donat, who had portrayed the hero in *The Count of Monte Cristo*, had dropped out of *Captain Blood* following a disagreement with Jack Warner over his contract, and the studio had flown into a panic: 22 actors were selected to make screen tests from an original list of over 50, an operation unheard of in those days, and one which would only be capped by the Scarlett O'Hara hunt a few years later. The director of the film was Michael Curtiz who, though he could never forget a female face – especially one as pretty as Lili Damita's – could not remember her husband's fleeting appearance in *The Case of the Curious Bride*. Indeed, it is said that he actually had to check to see if Errol was still on the studio's payroll. Persuaded by Damita, however, he invited Errol to make a test – and offered him the part.

Errol's test scene was with Olivia de Havilland, the nineteen-year-old actress he had met while being considered for *A Midsummer Night's Dream*, who had already been signed to play Peter Blood's love interest in the film. Both were shot in full costume, but whereas Curtiz was thrilled with his discovery, Hal Wallis, the studio's head of production, had some reservations. The next day he summoned Errol to his office and told him that the frilly cuffs and shirt-front he had worn for the test had made him look like a 'pansy'. For once, Errol kept his counsel and agreed to make whatever adjustments to his costume, or himself, the studio deemed necessary. He needed the part...and the money.

Captain Blood tells the story of the young Irish pacifist doctor who, after treating a wounded enemy leader during the Monmouth Rebellion of 1685, is accused of treason against King James II and condemned to be hanged by the infamous Judge Jeffreys, along with a number of others. The sentence is then commuted to deportation, and Blood and his friends are dispatched as slaves to Port Royal in Jamaica. Here, having been bought by the lovely Arabella (de Havilland) to save him from being sent to the mines by her ruthless plantation owner uncle, Colonel Bishop (Lionel Atwill), he becomes a favourite of the ageing governor after curing him of his gout, and also falls in love with Arabella.

When pirates attack the town and the boat which Blood and his men have been about to make their escape in is destroyed, they seize the marauders' vessel and as pirates themselves become the scourge of the high seas. A series of adventures follow: a 'partnership' between Blood and the cunning Captain Levasseur (Basil Rathbone) which ends with a duel to the death and a spectacular sea battle (using eighteen-foot scale models, and footage from the film of 1923 to cut down on costs), wherein Blood and his men save Port Royal from the invading French. Blood is aware that if he is captured by Colonel Bishop, now the new governor, he will hang – but *unaware* that England has a new

King, William III, who has pardoned them. All ends well when he is appointed Governor of Jamaica and, of course, he gets his girl.

Captain Blood was not, however, without its quota of production problems. Two days into shooting, Errol collapsed with a recurrence of the malaria that had plagued him since his days in New Guinea, but when the studio nurse told him that filming would have to be wound up for the day if he left the set, he downed a bottle of brandy and returned to work. That same evening, he was summoned to Jack Warner's office and accused of being drunk on duty. His reaction was to tell Warner, 'Sport, go fuck yourself!' before adding, and setting what would be a Flynn precedent, that unless the studio offered him a substantial salary increase, he would not be returning to the set at all! In these, the halcyon days of the studio system, any other actor would have been fired on the spot for insolence. Everyone at Warner Brothers knew only too well, however, that Errol *was* Peter Blood, and that to begin looking for a replacement at this stage in the production would have been courting financial disaster. His salary went up from $150 to $750 a week.

Neither did the young Australian get along with Michael Curtiz, who always pretended that his command of the English language – aside from the expletives which he seemed to thrive on – was so bad that he could win any argument by 'not understanding' what the opposition was yelling about. Curtiz could not stand Ross Alexander, the young actor playing Blood's side-kick, Jeremy Pitt. Tall, dashing, extremely handsome and muscular, Alexander had made a name for himself on Broadway in the perhaps now appropriately titled *Let Us Be Gay*, during the run of which he had had an affair with the leading man, Rod La Roque. After that, Alexander had played Demetrius in Reinhardt's *A Midsummer Night's Dream*. When the homophobic Curtiz suspected that Alexander and Errol may have been getting a little too 'close' – this was true, though they were very discreet – he told the rest of the cast, in front of them, 'Those two are just another couple of no good son-of-a-bitch faggots!' Errol exploded, 'Shut your mouth, you Hungarian motherfucker, or I'll shut it for you!'

An uneasy truce was maintained between Curtiz and the two actors when Jack Warner had intervened, though this did not prevent the pair from camping it up on the set, and one or two of their more homoerotic scenes actually made it past the censor. 'What's going *on* between you two?' barks Colonel Bishop, while Blood tends Jeremy's injured knee, massaging the shapely limb perhaps a little *too* sensually, while elsewhere the equally homophobic Atwill was outraged to find Blood stepping out of character and addressing him as 'my dear' and 'darling'. There was also a tremendous bust-up between Errol and Curtiz over Ross Alexander's somewhat exuberant armpits which, Errol declared, 'turned him on like hot twin fannies'. These became the focus of the cameraman's attention when, having been stripped to the waist, Jeremy is shackled to the stocks and whipped before being rescued by his friend. Curtiz was so paranoid that the scene would get him into trouble with the Hays Office that he turned up on the set with a razor. Errol grabbed this and threatened to slit the director's throat should he remove so much as one hair from Alexander's 'magnificent oxters', so the scene was left uncut, and received few complaints.

Atwill also complained to Curtiz about Errol's 'attempted philandering' with Olivia de Havilland. Errol apparently *wanted* to have an affair with her, but for once was unsure how to make the first move. Unlike Lili Damita and most of the other women he had slept with, de Havilland was neither earthy nor worldly, though she admitted to appreciating his 'Tazzie' sense of humour – which included turning his back on Curtiz and loudly breaking wind, or silencing the director's insults by calling him a 'bollockless scrotum' or a 'frog-eyed gallah'. She did not, however, take too kindly to some of the stunts he pulled on her – such as stealing into her dressing room and nailing her shoes to the floor or hiding a dead snake inside the voluminous pantaloons she wore under her costume. 'I had a lot to learn about the sensibilities of young ladies,' he later recalled, after she had rebuked him for the latter incident, adding, 'I must have spent too much of my early life with men.'

Long before *Captain Blood* had finished shooting, word spread around the film community that a new star was in its ascendancy. 'His name is on every wagging tongue in Hollywood,' observed *Film Weekly*'s W. H. Mooring. 'Experts forecast for him a career in romantic roles comparable with that of Ronald Colman.' When he read this, Errol invited the journalist to lunch with him at the studio canteen. Mooring, when asked to make a choice from the menu, quipped that he would have whatever Errol was having. This appealed to the actor's offbeat sense of humour and he ordered fillet steak, preceded by raw eggs in tomato and Worcester sauce! Mooring was permitted to watch the afternoon's filming, and wrote in his column:

> The eggs must have been good ones, for he put in a performance that for sheer agility and energy wouldn't have shamed Douglas Fairbanks in his prime. Cutlass smote cutlass with a clash of steel; shrieks and groans (not all of them acted) arose in all directions; full-throated yells mingled with curses; and an appalling stench of sizzling greasepaint, sweat, kerosene and gunpowder filled the set.

At another 'press' lunch, this time with *Picturegoer*'s Frederick Russell, Errol spoke frankly of his likes, dislikes and foibles picked up during his years as a student at the prestigious Lycée Louis le Grand in Paris, a fabrication of his own, along with the admission that Peter Blood's sword was the same one that had been given to his ancestor, Lord Terence Flynn, by Monmouth in 1686, which had been added to the impressive list supplied by Warner's publicity department:

> I'm afraid that I can't paint, sketch or play any musical instruments. I hate alarm clocks and weddings – well, my own was okay, I guess – and I'm terrified of dentists and spiders. Thunderstorms and heavy rain, I adore! How do I keep fit? By breathing through my *nose*, sir! And my burning desire, were I not an actor, would be to become a bartender! I like all kinds of sports, boxing mostly, and my preferred indoor sport is poker. Strip-poker is best when there are two gentlemen and a lady – you strip her, I'll poke her! And my most prized possession apart from my sword is a gold cross given to me by a dying missionary in New Guinea.

Captain Blood was a phenomenal success at the box office, turning Errol Flynn into an overnight sensation. The usually hypercritical Warren Reeve of *Photoplay* enthused:

> When people watch him, Clark Gable suddenly seems a little old, Leslie Howard perhaps is stodgy after all, and Herbert Marshall's

suave charm all at once seems empty and dull. For this youth's blood races and his eyes slash and his muscles *move*. The restless swell of far away seas is in the curve of his hair, the tense threat of the jungle is in his quick, smooth stride, distant sunswept horizons lie in his eyes. Only the gods know what lies ahead of a fellow who makes good and becomes the greatest shot in the arm this town's had for years.

Many of those involved with the production of *Captain Blood* – Guy Kibbee, Henry Stephenson, Basil Rathbone, Robert Barrat and of course Olivia de Havilland – became Flynn 'regulars'. Michael Curtiz would be regarded as 'his' director, though they rarely had anything but contempt for one another. Erich Wolfgang Korngold would be seen as 'his' composer. Already known in Austria and Germany for his operas and theatre scores, particularly his music for Max Reinhardt's productions, Korngold had fled the Nazi persecution of the Jews in 1934, having been invited to Hollywood by Reinhardt to arrange Mendelssohn's score for his *A Midsummer Night's Dream*. Were it not for his 'Flynn' scores, it is unlikely that Korngold's career in America would have endured.

Errol's relationship with Ross Alexander did not survive. The reckless young star's first 'lavender' marriage to actress Anna Freel came to a bloody conclusion shortly after *Captain Blood* was completed when she blew her brains out. Alexander then married Anne Nagel, who appeared in several of his films, but this union too was doomed. In January 1937, deeply in debt and his career on the skids, Alexander shot himself on his ranch. He was just 29, and soon after his death it was rumoured that he had taken his life because he believed Ronald Reagan had been signed to Warner Brothers to replace him. Although he would work with Reagan in the future, Errol would always detest him and hold him personally responsible for his lover's death.

The success of *Captain Blood* prevented Errol from being fired by Warner Brothers. Jack Warner would never forgive him for his 'more-dosh-or-I-quit' ultimatum, yet now he was forced into swallowing humble pie, knowing that he was on to a surefire winner. On the other hand, Errol's new celebrity status heralded the collapse of his marriage. Even at the film's première, Lili

Damita expressed her sadness at all the attention her husband was getting, telling reporters through her tears, 'I'm crying because now that he's about to become famous, he won't want me any more!'

This was perfectly true, though even by Hollywood standards the couple's separation was bizarre. Errol and Damita had recently leased a house at 8946 Appian Way, overlooking Laurel Canyon. She stayed on there until the lease ran out at the end of the year, while Errol moved into the property at 601 North Linden Drive which David Niven had just begun renting from Rosalind Russell, sharing the expenses, and sometimes the lovers, on a 50-50 basis. 'He was not a kind man,' Niven reflected, 'bu+ ·n those careless days he was fun to be with, and those days were the best of Flynn.'

The acid-tongued gossip columnist, Louella Parsons, wrote at the time that Niven and Flynn could not have been better matched room-mates because both were so overtly macho and 'connoisseurs of the fairer sex'. 'They said the same thing about Cary Grant and Randolph Scott, and those two were lovers for donkey's years,' Marlene Dietrich said, with a chuckle. 'And the way they treated the women in their lives, Flynn and Niven *deserved* each other.'

Errol's sex drive at this time is said to have been astronomical: a suntanned, muscular, drop-dead gorgeous young actor who had suddenly been catapulted to stardom could hardly go wrong in a town which was *full* of beautiful people, and he exploited himself quite unashamedly. He and Niven shared lovers of both sexes, sometimes several in a single night, and at least twice a week he drove over to Laurel Canyon to 'see to' his wife, with whom he still insisted upon attending society functions, where they would put on tremendous shows of disaffection, each trying to out bitch the other. After an argument, Damita would pout her lips and Errol would blurt out one of his plum 'pulling' lines, such as, 'I'm feeling as horny as a three peckered billy-goat!' and the pair would rush off and have sex somewhere, only to return half an hour later and start all over again!

Warner Brothers, meanwhile, set about deciding upon Errol's next film. He had been pencilled in for two, *Anthony Adverse* and *The Charge of the Light Brigade*, and Lili Damita secured him an audition with *Boy Wonder* producer Irving Thalberg, then casting for *Romeo and Juliet*. Thalberg's wife, Norma Shearer, had been signed to play Juliet, and John Barrymore to play Mercutio, but as yet Thalberg and the director, George Cukor, had not agreed on a leading man. Neither of them, however, wanted Errol Flynn. 'Too tall and too brash,' was how Cukor saw him, and Romeo went to the more 'refined and genteel' Leslie Howard, regardless of the fact that at 42 he was far too old for the role. (This was no problem for Hollywood, of course, who simply 'aged up' everyone else in the film.)

To quell the rumours – which were of course true – that Errol and Lili Damita had split up, the pair were rushed into a two-reeler entitled *Pirate Party On Catalina Island*. This short, filmed in Technicolor, had no storyline as such, but boasted a whole galaxy of Hollywood stars including John Gilbert, Marion Davies, Virginia Bruce and Cary Grant, who all appeared to be having a lot of fun. And by the time this was in the can, Errol had been informed that he would be playing Major Geoffrey Vickers in *The Charge Of The Light Brigade* – a large chunk of Hollywood hokum which gloriously fictionalises one of the key events in the Crimean War, in which Britain, France and Turkey go against Russia.

Anita Louise was to have been Errol's love interest in the film, but following a contractual hitch she was replaced by Olivia de Havilland. Patric Knowles, a twenty-four year old British actor recently arrived in Hollywood, was engaged to play Errol's brother. Tall, extremely handsome but somewhat naive, Knowles fell under Errol's spell at once and became part of the gang – attending the drunken revelries and same-sex parties, never afraid of letting his hair down, but stopping short of having an actual affair with Errol, much as he is alleged to have wanted to, terrified that if a scandal erupted he would be forced to give up his career.

Another British star who appeared in the film was fellow rebel rouser was David Niven, who in one of his first major Hollywood roles portrayed Captain Randall. Niven would fondly remember two incidents which occurred during shooting. The first took place when the English-language-murdering Michael Curtiz summoned the riderless mounts in preparation for the film's final scene – bellowing down the megaphone, 'Bring on the empty horses!' Forty years later, Niven would use this as the title for a volume of his autobiography. The second incident was Curtiz's *classic* outburst when, during one of their not infrequent on-set blues, Errol had called the director 'a thick as pig-shit bowl of goulash.' Curtiz had yelled back, 'You lousy faggot bum, you think I know fuck nothing. Well, let me tell you something – I know fuck *all*!'

The famous charge had taken place on 25 October 1854 during the Battle of Balaclava, when owing to an error of command 673 soldiers of the British Light Brigade had galloped the one and a half miles towards the entrenched Russian artillery, suffering 244 casualties when they had been fired on from all sides. In 1929, a young reporter and historian, Michael Jacoby, began researching the event, and five years later had completed a screenplay, accurate in every historical detail. This had, however, been rejected by every major studio in Hollywood – the general opinion being that few Americans would be interested in seeing a film about a war they had not helped to win – Jack Warner made an offer for the script after the huge success of *The Lives Of A Bengal Lancer*. In doing so, he enabled Hollywood to rewrite and glamorise one of recent history's most tragic episodes.

The greater part of the action takes place in India. Geoffrey and Perry Vickers (Patric Knowles) are dashing officers with the British Army, and both are in love with the same woman (de Havilland). They quarrel, and for a time go their separate ways. Geoffrey saves the life of the chiselling Surat Khan, the Amir of Suristan (C. Henry Gordon), who swears eternal gratitude, only to go back on his word and annihilate Geoffrey's garrison at Chukoti on the Northwest Frontier. Khan then adds insult to injury by rushing off to the Crimea to fight on the side of the Russians, an action which sees the Vickers brothers reunited in revenge. Geoffrey ensures that Perry does not take part in the charge – he has given him and his sweetheart his blessing and knows that there may be no survivors. He (and not Lords Raglan and Cardigan, relegated to bit-parts in the film) then orders the men of the 27th Lancers to advance, while Tennyson's poem flashes across the screen, and they ride to their doom, with the hero plunging his lance into the hated Khan, seconds before he himself dies.

The Charge of the Light Brigade should be considered one of the greatest action films of the thirties, especially on account of its magnificently shot final sequence. The sheer spectacle and magic of this may only be condemned, however, when one learns *how* some of these effects were achieved. Working in close conjunction with Michael Curtiz, the action specialist in charge of the horses was B. Reeves Eason, and between them they devised the appalling 'running W' system which enabled the horses to be brought down on cue. Tripwires were attached to the animals' front legs and connected to wooden posts which were hammered into the ground below camera-line, and once the horse had run its appointed distance, the wire would tauten, causing it to stumble head first and throw its stuntman rider, who of course was *trained* how to fall. During this one sequence alone, filmed in the picturesque San Fernando Valley, over 50 horses were badly injured, and many had to be destroyed. This and the film's glorification of leopard hunting brought so many complaints from anti-animal cruelty organisations – anger which was still widely felt in the fifties, when this was one of the few Flynn films *not* to be rereleased by Warner Brothers – that this quite despicable system was never used again.

The film also provided Errol with his first, though by no means last, on-set brawl. During a rehearsal for the charge, one of the extras, a burly man who for some reason had taken a dislike to him, stuck the point of his lance into Errol's horse's flank, causing the animal to rear up and throw him to the ground. Once he had recovered from the initial shock – and the guffaws of the other extras – Errol marched up to the man, hauled him from his mount, and gave him such a pasting that he had to be taken to hospital.

Two days later there was a second incident in the bar being used by the cast when the bartender, another big man, took exception to Errol's dog, Arno, a schnauzer given to him by Robert Lord, a producer pal. Tired of Arno's persistent cocking of his leg outside his hostelry, the bartender nailed a metal plate to the doorpost, to which he connected a battery-operated device. Upon hearing his dog's hysterical yelping, Errol grabbed the man by the scruff of the neck, dragged him outside, then made *him* urinate against the doorpost!

A frequent visitor to the set was *Motion Picture*'s James Reid, a timid man who was initially shocked by Errol's behaviour and his scathing attitude towards his peers – practising the lance by hurling it at a dummy dressed up as Michael Curtiz – disappearing into his dressing-room with a young woman and purposely leaving the door ajar – telling Jack Warner in front of everyone that he would be leaving Hollywood the moment the picture was finished...*before*, if he met with any opposition, and that he might not return. In his feature headed, *Can Hollywood Hold Errol Flynn?* Reid observed,

Acting, to Errol, is just another adventure in an adventurous life...and he isn't sure that acting, in some of its aspects, is a man's job. Standing in front of a camera, pretending undying love for a girl, speaking soft words to her, makes him uncomfortable. It isn't his idea of a he-man's way of earning a living. That's why he's so convincingly reckless in physically difficult scenes...he's getting twice as much he-man enjoyment out of them. Here is one hero who could give them thrills even if he *never* made love on the screen. When I asked him how long Hollywood would be able to hold him, he looked at me quizzically. Was I joking or serious? 'I'm likely to decide to quit Hollywood any day,' he said, simply and succinctly. He hasn't worked the wanderlust – or the fever for new adventures – out of his system. 'I won't be content,' he replied firmly, 'Until I can live a free life – do the things I want to do, when I want to do them – preferably in the South Seas.'

Jack Warner hit the roof when he learned what his investment had told the press – and so did Errol when Reid reported in his column, 'Errol has very little English accent, The dialogue coach has to groom him, as well as Olivia, in English intonations.' Collaring the journalist in the same bar where the debacle with the barman had occurred, Errol threatened him with a good hiding unless he printed a retraction – until Reid reminded him that, not only had Errol spoken throughout their interview with a thick Irish brogue, he had 'confided' that he had been born in a little town near Belfast! Errol apologised profusely for leading him on, and invited Reid to join him and his friends for a 'tipple' once they had wrapped up the 'Lancers' Quadrille' dance sequence which Curtiz had wanted to shoot in a single take on account of the heat.

Reid accepted – and ended up legless after an eight-hour bender.

Errol's next two films – *Green Light* and *Another Dawn* – would be released during the first half of 1937 when he was not in the United States to read the generally dismissive reviews. The former, providing one does not take the medical details too seriously, was a very *good* film. Based on the novel by Lloyd C. Douglas and ably directed by Frank Borzage, it finally teamed Errol with Anita Louise, a talented and much under-rated actress who would die tragically young. It also featured Margaret Lindsay, who had portrayed Errol's wife in *The Case Of The Curious Bride*, and the distinguished British stage-actor, Sir Cedric Hardwicke.

Errol played ladies man Newell Paige, a surgeon described by himself as, 'The young fellow without too many scruples and not very much courage,' – faults which by the end of the film he has rectified. The deeply-religious Mrs Dexter (Spring Byington), the Bay Tree Hospital's wealthy benefactor, is in need of a life-saving operation which only Dr Endicott (Henry O'Neill) the senior physician and Paige's mentor, is qualified to perform. When he fails to turn up on time Paige steps in, and he is doing well until halfway through the procedure when Endicott arrives. Taking over, he bungles the surgery and the patient dies.

To save his career, Endicott declares that Mrs Dexter's death was an accident, leaving Paige – the only surgeon to be seen going into theatre – heroically shouldering the blame. He is allowed to resign his post rather than suffer the humiliation of dismissal and meets Mrs Dexter's daughter, Phyllis (Louise), who initially does not know his identity – like his pretty assistant, Nurse Ogilvie (Lindsay) she falls in love with him.

Near the end of his tether, the agnostic Paige visits the polio-stricken Dean Harcourt (Hardwicke), Mrs Dexter's spiritual adviser who pontificates on faith and everlasting life, telling Page of the radical changes these effected on his life when he too had been at an all-time low,

> I had ambitions once, and then I became as I am. I preferred death to wasting my life as an impotent cripple. Then suddenly I discovered that my course is upward – in spite of everything I get the signal to go forward. I've been delayed there's no telling how

long, but eventually I get the green light and I know that once again I have commenced that irresistible onward drive!

Spurred on by Harcourt's diatribe – though feigning indifference –and the fact that Phyllis now knows who he really is and holds him responsible for her mother's death – Paige leaves for Montana, where he joins a former colleague, Stafford (Walter Abel) in his development of a vaccine for spotted fever, a malady which has claimed the lives of all those who have previously searched for a cure. Paige is against animal experimentation – 'They don't have to justify *their* lives, I do!' – so he injects himself with the disease (this does not happen in the Douglas novel) to see if his serum works, and develops a raging fever. All ends well, however. A distraught Endicott confesses his faux-pas at the sick-bed: if his protegé dies, he says, *he* will be as responsible for his death as he was Mrs Dexter's. And in the final frame we see the reformed agnostic attending one of Dean Harcourt's sermons at the cathedral.

Although the film was a big success, mindless of the critics, today it appears terribly dated and sadly is chiefly remembered for its music by Max Steiner, whose superb score for *The Charge of the Light Brigade* had added much to *its* impact with cinema audiences.

Born in Vienna in 1888, as a child prodigy Steiner had been a pupil of Mahler. At fourteen he had composed his first opera, and in the Twenties he had arrived in New York to write and conduct for Florenz Ziegfeld's 6th Avenue Theatre. With the advent of sound he had moved to Hollywood, where an early success had been his score for *King Kong* – the first of his *twenty-six* Oscar nominations. His most successful scores would be those he composed for *Gone With The Wind* and *Now Voyager*. Errol was *so* captivated by Steiner's music, he declared at the time, that he was 'willing to overlook' Steiner's Jewishness – an uncalled for, immature statement which nevertheless resulted in this phenomenally talented man becoming a Flynn regular, working on thirteen more of his films.

The second film released in 1937 was *Another Dawn*, an atmospheric, tangled tale of unrequited love set in a remote Sahara outpost – 'A long, long way from Tipperary,' the opening credits proclaim – directed by William Dieterle and with Kay Francis's name, not Errol's, heading the bill.

The dashing, almost annoyingly polite Captain Roark pilots his own plane into the outpost just as his commanding officer, Colonel Wister (Ian Hunter) is about to go home on leave. Errol's character is not seen on screen again until a third of the way into the film. En route to England, where with some improbability they also happen to be staying at the same country manor, Wister meets and falls in love with Julia Ashton (Francis), though he knows that their union will always be one-sided – she tells him that the great love of her life has been shot down in a plane during World War I, and that she will never feel so deeply for anyone else. Despite this, the pair return to the outpost as man and wife.

Here, Julia is virtually thrown into Roark's arms by her husband's persistent absence with his cavalry division, fighting the Arabs. Everything about Roark reminds her of her lost amour, yet even though she is hopelessly attracted to him – and he her – morality prevails because they both respect Wister too much to ever wish to hurt him. This persistent denial naturally makes them miserable. When Roark is badly wounded during a skirmish, Julia's distress is such that she feels she must leave the Sahara before all *three* lives are destroyed – Roark's, upon his recovery, to request a transfer which Webster denies him. It then emerges that Roark's sister (Frieda Inescourt) has secretly loved Wister for years, that to cope with this she has contented herself with watching and sharing his life as an outsider without his knowledge. Wister then becomes aware of the truth and pays the ultimate sacrifice so that the lovers might be together – stealing Roark's plane, he goes out on a mission to bomb an enemy dam, and is shot down.

Another Dawn, melodramatic and dated perhaps, is like its predecessor chiefly remembered for its haunting score, this time by Korngold who the previous year had won an Oscar for his music for *Anthony Adverse*. Korngold would later incorporate much of the theme for the Flynn picture into his violin concerto, immortalised by Jascha Heifetz.

Errol's next film, Mark Twain's *The Prince And The Pauper*, saw him in a role which the critics declared to be a return to form. He played Miles Hendon, the irascible young soldier who allies himself to the future King Edward VI in the England of 1547, when the tyrannical Henry VIII lies on his deathbed deliberating over who will become Lord Protector – the kindly Duke of Norfolk (Henry Stephenson) or the calculating Earl of Hertford (Claude Rains).

As a prank, Edward changes clothes with Tom Canty, a beggar-boy lookalike, but their game turns sour when Edward, disguised as the pauper, is driven from the palace by the Captain of the Guards (Alan Hale), and discovers what life is really like in the London backstreets. While the mob is beating him for asserting his royal authority – which he lauds over the people upon hearing of Henry's death – he is rescued by Hendon, a spectacular entrance by Errol in the film's 50th minute.

For a while, Hendon thinks this boy is mad, until he learns who he really is, and henceforth becomes Edward's protector, while the evil Hertford susses his boy's identity: sending the hapless Norfolk to the Tower, he convinces the court that Edward/Tom is acting strangely because he is mentally ill, dupes him into naming him Protector, arranges the coronation, then sends out the Captain of the Guard to kill the real prince. All ends well, however, when Hendon uncovers the plot: after fighting and killing Tom Canty's brutal father, he engages in a duel to the death with the Captain of the Guard on the morning of the coronation, delivering Edward – rags and all – to Westminster Abbey, seconds before the Archbishop is about to place the crown on the impostor's head.

The true stars of *The Prince And The Pauper*, of course, were Billy and Bobby Mauch, the twins who played the boys. Throughout much of the action, Errol appears as little more than an attractive bystander, though he does get to play a brief romantic interlude with a barmaid (Phyllis Barry), tossing a coin to decide if he is to spend the night with her, but leaving her when duty calls. Errol and Alan Hale also became close friends while making the film – a friendship which would endure for life and see the pair starring together in eleven more films, though this was the only one where they were enemies. The stretched-out coronation scene was also a clever marketing ploy by Warner Brothers to cash in on the tremendous publicity being effected by the soon-to-be coronation of King George VI, following the abdication crisis, and it worked. The film was a huge success on both sides of the Atlantic.

By the time he had completed this film, however, Errol had grown restless and longed for an adventure that could not be found on any Hollywood backlot. 'The sea raged inside me – I still had difficulty realising I was here in the mixed-up world of Hollywood,' he would recall, adding how, when he went to sleep at night he could still hear the sounds of the ocean that had lulled him to sleep as a boy. Astonishingly, 'between working, socialising and screwing', he managed to rattle off a series of reports about the so-called Hollywood jungle for the *Sydney Reporter*, as well as a number of poems, a clutch of short stories and a full length novel.

Beam Ends, published in 1937, was a largely autobiographical account of the *Sirocco*'s 1930 journey from Sydney to New Guinea. The book was not a massive seller, though it did spark off a storm of controversy when the press realised that the cinema's newest hero had lived a life way beyond the imagination of any Hollywood public relations man. And for reasons which no-one quite understood, not least of all its author, the book was banned in Germany when Hitler declared it 'unfit for the consumption of young Nazis'.

W. H. Mooring, who had championed Errol during the shooting of *Captain Blood*, visited the set of *The Prince And The Pauper*, and was surprised by Errol's attitude towards the Hollywood hands which were feeding him.

Errol Flynn is in a dangerous position. He got to the top almost in one leap, and in Hollywood, for a variety of reasons, it is risky to do this trick too quickly for it naturally creates a certain feeling of acute jealousy amongst those who haven't had such fine luck. But, unfortunately, something else has happened to Mr Flynn. He has been seized with a new ambition – he wants to be a screen writer! Now he has fine muscle, a clear brain and unlimited energy. He has handsome features and a screen way with the ladies. But he will need more if he is to consolidate his position at the top of the Hollywood tree. His flair for writing may be indulged as a nice sort of pastime when he retreats to his own fairy castle in the hills – a castle he made in and OUT of Hollywood . . . Yet he simply cannot be satisfied with what life has to give. Success to Errol Flynn is nothing compared to the thrill he can find in seeking it. He is a hunter after hidden treasure which, once found, loses all its glamour. I hope he will calm down and stick to his acting, but I have my doubts.

In September 1936, Errol's prayers were effectively answered by the arrival of a telegram from Herman F. Erben, announcing that his old chum was on his way to California with a cargo of 1,200 monkeys. The animals, his only assets, were to be sold to the Rockefeller Institute for experimentation, and the money raised was to go towards the 'mission' Erben planned for Errol and himself. Errol, it would appear, had written to Erben about his marital problems and the tediousness of the film world, and Erben had come up with the ideal solution. Erben was about to embark on a medical expedition to South America and was expected to be away for several months. This, the Austrian declared, would allow Errol ample time to propose to the newspaper magnate, William Randolph Hearst, that the two of them should be employed as official correspondents of the Spanish Civil War!

3

Swinging Swords and Grappling Hooks

'In the Hollywood jungle it was no trouble for me to say with a laugh,
and mean it, "You can stick this place where the monkey stuck
the coconuts!"'

In his memoirs, Errol confessed that he had sympathised with the
Republican government in Spain, but that he would have
augmented either side in the conflict just to get away from
Hollywood and his domineering wife. He certainly did not tell Lili
Damita about his plans, which was why she jumped to the
conclusion that a woman was involved, and an important one at
that if Errol was going to such lengths to cover his tracks,
something he had never done thus far in their marriage.
Therefore, when Errol and Erben checked into New York's St
Moritz Hotel, having flown to Chicago then completed their
journey by bus, Damita was already there with a Warner Brothers
publicity man.

Jack Warner, who had perhaps pushed the Flynns into getting
married in the first place, had been pestered by the press, having
heard that their marriage was on the rocks. The couple were
therefore obliged to pose for photographers, embracing and
smiling radiantly, to prove to the world that such rumours were
not true. *The Green Light* was about to receive its New York
première, and the studio could not afford the adverse publicity.

Warner, who had around $2 million invested in Errol's short-term future, *was* told that he was going to Spain – 'to follow in Hemingway's footsteps' – and *begged* him to reconsider before jeopardising his safety. As usual, Errol was only interested in pleasing himself: lingering in New York long enough only to receive treatment for another attack of gonorrhoea, he and Erben sailed for England on the *Queen Mary* on 24 February 1937.

Since their previous adventure, Erben had travelled extensively in his capacity as medical officer with the Austro-American TransAsiatic Expedition – through Palestine, Iran and Iraq and via the Khyber Pass into India, then on to Burma, Indochina and finally to Peking. So far as is known, Erben had convinced Errol that he had been invited to join the Spanish Medical Aid Committee – the organisation was in dire need of doctors to man the makeshift clinics and hospitals, mostly in convents and stately homes in and around Madrid – and there is no evidence whatsoever to suggest that Errol had any knowledge of his companion's *ulterior* motive in travelling to Spain.

Errol's indisposition allowed Lili Damita a little more time to attempt to outsmart him. She found out that he had planned on staying in London for several days before moving on to Paris, so when he arrived at the Plaza Athenée Hotel, again she was there before him, this time occupying his suite and with a press conference in attendance. Again, the couple put on an act for the photographs which were wired back to Hollywood, and for four days – leaving Erben to his own devices – the couple took in the city's nightlife.

Their first evening was spent at Chez Kornilof, a Russian-styled cabaret-restaurant much favoured by émigrés: Marlene Dietrich had sung there in 1933, as had Gracie Fields, and one of the regulars in 1937 was the Russian bass, Fyodor Chaliapin, for whom Errol had tremendous admiration. 'Chaliapin could, if he'd wanted to, have had a voice as big as Trotsky's during the Russian revolution, but he chose to remain an artist,' he recalled. Another regular was Chaliapin's common-law wife, Damia, between the two wars the greatest chanteuse in France, if not in the whole of Europe. In 1974, four years before her death, Damia remembered the couple. She told me: 'Damita, I never liked. She was terrified that somebody would run off with him, yet she did little to encourage him to love her because she was so nasty towards him. Some years before, I had recorded a song called "Celle Que Vous Attendez", an adaptation of an Irish ballad, "My Little Cottage In Kildare", which Flynn knew well. I even managed to get him to sing a couple of verses along with me – after he'd had a few drinks, of course!'

During their second evening in Paris, the Flynns visited an altogether less respectable establishment: the infamous, gay-patronised Jockey Club, where the artiste-in-residence was the outrageous Kiki de Montparnasse, arguably the most vulgar woman to have ever trodden the boards of a music hall. Errol was far less interested in her *cafardiste* songs than he was in her 'candle-snuffing' routine after her act, using the lips of her vagina. These outings aside, however, his sojourn in Paris was not a happy one. Each time the couple returned to their suite, the arguments would begin, with Errol cursing so profanely and Damita smashing so much crockery that they were told never to return to the Plaza Athenée.

On 26 March, Errol and Erben arrived in Barcelona, where they stayed for six days as guests of the Warner Brothers office there before moving on to Valencia, then Madrid, where they publicly declared their opposition to General Franco – and Errol gave a brief radio announcement detailing the Hearst commission. Erben, he stressed, was his official photographer and closest friend. What also seems certain is that someone – with his record for conning people, possibly Errol himself – had promised the Loyalists $1 million, collected from sympathisers in Hollywood, in return for the privileged treatment he and his friend were receiving at a time when virtually no Americans were allowed into Spain: the very best hotels and food, as much drinks and cigarettes as they wanted, a chauffeur-driven car, and access to the classiest whores in town.

In 1959, Errol would include an 'over-Hemingwayed' account of his adventure in *My Wicked, Wicked Ways* – of how he and 'Gerrit Koets' had narrowly missed being blown up by a car bomb (untrue) and of how he had been injured in a skirmish after dining with General von Helmuth, who had defected to the Loyalists (partly true). And of course, there had been a young woman to add a little romance to the proceedings – this one's name was

Estrella, and baptised his 'symbolisation of Spain'. However, once Errol had bedded her in the heat of the battle, and when Loyalist officials began enquiring after their $1 million, Errol decided that there would be little point in outstaying his welcome. 'Now I could leave Spain,' he recalled. 'It was all out of me, the deep melancholy, the flight from Lili, from the studio tension, the death-wish.'

The report which reached Jack Warner in April 1937, however – in Errol's own distinguishable handwriting – told a far different and, it would appear, more truthful story. For one thing, Erben's real name was used throughout. Errol explained how the pair had been ensconced on the third floor of Madrid's Grand Via Hotel, a plush establishment opposite the imposing Telephone Building, and one whose rooms were considerably cheaper than others in the city.

At nine-thirty the next morning I found out just why it was so cheap. If you've spent the last twenty hours riding over shell-pitted roads at 80 mph, you rather like to lie abed for a while the next morning, so I was in no mood for levity when awakened by a sibilant *whoo-ooshing*, followed by a loud crash. I opened a tentative eye and peered through the window. A few yards away, bathed in the morning sunlight, stood the huge Telephone Building – it had holes in it, large gaping holes, and from one of them dust, bricks and debris were at that moment still falling. I rose and left my bed rapidly. Arriving in the lobby, we wrapped ourselves in bathrobes and dignity and approached the clerk ... who expressed polite interest when we informed him that the view had three spanking new holes in it.

He glanced at his watch. 'Ah, yes! Nine forty-five. The enemy warm up their guns with three shells at the Telephone Building every morning. You may return to your rooms now in complete safety. There'll be no more bombardment until tomorrow morning at the same time!'

Errol and Erben did not go back to their rooms, but moved to the cellar, where they spent much of the next few weeks camped out with other foreign correspondents, deposed government officials and wounded soldiers. Errol befriended a middle-aged Spanish revolutionary named Pedro, and appointed him his driver.

All the guns and bombs in Spain only frightened me half as much as Pedro. who wore an outsized revolver at the ready even when he went to bed. He piloted us around Madrid and the front sectors with unquenchable ardour... driving at 120 kilometres an hour over bad roads and turning around to the back seat for a friendly chat at the same time. When I add that he had the Spanish habit of talking with his hands you'll see what I mean. Just as disaster seemed inevitable, Pedro would take a casual glance at the road, see a shell-hole, and with one hand swerve expertly around it on two wheels, then return to the conversation, all without batting an eye. Once, coming back from the Guadalajara front, we looked out and saw a huge tri-motored bomber swooping down over the road. Pedro kept the car careening from side to side to make a more difficult target for the machine-gunners above, and just as I was about to feel I'd rather be bombed than drive on like this, Pedro jammed on his brakes. The car immediately turned around twice in its tracks like a top, and we wrenched open the doors and dove headlong into a ditch as a single burst of machine-gun fire cut a neat dotted line down the length of the automobile.

It was Pedro who secured Errol and Erben a virtually impossible-to-come by night pass so that they could cover the fighting around the University City area after curfew. This was dangerous stuff indeed. On every street corner the pair were accosted by 'committees' – gun-toting officials who examined their papers, usually after manhandling them and adding a few more bruises to their already impressive collection, and were known to fire indiscriminately at anyone attempting to cross the front lines during the blackout. Erben was particularly interested in visiting the Rosales, one of the city's most colourful districts which was now reduced to little more than a pile of rubble. And it was here, in the wide-open plaza, that Errol's career almost came to an abrupt halt.

A few hundred yards away, a machine-gunner sent blasts of flame and lead whipping across every few seconds. Almost immediately, from across the valley a couple of kilometres away, would come the answering flash from the opposing artillery position. Nearly a full second would elapse after we saw the flash before hearing the dull boom, then the whine of the shell as it hurtled overhead into the heart of the city. Erben and I took shelter around the corner of a ruined building. As far as we knew, no shells had landed there for about two weeks. I took a last look at the lines. Across the valley, I saw the now familiar flash, waited for the boom and whine. It came closer. Paralysed, I suddenly knew that this one wasn't headed into town. Erben opened his mouth to yell, but no sound issued. I'll never know whether some spontaneous muscle convulsion or the concussion of the shell itself threw us flat, but whatever the agency, it is to that we owe our lives. The shattered wreck of the wall at our backs was a tottery shield. In the split second before I lost consciousness, I heard the sickening sound of shrapnel smacking up against the wall, like fifty eggs cracking on a footpath.

After the skirmish at the Rosales, one Spanish newspaper erroneously reported that Errol had been killed in action, news which was first relayed to Lili Damita in Paris. The telegram, sent on behalf of the Loyalists, read, 'IN THIS YOUR HOUR OF SADNESS, WE SYMPATHISE WITH YOU OVER ERROL'S LOSS. WE FEEL SURE HIS DEATH WAS NOT IN VAIN.' Errol's 'little French pal', however, was the last person on his mind. Suffering from concussion and lacerations to his shoulder, he had been dragged from the rubble and taken to a local hospital, where he had quickly recovered, and was soon able to seduce his nurse – possibly the Estrella he refers to in his autobiography – and cable Jack Warner with the news that he was very much alive. Warner ordered him to return home at once.

For decades there has been considerable speculation as to whether Errol was in awe of Herman Erben's *real* motive for covering the Spanish Civil War, or whether he was merely an innocent bystander. He was certainly a highly intelligent and resourceful young man, one who was so adept at spinning yarns and pulling the wool over other people's eyes that one might have expected him to have worked out for himself what was going on. On the other hand, however, he did not understand the language, and Erben was a devious individual who had been trained to outfox even his closest friends.

The largely idle speculation that Errol actually *worked* as a Nazi spy – an accusation which remains today in some circles – was originally activated in 1979 when the biographer Charles Higham claimed in *Errol Flynn: The Untold Story* that he had located some 5,000 documents alluding to the fact from sources in Washington. The US State Department later confirmed that there had in fact only been around 250, mostly relating to passport and visa applications, and that these were 'open to any form of interpretation'. Higham substantiated his charges by supplying statements allegedly made by reliable sources – all dead or requesting that their names be withheld.

Charles Higham described Herman Friedrich Erben as 'one of the most important and ingenious Nazi agents of the twentieth century'. That Erben was a Fascist cannot be denied, but he was hardly big league – indeed, perhaps his only true claim to notoriety is that he was a friend of a famous movie star and almost certainly would have been swallowed by the annals of history were it not for this fact. Higham further augmented Erhen's high status by informing his readers that he was a member of the powerful Sturmabteilung – the Stormtroopers, a branch of the SS – which brought the acid comment from Errol's staunchest defender, Tony Thomas, 'With Jewish blood, Herman Erben had about as much chance of becoming a member of the SS as Martin Luther King would have had being elected an officer in the Ku-Klux-Klan.'

Thomas, whose *Errol Flynn: The Spy Who Never Was* was published in 1990, found substantial evidence to contradict Higham's further accusations that Errol had never gone on Bond tours or even entertained the troops during the war, and that he had been so virulently anti-Semitic that he had only allowed himself to be photographed once with Jack Warner. Thomas's proof was a simple scrapbook of newspaper articles and photographs which Higham had clearly overlooked.

Others, myself included, have argued that Errol's character alone would hardly have attracted him towards the Hitlerian doctrine, for here was a man who had spent his whole life rebelling *against* authority and discipline. This point was emphasised by Errol's second wife, Nora Eddington, in an irate letter to the *Los Angeles Times*, part of which read:

Errol was a wild spirit and about as unconventional as any man ever born. He hated authority, particularly policemen, so the idea of him being attracted to the Nazis is absurd...in fact, if he hated anyone he would refer to them as a blankety-blank Nazi. Errol even resented being told what to do by Warner Brothers. Can anyone seriously imagine wanting to live under a dictatorship?

Tony Thomas, who also accused Higham of falsifying government documents, added:

Flynn's playboy philosophy, his hedonism, were about as far removed from the humourless demarcations of Hitlerian socialism as could be imagined. He was, after all, an Aussie. Of all the people I have met in the world it seems to me that the Australians, with their cheerful disdainful attitude towards work and their lusty bent for sport and fun would be the last group Hitler would be able to entice into his constipated concept of Utopia.

Thomas also drew attention towards the obvious, regarding the artificialities and divided loyalties of the film capital where making a fast buck were concerned:

Had Flynn actually been involved in espionage in Spain, it would have surfaced long ago in the plethora of memoirs and histories written by people who took part in the Spanish Civil War and in Second World War intelligence activities. Ex-Nazi intelligence agents have been prolific in writing about their adventures. The involvement of a famous Hollywood personality would have been impossible to suppress...If the charges had been true, the book would have been a sensational exposé of a man operating behind a magnificently false facade, and the basis for a spectacular and juicy movie. Hollywood has little pity. For the sake of a good story it will eat its own. But for that to have happened the charges would have had to be beyond refutation, instead of tissues of supposition and implication.

In Madrid, using Errol as his cover, Erben photographed literally thousands of German émigrés who had defected to the International Brigade. Some of the more prominent ones, including General von Helmuth, were delighted to pose with Captain Blood, and these pictures were handed over to the Gestapo, resulting in large numbers of these unfortunate people being persecuted just as cruelly as the Nazis later persecuted the Jews.

Bidding farewell to Erben, Errol sailed to America at the end of

April. His first port of call was the White House and an audience with President Roosevelt, who was interested in hearing first-hand of his Spanish adventure. What was actually said within the portals of the White House is not known, though the President – ailing and confined to a wheelchair – was sufficiently impressed to want to present Errol with a signed portrait of himself. The FBI, on the other hand, ordered a thorough investigation into the affair – one which would continue for several years and ultimately conclude that Errol's only culpability was that he had been stupid not to have seen through Erben's charade. Basically, though he had conducted his business in Spain with impartiality, save for one occasion when, veering away from his apolitical stance, he had accepted a dinner invitation from General von Helmuth because, he claimed, he had 'liked the guy'.

Errol would see little of Herman Erben following their Spanish adventure. In September 1938 the Austrian was photographed with Errol at a Warner Brothers party, and Erben later snapped him on the set of *The Sisters* with Bette Davis. Soon afterwards when the American authorities learnt of his involvement with the Sepik expedition, Erben's US citizenship was suspended and he once again embarked on a series of perigrinations around the world. At the end of 1939, as surgeon on the *Admiral Graf Spee*'s supply ship, he was at hand in Montevideo harbour to photograph her scuttle. The next year, following a brief internment in Argentina on account of a forged visa, he returned to the United States to face a governmental hearing over his suspended citizenship, staying long enough to spend a few days on Errol's yacht before being advised by his lawyer to leave the country because he believed he would lose his case and be arrested. The fact that Errol is supposed to have personally driven him to the border does not necessarily mean, however, that he knew what Erben was actually suspected *of*: to his way of thinking, he was simply helping out a pal who was in a fix.

After spending some time in Mexico, Erben travelled to Shanghai, where he was arrested and imprisoned by the US Army on suspicion of being a double-agent. He and Errol would never meet again, though they would exchange letters for a number of years. Erben never regained his US citizenship and was forbidden from ever entering the country again. In 1980, when he was 83 years old and only recently retired from his medical career, he agreed to be interviewed in Vienna – in response to the Higham allegations levelled against Errol – for ABC Television's *20-20* programme. Snarling defensively at the camera, he pronounced in a thick accent:

> If I had been a Nazi spy, then I might have been very careful to disguise this until such time as I would have snared him or brainwashed him. Neither snaring Errol Flynn nor brainwashing him as a friend was ever attempted by me and never considered.

William Donati, the young American writer-investigator who interviewed Erben for the programme, came to the same conclusion as Tony Thomas – that there was no incriminating evidence against Errol. Intimating that such was Errol's flair for never accepting second-best, Donati concluded, 'If Flynn had been pro-German, then he would have lent himself to the Nationalist side as a propagandist. That's where his *true* value would have been, *not* as an agent.' Donati's theory would be supported by Sir William Stephenson, the head of British Intelligence, who carried out an independent investigation and concluded, 'In my professional opinion Mr Errol Flynn was *not* a Nazi spy.'

From Washington, Errol travelled to Hollywood, lingering there just long enough to pick up the pay cheques which had accumulated in his absence, and to tell Jack Warner, who rebuked him yet again for interfering in another country's politics when he should have been making films, exactly what to do with the script he had set aside for him to read. Then, promising Lili Damita that this would be their second honeymoon, he took her to Boston. On the day of their arrival they had an almighty row which resulted in Errol storming out of their hotel and, for the second time, purchasing a sailboat on impulse. The cost, a mere $17,000. He baptised this one the *Sirocco* – ignoring the mariner's time-honoured superstition that in using the same name twice he would be courting bad luck. With Damita forgiven once more and reluctantly on board, the Flynns set sail for the West Indies.

Errol often referred to the *Sirocco* as his 'floating bag-shanty', and the longer he had the boat, the wilder the high-seas parties became. Initially, he bedded women indiscriminately and sometimes did not even bother asking their names. Indeed, there were so many of these, picked up just about anywhere, that he would line them up for 'muster', selecting one or two for his own use, then distribute the rest among his friends and the crew. Each wore an enamel badge emblazoned with his emblem – an erect penis and testicles, and the initials FFF which stood for Flynn's Flying Fuckers.

Neither were all of Errol's conquests women. He had slept with several men at David Niven's apartment, confessing that at the time there had been no women present to satisfy his urges, but he had been too drunk to tell the difference anyway. A little later, at one of Carole Lombard's infamous parties at her St Cloud home, off Sunset Boulevard, he met William Lundigan – a blonde, ethereal-looking former radio announcer who had recently signed up as a bit-part actor with Lombard's studio. Encouraged by the future Mrs Clark Gable, the undisputed doyenne of Hollywood's so-called lavender set, Errol spent the night with the young man – deliberately staying sober so that his 'judgement' of the event might remain unclouded. Afterwards, he had told his hostess that sex with Lundigan had been as pleasurable as it could have been with any woman, and he elected to search for more of the same – but not in Hollywood, where the slightest indiscretion could spell career suicide. He therefore began 'recruiting' young men to augment his crew, who after lights out secreted themselves into his cabin and always disappeared before dawn, Many of these young men were so in awe of Errol that they would have slept with him for nothing. Others were given money or offered parts in imaginary films, while 'good lays' such as Bill Lundigan really did get to work with him.

At the *Sirocco*'s first port of call on its maiden voyage, Havana, Damita stayed on the boat and Errol went off in search of a brothel, recommended by a friend, which specialised in under-aged girls. Damita also stayed behind in Nassau, while Errol spent several days underwater fishing. Back on board the couple argued more than they ever had, and after two weeks of this Errol headed back to Hollywood, where for a second time he moved in with David Niven, this time into Niven's recently acquired beach house in Malibu, aptly nicknamed 'Cirrhosis-by-the-Sea'.

Soon after settling in with Niven, Errol again teamed up with

Michael Curtiz, for his comedy debut. *The Perfect Specimen* was based on a 'slushy' story by Samuel Hopkins Adams which had recently appeared in *Cosmopolitan*. Gerald Beresford Wicks, the heir to a vast fortune, has been raised by his aunt (May Robson) so that, in her eyes at least, he will one day enter society as the model citizen: refined, charming, knowledgeable and an all-round sportsman. Unfortunately, while acquiring these essential skills, Gerald has never once been allowed outside the gates of the family mansion and knows nothing about contact with other human beings...until a young woman reporter (Joan Blondell) crashes her car through the fence. It is she who introduces him to the outside world, with its pitfalls, though all ends well and the couple fall in love.

The general consensus of opinion with this film was that Errol had insufficient acting experience behind him to take up an articulate comedy role, and he himself admitted that he was out of his depth. A naturally witty man off the screen, and a riotous teller of bawdy jokes, he simply could not make someone else's material *sound* funny, particularly when it was not very funny to begin with.

What Errol did enjoy about *The Perfect Specimen* was the boxing sequence, where he was allowed to show off his superb physique, and could boast once more to the press about his 'success' in the 1928 Olympics. His opponent in the scene was a character named Pinky, which brought Allen Jenkins, the actor playing him, a few ribald comments from Errol. 'Might as well just call him Faggot and have done with it!' he told Michael Curtiz, who lost his temper with Jenkins on the set when he kept ducking the much bigger, tougher and agile Australian's punches.

It was while Errol was working on this film that Lili Damita introduced him to her friend and sometime co-star, Lupe Velez, whose tempestuous love affairs with several of Hollywood's leading men had earned her the nickname 'Mexican Spitfire'. Such was Lupe's appetite for sex that some of her victims had never recovered from their ordeal. John Gilbert, who had fallen for her on the rebound after being jilted by Garbo, had ended up a shivering wreck whose only solace had come from the bottle. So too had the opera singer Lawrence Tibbet, and in 1928, on the set of *Wolf Song*, she began her most disastrous relationship with

Gary Cooper. The archetypal, blue-chinned, strapping, all-American hero suffered a nervous breakdown and lost 35 lbs in weight after six months of public tantrums and innumerable sex-sessions during which Lupe had tied him to the bed for hours at a time and 'ridden' him until he passed out.

By the time she got around to Errol, some twenty lovers later, Lupe was coming to the end of her stormy marriage to Tarzan actor Johnny Weissmuller. She had also developed an annoying habit of standing on restaurant tables, hoisting up her skirt, and displaying to all and sundry that she was not wearing panties. She also had a 'party trick' – an ability to rotate one of her breasts, which were, Errol recorded, 'The most beautiful that Hollywood had ever seen.'

At first Errol, who could out-vulgar anyone, and frequently did, found Lupe's antics highly amusing, particularly as she was also a devout Catholic. In his memoirs he writes of how she was once on her knees in front of him, performing oral sex, when she paused for a moment to beg forgiveness from a statuette of the Madonna and Child which he kept on his dressing table! It was she, too, who taught him how to enhance his lovemaking – as if he needed any lessons – by applying a pinch of cocaine to the tip of his penis, a practice he would continue for the rest of his life.

Both Johnny Weissmuller and Lili Damita begged Errol to end his relationship with Lupe Velez. The former was genuinely concerned for his health and sanity, while Damita threatened him with a divorce which would cost him every cent he possessed. It was Jack Warner, however, who finally wrestled him from her clutches by offering a 'take it and drop her – you can't have both' ultimatum for the role all Hollywood had been talking about for months – *Robin Hood*. Errol did not even bother saying goodbye to her.

There were so many Flynn regulars lined up for *The Adventures of Robin Hood* that, in retrospect, it could not have been anything *but* dazzling: Curtiz, Korngold, de Havilland, Rathbone, Hale and Knowles, not to mention Sol Polito's sublime photography. Warner Brothers had first considered making the film while awaiting the release of *Captain Blood*, with James Cagney, fresh from his success in *Midsummer Night's Dream*, in the lead. This potentially woeful exercise in miscasting thankfully never took place, and now Warner allotted an unprecedented $1,600,000 to the budget, making it the studio's most expensive movie to date. In actual fact the costs would have surpassed the $2 million mark by the time of its completion.

Many cinemagoers and critics firmly believed that Douglas Fairbanks' Robin Hood of 1922 would never be surpassed, and so had Fairbanks, who had copyrighted not just his script, but his ideas and locations. Warner's researchers and scriptwriters, however, did not have to tamper too much with the Robin Hood legend: Fairbanks' desire to be original had resulted in him virtually ignoring the ballads – the stave-fight with Little John on the narrow bridge, Will Scarlet's plucking of his lute and Friar Tuck's piggy-back ride across the river are all here, though this new 'Protector of the People' has become a Saxon knight, fighting Norman oppression half a century too late, while the rapscallion challenging him for the affection of the lovely Lady Marian (de Havilland) is not the Sheriff of Nottingham but the leering, conniving Sir Guy of Gisbourne (Basil Rathbone).

As with *Captain Blood*, Errol's new epic had more than its share of on-set dilemmas, almost all of them exacerbated by the star himself. Hoping to reduce the risk of the usual walk-out, Jack Warner had offered Errol a new contract for $3,600 a week, putting him on a par with Clark Gable and Robert Taylor. This was resented by Basil Rathbone, who had never ceased to remind Errol during the shooting of *Captain Blood* that he had been earning more than the film's star. Since then, Errol had learnt of Rathbone's sexual preferences, and when the actor leered at him during their first rehearsal and snarled, 'I suppose you'll be satisfied now you're earning more than me, you dirty little Aussie!' Errol spat back, 'Never mind, sport. You're still getting to suck more dicks than me!' Surprisingly, this outburst resulted in these two very different men becoming friends.

Errol's bust-up with the director, William Keighley – a man he instinctively loathed because he did not consider him professional enough to be handling such a massive budget – occurred over his own decision to grow a short beard for his part. This, Keighley maintained, would be detrimental to his on-screen appeal and might even result in the film proving a flop with female admirers. Errol stuck to his guns, telling his on-off friendly journalist, W. H. Mooring,

'Whether the nomad of Nottingham had one or not is immaterial. But I suppose the safety razor, like Errol Flynn himself being then a thing unknown, and Sherwood Forest being a place for luxurious growth, our hero might most likely have sported at least a few days' beard-length at most times. And in any case, my beard will keep the flies off!'

 To make Keighley's life a little more difficult, Errol made a point of turning up late every morning, usually suffering from a hangover after one of his extended drinking sessions with Alan Hale, who was playing Little John, as he had in the Fairbanks film. Errol was also rude to studio personnel, and purposely fluffed his lines, telling Jack Warner, 'Blame the director, sport. The cunt's sending everybody to sleep!'

 Errol, though, was not the only one who complained about the director, and after an emergency meeting with studio bosses, Keighley was dropped and replaced by Michael Curtiz. This brought more screams of protest from Errol, who told Warner, 'The minute that Hungarian motherfucker walks on to the set, I walk off!' Errol did *not* walk off, though for two days he completely ignored Curtiz. As part of his deal, Curtiz brought in the fencing master, Fred Cavens, to put Errol and Basil Rathbone through their paces for the film's famous duel scene – though the technique he applied had not been used in England until the late seventeenth century – and Howard Hill, the champion bowman who 'covered' Errol's shooting during the archery contest. When Errol and Curtiz did begin speaking, it was mostly to insult each other and turn the air blue. The last straw occurred during the banqueting scene, an expensive one when Errol ruined the take by spitting out a mouthful of what was in his goblet, and demanding to know who was responsible for serving him such 'panther piss'. When Curtiz intervened, Errol flung what was left in the goblet into his face. And when Jack Warner threatened to fire him, all he did by way of apology was to crack, 'Sorry, sport, but I think I have a contract!'

 Warner was powerless to argue. That same week, Errol had made his debut on the cover of *Life* magazine, under the banner headline, 'ERROL FLYNN – GLAMOUR BOY'. The magazine's photographer had snapped him during a fishing expedition in Miami, and wearing a pair of skimpy swimming trunks he looked every inch the star Jack Warner predicted he would become in the accompanying editorial. This on-set vitriol, of course, only brought out the best in Errol – both Warner and Curtiz declared that he always worked better when fired up – and made *The Adventures of Robin Hood* perhaps the best swashbuckling movie of all time.

It is 1191, and while King Richard the Lionheart lies in an Austrian dungeon, England suffers under his tyrannical brother, Prince John (an outrageously camp Claude Rains), who has appointed himself Regent. The film opens with the peasant, Much the miller's son (Herbert Mundin) being apprehended by John's chief adherent, Sir Guy of Gisbourne, for stealing the royal deer – a hanging offence. Much is rescued by Robin and his men, and Robin audaciously delivers the deer to John's banqueting table – an effective entrance which earns him an invitation to stay for supper, and encouraging glances from the Lady Marian. It is a trap, the first of many from which he escapes with much thigh-slapping and sword play, unbridled athleticism, and with the odd phrase of Aussie twang thrown in for good measure! The scene in Sherwood Forest (California's Bidwell Park) where Gisbourne and his entourage, including Marian, are captured and relieved of the huge amount of purloined money and food they are transporting by the dozens of Lincoln Green-clad men who drop noiselessly from the trees is particularly appealing.

It is at this stage that Marian becomes involved with Robin's cause, and with him, when she witnesses first-hand the poverty and destitution wrought upon the Saxons by her own people. Her subsequent actions lead to her arrest for treason, on the eve of John's hoped-for coronation. Her intervention has already saved Robin from the hangman's noose, and his rescue of her from Nottingham Castle is truly spectacular, coinciding with King Richard's return to England. The coronation is disrupted by the King and Robin's combined forces, disguised as monks, and after a roisterous free-for-all skirmish, Robin and Gisbourne fight it out with broadswords, while Korngold's stunning score hilights the scrapping and clashing of steel. The panted dialogue is slushy. Gisbourne, 'You've come to Nottingham once too often!'; Robin, 'When this is over, my friend, there'll be no need for me to come again!' Then the hero plunges his blade into the villain's heart, and it is indeed over. Richard reveals his identity, John and his followers are banished from the land, and among the honours heaped upon Robin is the hand of the Lady Marian. A masterpiece!

Errol's next film, which once more teamed him with Michael Curtiz, de Havilland, Patric Knowles and several of the minor actors from *The Adventures of Robin Hood*, along with Rosalind Russell, could not have been more different in its approach and content. Curtiz had dismissed his and Errol's earlier comedy attempt as 'claptrap', but only on account of the second-rate material. Errol was, the director maintained, a natural 'screwball', and *Four's a Crowd*, based on a story by Wallace Sullivan, would prove to the world just how funny he could be.

Errol played public relations man Bob Lansford, whose previous position has been editor-in-charge of a newspaper now run by his intellectually challenged arch-rival, Patterson Buckley (Knowles), of whom he quips, 'Born a half-wit and gradually making the other half match!' Lansford's *truc* is to sanitise the reputations of wealthy men of poor public esteem by bamboozling them into donating money to charity. One such is John P. Dillingwell (Walter Connelly), an eccentric millionaire pre-occupied with his model trains and caring for his pretty grand-daughter, Lorri (de Havilland). The farce which follows would have been worthy of Grant and Hepburn, then Hollywood's king and queen of screwball. Lansford falls for Lorri *and* one of Buckley's earthy reporters, Jean Christy (Russell), to whom he says, 'There are some things I don't know much about, but I have a knowledge of women that few men have possessed' – Michael Curtiz's way of assuring the public that Flynn's behaviour was every bit as rakish on the screen as it was off. Buckley, too, is in love with both women, but seems set to marry Jean – and Lansford, Lorri – but the double ceremony goes awry when everyone starts arguing, and partners are exchanged.

Four's a Crowd did sterling business at the box office, though it was much underestimated by Errol's fans and the media, who by this time were only really interested in seeing him typecast as a swashbuckler, officer or adventurer. This is a shame: throughout the film he is persistently on cue, his comic mannerisms are far from contrived, and his voice is certainly not as grating as Cary

Grant's. He also proved a talent for switching from sheer buffoonery – biting the tail of one of Dillingwell's dogs after the pack has chased him off the property – to pathos, as in the scene where he tells Jean that Dillingwell's wrenched wealth is going towards helping the sick. Warner Brothers, however, knew which side their bread was buttered on: if the public wanted to see their hero with a sword or a gun in his hand, then so long as the cinemas remained full, nothing else mattered.

Around the time that *Four's a Crowd* was being made, Errol and a group of male friends formed the Olympiads, a small society of anti-Semitic pseudo-intellectuals who spent much of their time behind locked doors, getting drunk, discussing who they had had sex with, exchanging jokes and ribald stories, and opining on art, travel, literature and letters. Most of these meetings took place at the Bundy Drive home of the avant-garde painter, John Decker, and the founder members included actors Alan Hale, Alan Mowbray, Grant Mitchell and Patric Knowles, still gently rebuffing Errol's advances. Occasional members included Bill Lundigan, John Barrymore, Gerrit Koets' aka Herman Erben, Bruce Cabot, W. C. Fields and the writer Gene Fowler. Among those *refused* admission to the Olympiads were Edward G. Robinson and Jack Warner – for the simple reason that both were Jews.

Occasionally, the Olympiads would be invited to spend a few days aboard Errol's yacht, with its endless supply of women, booze and cocaine, and it was probably one of those who had been rejected for membership who now reported him to the authorities. In those days, foreigners residing in the United States were prohibited from owning boats over twenty feet in length and in excess of five tons. Therefore, as the *Sirocco* weighed over 30 tons and was three times its permitted length, Errol was told to get rid of it. *He*, however, proffered a more practical solution: as his boat was infinitely more important than his British Empire passport, he put in an application for American citizenship!

At the end of 1937, Errol spent two weeks in London, and he would later boast that during this trip he had had a passionate affair with the Duchess of Argyll. 'My very own Duchess,' he told Earl Conrad, adding how he had 'bowed and scuffed' to the essential protocol assigned to such meetings. The moment her husband's back had turned, he said she made her move. Putting on a Scottish accent, Errol continued the story:

> She started dragging me, as if I were a Bengali rebel, to her gallows in an adjoining room. I let myself be dragged and managed to get my fingers into the back of her dress at the neck, where I could tear it off with the most ease ... In a moment we were there on the Duke's bed. All I can remember the great lady saying before the bout began was exactly what Rosie O'Grady must have said in similar circumstances: 'Oh, Ehrell! Oh Ehrell! Fook me! Fook me!'

Returning to Hollywood, Errol inadvertently found himself involved in the *Gone With the Wind* star-search fever which had gripped the film community for some time. Margaret Mitchell's million-selling novel had been read by David O. Selznick *before* publication, and upon purchasing the screen rights in July 1936 he had boasted that the film would prove the zenith of his achievements since leaving MGM the previous year to set up his own company. Unable to finance the film himself, however, he had approached Louis B. Mayer – his father-in-law. Mayer had immediately injected $1.25 million into the production, and as part of the deal had brought in Clark Gable to play the film's hero, Rhett Butler.

Initially, the tempestuous heroine, Scarlett O'Hara, was to have been played by Norma Shearer, but a change of heart from her had led to the longest search in movie history: 1,400 actresses were interviewed, auditioned and tested, ranging from unknown hoofers to the very biggest of the Hollywood legends. Katharine Hepburn, Claudette Colbert, Joan Crawford and Margaret Sullavan had all been shortlisted, but for a time the clear favourites had been Tallulah Bankhead – an *authentic* Southern belle who had filmed her test wearing one of Garbo's gowns from *Camille* – and Olivia de Havilland. Tallulah had subsequently been dropped when in a drunken outburst she had threatened to spill the beans about the director George Cukor's earlier relationship with Clark Gable, and de Havilland had been relegated to the film's second lead. By the spring of 1938, however, Bette Davis was heading the runners for the 'Scarlett Sweepstakes', and was pleading with Jack Warner to loan her out to MGM.

Warner considered his options. From his point of view, Davis was even more difficult to get along with than Errol – and like Errol, always complaining that she was underpaid. Warner also knew that if either star left his studio, they would find some way of not coming back. For this reason, Warner made David O. Selznick an offer which he assumed he would only be able to refuse, considering that Gable had already signed his contract: Warner Brothers would allow MGM to have Bette Davis, but only if they signed Errol Flynn for the role of Rhett Butler!

Much to everyone's surprise – and horror! – Selznick was in favour of the proposal, and so too was Jack Warner when he realised that there would be a great deal of money in it for himself. Davis, however, was appalled that – despite Gable's famed halitosis and lack of personal hygiene – she would be 'expected to have lip contact with a man who's been inside every cathouse between here and Timbuktu,' and told MGM exactly what to do with their offer. Not to be outdone, Warner then informed *her* that she would be working with Flynn whether she liked it or not, for he had decided to exact his revenge by putting them together in *The Sisters*, adapted from the novel by Myron Brinig.

The film, which began shooting in June 1938, did not cut much ice with Flynn fans and the critics, primarily because he was once more cast against 'type', though in this production his peers must have observed the similarities between the actor and the part he was playing. Frank Medlin is the cynical, hard-drinking sports writer and would-be novelist who meets Louise Elliott (Davis), one of the three daughters of a Montana pharmacist, at a campaign ball on the eve of the 1904 Roosevelt election. 'I'm a lost soul who'll soon be vanishing into the wilderness,' he tells her, after cutting in on her dance with her intended.

Louise is promised to Tom Knivel (Dick Foran) who owns the town's first car. Within days, however, she and Frank elope to San Francisco, Knivel subsequently marries Louise's sister Grace (Jane Bryan), while the third sister, Helen (Anita Louise) enters a loveless union with Frank's wealthy pal, Sam Johnson (Alan Hale).

In San Francisco, Louise is forced to endure a lonely, frugal existence while her husband sinks to the depths of drunken despondency trying to provide her with the comforts she has been used to – unnecessarily, it would appear, for all she really wants is him, for richer or poorer. When she falls pregnant, Frank temporarily reforms, only to fall back on his vices when Louise suffers a miscarriage after accompanying him to a boxing match. Increasingly in debt, Frank demands a pay rise from his editor: when this is refused, the pair argue and he is fired. Louise does not mind this. She is confident that her husband will complete his all-important book and that this will be the answer to all their problems, so she takes a job in a department store. Her staunch independence, however, clashes head-on with Frank's increasing fallibility until he reaches such a low ebb that escape is his only option. The actor merges with the character again when Frank is bitten by the wanderlust, though the addition of a five o'clock shadow as an accoutrement to his neurasthenia only succeeds in making Errol look even more dishy than ever.   •

Frank sets sail on the Singapore-bound *SS Peralta* on an auspicious date – 18 April 1906, the day of the San Francisco earthquake which left more than 400 people dead. The Medlins' apartment block is reduced to a pile of rubble – a brief but dramatic sequence which incorporates footage from the 1927 film, *In Old San Francisco*. Bette Davis's wounded, tragi-camp expression while she sits dishevelled among the ruins is an image not easily forgotten. Louise then suffers a complete mental breakdown, and is recuperating at a friend's house when Frank returns from his overseas adventure.

Until this stage in the shooting schedule, director Anatole Litvak's only on-set difference of opinion with his leading man had been when Bette Davis had complained about Errol being more interested in ogling the continuity girls than in learning his lines. Errol did not have to make a supreme effort to seduce these: he always made a point of leaving his dressing room door wide open while he was changing, and always stripped naked – 'To enable the wenches to engage in a little window-shopping.' The first time Anatole Litvak saw him doing this he yelled, 'For decency's sake, Flynn, *cover* yourself!' Errol merely grinned, then draped a handkerchief over his erection.

In the Brinig novel, Frank suffers rejection when Louise marries her kindly boss (Ian Hunter), and upon Errol's insistence this scene was shot. Jack Warner, however, was afraid that this might have an adverse effect on the box office because the public might believe that, in view of some of the rumours concerning his private life, Errol Flynn himself was being humiliated on the screen, other than some fictitious journalist. The studio chief therefore commissioned an 'alternative' ending, wherein the couple are reconciled in the manner they have met, at another electoral campaign ball. Errol hit the roof over this, and only agreed to complete the film once Warner had given his word that the final decision over which ending to use would be left to the 'hand-picked' preview audience. Warner's scene was given the thumbs-up.

Bette Davis later confessed that, despite her loathing of the man, she had *wanted* to work with Errol because to do so at that time – when she was yet to hit her peak and he was by far the bigger star, earning twice as much as her – had done wonders for her prestige and confidence. 'Without him, I doubt the picture would have amounted to much,' she said. Davis was also complimentary about Errol's looks, though not about his talent, concluding, 'He was one of the great male beauties of his time, but a lousy actor because he never took himself seriously – and because he was so goddam lazy!' Both stars denied, however, that when Errol had made an attempt to kiss her for real, away from the film set, Davis had shoved him away.

Errol's next film *was* a return to form, and a spectacular one at that. 'In *The Dawn Patrol*,' wrote *Film Weekly*'s R. Ewart Williams, 'Errol Flynn not only gives the best performance of his career, but also turns in a character study which is notable for its sincerity and restraint.' Based on the novel *Flight Commander* by John Monk Saunders and Howard Hawks, it had first been filmed in 1930, three years after the spate of World War I aviation movies had been launched with *Wings*, another Monk Saunders and Hawks story. Then, the leads had been played by Douglas Fairbanks Jr, Richard Barthelmess and Neil Hamilton. Now, supporting Errol in an all-male, all-British cast were David Niven and 'arch-villain' Basil Rathbone. Edmund Goulding was brought in to direct, and to cut costs Jack Warner insisted upon using the flying scenes from the original film, superimposing the new actors on to somewhat amateur process shots. Even so, after *Wings* this one is generally regarded as the best World War I movie ever made. It was also one of the few Flynn films where he has no female love interest.

'A great big, noisy, rather stupid game that doesn't make any sense at all,' is how Errol's semi-pacifist hero, Captain Courtney, dismisses the war after witnessing the deaths in action of so many young men, and erasing their names from the blackboard in the headquarters' bar, while 'Poor Butterfly' drones on in the background and the flyers belt out a chorus of 'Hurrah For The Next Man Who Dies!'

Courtney's best friend is Lieutenant Scott (Niven), who shares his interest in the bottle and generally having a good time, even when this amounts to boozing with an amicable German prisoner-of-war. This air of bonhomie changes, however, when the force's hard-bitten commander, Major Brand (Rathbone) is promoted and nominates Courtney as his successor. Every mission across enemy lines against the might of the famous German ace, von Richter, fails on account of the squadron's inexperienced airmen and out-of-date planes. Scott himself is reported killed in action, but returns drunk, and one of the replacement recruits turns out to be his young brother, Donny (Morton Lowry), fresh out of school and like all the others hopelessly green. Courtney and Scott fall out over the former's decision to send Donny out against von Richter. Courtney, however, has explicit instructions from *his* superior, and when the youngster is killed, Scott hits his friend and calls him 'dirty butcher'. Courtney then exonerates himself by making the ultimate sacrifice: when Scott volunteers for a suicidal attack on an enemy ammunitions base, Courtney gets him drunk and goes in his place. The mission is a success, though he is shot down, and the film ends with Scott being appointed commander as more recruits arrive with little or no knowledge of combat tactics.

While shooting *The Dawn Patrol*, Errol had a brief affair with Edmund Goulding, who had never made a secret of his homosexuality. Eighteen years Errol's senior, the British-born director of such classics as *Grand Hotel* had emigrated to the United States soon after serving in World War I, and although he eventually entered into a 'twilight tandem' marriage with the dying ballerina, Marjorie Moss, to curb the gossips, this rotund man with the Noël Coward mannerisms and an absolute mania for the casting couch had, during a lengthy career, relationships with dozens of

Hollywood hopefuls including Robert Taylor, Edward Everett Horton and Tyrone Power.

On the negative side, Goulding had single-handedly provided Hollywood with the stereotyped homosexual man by having Jed Prouty play a 'bumbling nervous Nellie' in MGM's first talkie, *Broadway Melody*, shot in 1929. His good points, however, more than made up for this and Errol said of him, 'Eddie had more friends in Hollywood than any man I ever knew, simply because he was so kind towards everyone that *he* knew. What a pity there weren't more around like him.'

For some time, it would appear, Errol had been longing to 'get to know' Tyrone Power, then 26 and at the height of his popularity. Of almost ethereal beauty, with sallow skin and long, dark eyelashes, Power had recently entered into a 'lavender' marriage with the French actress, Annabella, a feisty woman who would later boast to the world that he had been a coprophiliac. When the two actors met at one of Edmund Goulding's all-male parties and Errol told Power, point-blank, that he wanted to sleep with him, they retired to an upstairs room and were not seen for two days. Their relationship, however, though it dragged on for six months, was doomed almost from the start. Power, a shy, nervous man, disapproved of Errol's roughness and vulgarity. He disliked his 'running commentary' during their most intimate moments, and his insistence on repeating to his drinking pals, in graphic detail, what had transpired in the bedroom. Most of all, however, he cringed at the way Errol announced, whenever the mood took him and no matter who might have been listening, 'Fancy a poke, sport?'

Despite this, Tyrone Power made the mistake of falling in love with Errol, while all Errol wanted was the raw sex and to add another notch to his bedpost. Power longed for a tender, one-to-one relationship whereas Errol, mere days into their affair, wanted Goulding and their other gay or bisexual friends to *watch* them having sex. Even so, the two remained close friends until Power's early death, at 45, in 1958.

'Reluctant, half-pissed and only paying cursory attention to a half-baked script,' was how Errol described his experience on the set of *Dodge City*, which was released in 1939. Inasmuch as the previous year had been a good one for the revival of the swashbuckler, this was the year of the big-budget Western. *Jesse*

James, *Union Pacific* and *Stagecoach* were all mammoth hits, James Cagney triumphed in *The Oklahoma Kid*, and *Destry Rides Again* with James Stewart in the title role resurrected Marlene Dietrich's ailing career, and gave her a record success with *The Boys in the Backroom*.

Dodge City, set in Kansas shortly after the American Civil War, was in many ways an amalgamation of these films. On the positive side, Errol was able to hold his own against any of his contemporaries, and once again he had Olivia de Havilland as his leading lady. Also, the film was in breathtaking Technicolor and boasted one of the most sensational bar-room brawls ever seen in a Western, wherein the Gay Lady Saloon is virtually annihilated, while Ann Sheridan croons indifferently. Recently voted The Oomph Girl by 'Hollywood's Ten Most Eligible Bachelors' – including Errol, David Niven and Edmund Goulding – Sheridan does not merit second female lead. She is wholly superfluous to the plot and is certainly no Dietrich with her half-hearted attempt at portraying a brassy saloon girl. The script, too, left much to be desired.

Errol played Wade Hatton, a been-everywhere-done-everything young Irishman whose clipped colonial accent is explained by his side-kick (Alan Hale) shortly before the real action begins: 'He's the most moving-on young man you ever saw,' he says, when Hatton turns down an offer from the town's patron, Colonel Dodge, to restore law and order. 'First off he was in the English Army over in India, then he got mixed up in some kind of hoo-ray revolution down Cuba way, then he started punching cattle in Texas – that is of course before he enlisted in the war. So you see, he's either the greatest traveller who ever lived, or he is the biggest liar!'

The storyline of *Dodge City*, henceforth, is archetypal. Hatton meets the waggon-train conveying the lovely Abbie Irving (de Havilland) and her reckless brother (William Lundigan), whose unruly behaviour starts a cattle stampede which tramples him to death. He makes an enemy of the town mouthpiece, Jeff Surrett (Bruce Cabot), who has turned the place into 'a Babylon of the American Frontier, packed with settlers, thieves and gunmen ... the town that knows no ethics but cash and killing'. At first, the locals are indifferent towards his refinements. 'Shakespeare?' someone asks. 'What part of Texas is he from?' Yet Hatton *does* become sheriff when Surrett's men kill a child, and under his regime the jails are full, taxes and liquor regulations are imposed, and firearms are banned in the main thoroughfare. He finally gets his man during a shoot-out on a burning train, he ends up marrying his sweetheart. Abbie, who has reacted coldly towards him throughout most of the film, has latently recognised the hero in him, and as the credits are about to roll the pair leave town for Hatton's next 'assignment', the cleaning up of Virginia City.

During the shooting of *Dodge City*, Errol, Bruce Cabot, David Niven and John Barrymore embarked on a series of all-night benders which became the talk of the town. Marlene Dietrich, witness to several of these escapades, told me:

> They were all incredibly bitchy towards each other. Flynn absolutely adored Barrymore and could see no wrong in him, but the other two couldn't stand him, or one another. Niven of course was always the perfect gentleman, whereas Cabot, the stupidest actor in Hollywood who couldn't even *read* his lines, let alone remember them, always acted like a complete shit. And so far as any of us ever knew, whenever he turned up at a party he *never* put his hand in his pocket.

Niven too later complained about Cabot's 'sponging', and also said that he had never been able to comprehend Errol's fascination for 'The Great Profile', as Barrymore had been known in his heyday, claiming that he had found him 'coarse and conspicuously unclean'. Coarse he certainly was, though almost always poetically so, as was proved during one of the quartet's visits to the Mocambo. Though he was easily outvulgared by Errol, when Tallulah Bankhead, the undisputed queen of one-liners, asked the two men if they could come up with a novel way of describing the most intimate parts of their wives' anatomy, Barrymore replied:

> It's like this. You push it in, and after it has entered the main saloon and the gallery, a cabin-boy descends a ladder and tinkles a bell. *That's* how big her Venus's fly-trap is!

To which Errol added:

> Oh, I think I can put it simpler than that. In layman's terms, my wife's honey-pot is *so* big that it will stretch a mile before tearing an inch!

Errol's friendship with Niven, however, took a serious nosedive at around this time when Errol drove him to the only place in town where, he declared, one could find 'really tight pussy' – Hollywood High School. And when Niven commented that a man could end up in prison for even *thinking* such a thing, all Errol could say was, 'San Quentin Quail. Now, why didn't I think of that?'

Henceforth, Bruce Cabot would replace Niven as Errol's 'fuck-buddy', and though Cabot's sexual proclivities had never gone as far as under-aged girls, he was bisexual and heavily into voyeurism. Therefore, when he suggested that it might prove something of an educational experience to watch each other in action, Errol was more than willing. Off and on he was still seeing Bill Lundigan – good to his word, he had persuaded Michael Curtiz to cast the young man as Olivia de Havilland's brother in *Dodge City* – but, as he was still a little shaky about letting even his best friends in on this side of his life, he told Cabot that he would not allow him to watch him having sex with a man. The older actor arranged for them to visit a downtown brothel, where they shared a whore and, after she had been dismissed, one another. Henceforth, for obvious reasons, Errol would always refer to Cabot as Big Bruce.

News of Errol's adventures – though not necessarily the ongoing one with Cabot – was conveyed to Bette Davis, the undisputed queen of Warner Brothers who had just agreed to play Elizabeth I in the screen adaptation of Maxwell Anderson's *Elizabeth the Queen*, a Broadway success in 1930 for husband and wife team Alfred Lunt and Lynne Fontanne.

Since working with Errol in *The Sisters*, Davis had hit the box office jackpot with *Jezebel*, and she could now afford to be more demanding when it came to co-stars. Therefore *her* choice for the role of her love interest in the film, Robert Devereux, the ill-fated Earl of Essex, had been Laurence Olivier, but as he was busy filming *Rebecca* for Alfred Hitchcock, Jack Warner informed her that he had signed up Errol Flynn...and waited for the fireworks. These were not long in coming. Davis told Warner that she had suffered near-martyrdom while shooting *The Sisters*, when Flynn's behaviour had been merely lamentable. Now, she added, he was positively immoral and she wanted absolutely nothing to do with him, even if it meant giving up the part the critics were already saying she had been born to play. After several heated arguments – which took place while Errol went off on a trip to Mexico aboard the *Sirocco* with Bruce Cabot and Bill Lundigan – Jack Warner managed to get Davis to change her mind.

More sparks flew when Errol returned to Hollywood. To him, the mere mention of Bette Davis's name was akin to waving a red rag in front of a bull, yet he could not ignore the fact that appearing with her in such a film would move his own career to unprecedented heights. Even so, he made it clear that she would not be getting all of her own way. Firstly, he objected to Maxwell Anderson's script, which comprised alternating couplets of blank verse and prose. He was not Olivier, he maintained, and not only would he never be able to remember such 'long-winded piffle', but the public would not understand it. The script was therefore subjected to a hasty rewrite by Norman Reilly Raine and Aeneas MacKenzie.

Having won this first round, Errol next went into battle over the credits. He had asked for top billing in *The Sisters*, and he demanded it now. When Jack Warner pointed out that the playbills would look rather silly emblazoned with 'Errol Flynn in *Elizabeth the Queen*', his irate response was that the title would have to be changed, and suggested *The Knight and the Lady*, adding that he was sure his co-star would not object to being called a lady for once. Upon hearing this, Davis threatened to tear up her contract, and a disaster was only averted when someone at Warner Brothers announced that the film would be called *The Private Lives of Elizabeth and Essex*. Seven years previously, Charles Laughton had won an Oscar for his portrayal of Elizabeth's father in *The Private Life of Henry VIII*, and this one, the studio's publicist promised, could be loosely regarded as a sequel. The problem over credits was ultimately solved by billing the two sparring stars alphabetically as 'Bette Davis and Errol Flynn'. The 'and', both agreed, was of the utmost importance. What *really* rankled Davis, however, was the fact that Errol, on $6,000 a week, was still earning $1,000 a week more than she was.

The film proved no sequel. It opens in 1596, when Elizabeth is 63 years old, and Essex almost 30. The age difference shocked her courtiers, but not Hollywood, who conveniently and considerably reduced the gap by not giving the queen too many wrinkles, and by declaring in every press release that in civilian life, Davis and Flynn were the same age, give or take a few months. The film also presented Sir Walter Raleigh (Vincent Price) as a villain. Otherwise, the settings and real-life characters were more or less spot on.

Having defeated the Spanish at Cadiz, Essex makes his triumphant entry into London, though his popularity with the people is not echoed at the royal palace of Whitehall. Elizabeth rebukes him for failing to capture the Spanish treasure, he turns his back on her, and she slaps him. Davis, wearing a great deal of costume jewellery, played the scene for real, and Michael Curtiz took sardonic pleasure from filming it several times. 'I felt as if I had been hit by a railroad locomotive,' Errol recalled, explaining how he had left the set three times to throw up in his dressing room 'Joe Louis himself couldn't give a right hook better than Bette hooked me with. My jaw went out. I felt a click behind my ear and saw all these comets, shooting stars, all in one flash.'

Another scene, which takes place in Elizabeth's private apartments, led to more violence when, upon seeing her make a difficult entrance – weighed down by one of Orry-Kelly's thick brocaded gowns – Errol ruined the take by barking, 'Bette, my dear. You're walking as if you've shit yourself again!' His protagonist picked up a cast-iron candlestick and flung it at him, missing his head by mere inches.

Banned from the court, however, Essex still professes his love for Elizabeth, saying, 'If she were my mother's kitchen hag, toothless and wooden-legged, she'd still make all the others seem pale and colourless!' In fact, this particular Elizabeth wears so much rice powder on her face that she could not be any paler, her hair has been shaved off at the front so that she appears bald under a gruesome red wig, her eyebrows have been removed and pencilled in, and the sheer beauty of those around her only makes her blithely aware of her ugliness. Therefore, when her ladies-in-waiting mock her by singing seditious rhymes – something which would never have happened at the real Elizabeth's court – she pauses for a moment to search for crow's-feet, then smashes every mirror in the room. 'To be a queen is to be less than human,' she laments, then in a moment of weakness summons Essex back to

London, where he is appointed Master of the Ordinance, a position which rankles his rivals but thrills her because it means that henceforth he will be based in England and never leave her again.

For a while, the lovers get on famously, exchanging sarcastic banter, frequently becoming quarrelsome, yet always knowing just how far to go with one another. Elizabeth gives Essex her father's ring: should she ever lose her temper with him, no matter the gravity of the circumstances, all he has to do is return this and all will be forgiven. The leg-pulling and kisses continue. When she pokes him playfully in the ribs, he gives her a whack on the backside which sends her sprawling. Then, he opposes her by accepting a challenge from his enemies at court and sailing to Ireland to quell the Tyrone rebellion – a six-month mission which fails when, instead of capturing the troublesome earl, he signs a truce. He then returns to London a changed man. His and Elizabeth's letters to each other have been intercepted: believing himself once more out of favour, he attempts to raise the City of London to seize power over the Queen's counsellors, and is arrested and charged with treason. Even so, there is a final reconciliation. Elizabeth asks for her ring back, and even offers to share the throne with him, but knowing that his quest is only for absolute power, both become resigned to the fact that the headsman's axe will be the only solution. And so Essex dies, while his queen sits and weeps alone in her 'widow's' weeds.

Some years later, both of Errol's films with Bette Davis would become elevated to the Camp Hall of Fame. 'The Sisters has plenty to offer the camp enthusiast,' Paul Roen wrote in his amusing and authoritative *High Camp: A Gay Guide to Camp and Cult Films*. 'It's got Bette Davis, Lee Patrick, Mayo Methot, Laura Hope Crews and the San Francisco earthquake.' In the same publication, Davis's portrayal of Good Queen Bess, with 'her cold, heavy-lidded fish eyes balefully glaring from a face of chalky, corpse-like whiteness' was proclaimed 'a lasting source of inspiration to female impersonators everywhere'.

The Private Lives of Elizabeth and Essex went on release in December 1939, three months after war had been declared in Europe, and still a British Empire citizen – although he had filled in all the necessary documents to become an American – Errol was anxious to play his part. He was therefore devastated when every single branch of the armed forces turned him down on account of his health, something which would profoundly affect him for the rest of his life and cause him to question his manliness. As far as the public was concerned, Errol Flynn was the perfect specimen, yet now it was revealed that this superbly packaged slab of Australian beefcake had a draft rating of 4F not just on account of recurrent malaria, but because he had a heart murmur and a slight touch of tuberculosis.

And if this was not *enough* for Errol to contend with, he then found out that his parents were about to visit Hollywood for the first time.

4

Ride, You Wolverines!

'The Christian concept of monogamy is to me nothing more than a
travesty of human nature. It doesn't work, never will.'

Errol was on the set of his second Western, *Virginia City*, when his
parents arrived in Hollywood, accompanied by his twenty-year-
old sister, Rosemary. Had Theodore been alone, Errol almost
certainly would have made the effort to meet him at the railway
station: the two did speak on the telephone to arrange a dinner
date but the younger Flynn completely forgot about it. Leaving his
wife and daughter at their hotel, Theodore therefore set off to
surprise him – only to receive the shock of his life. A studio
technician indicated Errol's dressing room, and as Theodore
pushed the door open he was met with the spectacle of his son,
trousers around his ankles, having sex with a naked young
woman up against the wall. 'Take a seat, Dad. I shan't be long!'
he panted.

Errol, who was experiencing one of his frequent, brief reunions
with Lili Damita, invited his family to stay with them at their
apartment, but was not impressed when Marelle declared in her
first press interview, 'I am disgusted that Errol wants to become
American. If my son had stayed in Australia, he would have joined
up by now, along with the other *men*.' Errol's reaction was to keep
on referring to his mother as 'The Cunt' whenever asked if he was
enjoying having his relatives stay with him, once getting his face

slapped in public, by his wife, for doing so.

It is not known if Errol's mother was actually implying that he was a coward – though she knew nothing of his health problems save his recurring bouts of malaria – but Errol's wife certainly thought she was. So did a young reporter from the *Los Angeles Times*, who suggested that maybe Errol had joined the ranks of the 'lazy sunbathers', a term coined by the intensely patriotic Marlene Dietrich for those Hollywood stars who were too busy making money to worry about the fate of the world. Marelle turned on the young man and snarled, 'My son's a *brave* young man, but he wants to become an American citizen because he's currently paying British and American income tax. That isn't fair. So, he's going to stay here in Hollywood and raise as much money for the war effort as he can.'

Errol certainly did not disappoint in this respect. He and Bruce Cabot organised a friendly mixed-doubles tennis match, for which privileged spectators – including Errol's parents and sister – paid $50 each to watch the two stars playing two busty blonde hoofers. And to make the event more interesting, all four contestants were stark naked.

Marelle's unexpected leaning towards him cut no ice with Errol, who continued telling reporters that he could not stand the woman. 'I remember when I was a child, at bath time,' he confided in one middle-aged man who was brought to the studio by Bruce Cabot to conduct what should have been an in-depth interview about life in Tasmania during the twenties. 'My mother used to point to my cock and say, "That thing there is dirty, it's disgusting, the same way that sex is disgusting!"' Then, taking out his penis, he demanded of the white-faced journalist, 'Tell me the truth. Does it look *dirty* to you?'

By staying out of his mother's sight as much as he could, Errol put in more time at the studio, and for once showed a little more enthusiasm for his work. On reflection, *Virginia City* should have been one of his better films. It certainly had all the right ingredients: direction by Michael Curtiz, stunning photography (albeit in black and white) by Sol Polito, and a supporting cast headed by Randolph Scott, Miriam Hopkins and, in the role of a half-breed outlaw, Humphrey Bogart! It was also forecast that the film would be a sequel to *Dodge City*, but while some of the actors from the earlier production were in it – including Errol's boozing pals Alan Hale and Guinn 'Big Boy' Williams – they all played different characters, and the action this time took place *during* the American Civil War. Sadly, the sets were mediocre, the scenario scarcely credible, and the dialogue dire.

Errol looked good as Kerry Bradford, the Union officer who has arrived in Virginia City, having escaped from a Confederate prison, to prevent a huge shipment of gold being smuggled across enemy lines by his former prison governor, Vance (Scott). Miriam Hopkins played a tone-deaf singing and dancing Southern spy who is amorously interested in both, but the worst example of miscasting was Bogart, whose Mexican accent seemed to change with each scene he appeared in.

Augmented by Bogart, who never really fitted in with Errol's so-called 'intellectual roistering', the 'Flynn Gang', comprising himself, Hale, Williams, Cabot, Lundigan and Knowles, proved themselves hellraisers par excellence during the shooting of *Virginia City*. Although the latter three did not appear in the film – indeed, it seems almost incomprehensible that Jack Warner never put Cabot into another Flynn picture – they visited the set regularly and each evening hit the town like a tidal wave. Errol and Bogart had much in common, not least the fact that both were married to tough, domineering women they despised yet could not live without. Errol, Cabot and Knowles had all slept with Bogart's third wife, Mayo Methot, who had had a bit-part in *The Sisters*, and whose unconventional behaviour made even that of Lupe Velez appear tame. Methot, who earned herself the nickname 'Sluggy', was also fond of fighting with her fists, and she usually won. During her stormy marriage to Bogart, she had beaten him up, stabbed him with a kitchen knife and set fire to their home. Bogart's escapades with Errol, however, for once did not involve women but getting *away* from them, and even Errol was astonished at the amount of liquor Bogart could consume and still stay on his feet.

After finishing the film, Errol purchased a large plot of land on Mulholland Drive, a beautiful location overlooking the San Fernando Valley. The cost was $35,000. 'I was living the life of a married bachelor,' he recalled in his memoirs. 'I had male pals around me for sports, athletics, gambling and fun, starlets for recreation, and the little woman at home.' Errol had already drawn up a plan of how he wanted his bachelor pad, and its construction began without delay while he flung himself into another swashbuckling adventure, *The Sea Hawk*, a thinly disguised exercise in anti-Nazi propaganda where the setting – Elizabethan England and much of the civilised world being threatened by the tyranny of one man, Philip II of Spain – brought inevitable comparisons with what was happening in Europe at that time. And who better to stamp out this 'oppression' than the archetypal English hero portrayed by Errol Flynn?

Rafael Sabatini's classic story had originally been filmed in 1924, with the heart-throb actor Milton Sills taking the title role after it had been rejected by Valentino. In this version, the scriptwriter adhered strictly to the book. The remake, however, had only one thing in common with the Sabatini work – its title – and was based on a screenplay by Seton I. Miller, *Beggars of the Sea*, which itself had been rehashed by Howard Koch, the man who had scripted Orson Welles' *War of the Worlds* broadcast of 1938. It was given a budget of $1,700,000, which this time was regulated by incorporating some of the sets and costumes from *Elizabeth and Essex*, along with clips of the battle footage from *Captain Blood*. However, while smaller models of ships were filmed in a studio tank – to cut down on costs – Jack Warner did commission two full-scale vessels for the protagonists, measuring 135 and 165 feet.

The Sea Hawk is regarded by many Flynn fans as the finest film he ever made. In it he played Geoffrey Thorpe, one of the numerous 'seahawks' or privateers then responsible for plundering Spanish ships and relocating their already purloined booty to the English treasury. The swashbuckling begins immediately when Thorpe's ship, the *Albatross*, encounters the galleon conveying the Spanish ambassador (Claude Rains, once again in high camp mode) to England. With him are his pretty niece, Dona Maria (Brenda Marshall), and a cargo of captured English mariners who have been forced to toil as galley slaves. In the ensuing battle, every conceivable weapon is put to the test – rapier, cutlass, cannon, dagger, musket and sword – and the enemy capitulate as their vessel sinks, only just preventing Thorpe from dispatching their captain (Gilbert Roland).

The freed slaves now become Thorpe's men, and the initially stand-offish Dona Maria – a common trait in Flynn movies – captures his heart after he has pronounced the plum line which Errol had to retake several times because he kept cracking up: 'We have an old proverb in England. It says, "Those who sail without oars stay on good terms with the wind!"' In London, Thorpe is disciplined by his queen (Flora Robson) for attacking what she believes was a peace-keeping mission. What she does not know is that there is a spy within her court – the creepy Lord Wolfingham (Henry Daniell), who learns of Thorpe's mission to ambush a Spanish treasure train in Panama. Dona Maria tries to warn him, but arrives at the port just as the *Albatross* is leaving.

In Panama, Thorpe loses half of his men in the jungle before running into an ambush: captured by the Spaniards, they are sent to the galleys, while the scene flashes back to Elizabeth's court, where Dona Maria sings her Korngold lament, 'My Love Is Far From Me'. All ends well, however, when the slaves break free of their chains and take over the ship, and once Thorpe has been reunited with his love, there is a final showdown between Wolfingham. This duel, again choreographed by Fred Cavens, is even more spectacular than Errol's earlier effort with Basil Rathbone – crashing through windows, up and down stairs, in and out of every room in the palace. Once he has rapiered his man, Thorpe barely pauses for breath before taking on Elizabeth's guards. This skirmish is curtailed by the Queen's appearance, however, and Thorpe hands her documentary proof of the skulduggery between Wolfingham and the Spanish king. In the film's closing scene, when Thorpe is knighted, Elizabeth delivers her famous speech which British audiences in particular interpreted as a strident anti-Fascist slogan:

> A grave duty confronts us all to prepare our nation for a war that none of us wants ... When the ruthless ambition of a man threatens to engulf the world it becomes a solemn obligation to all free men to affirm that the earth belongs not to any one man, but to *all* men, and that freedom is the deed and title to the soil on which we exist.

By and large, Flora Robson was a more effective Elizabeth than Bette Davis had been: whereas Davis had appeared corpse-like and neurotic, Robson's queen was more humane. On the set, too, Robson was less problematic than Davis had been, prompting Errol to declare that he would do anything to work with her again. He did, shortly afterwards, but only on the radio in the Philip Morris Playhouse production of Hitchcock's *The Lady Vanishes*.

Flora Robson's 'responsible' behaviour rubbed off on Errol, resulting in just two tantrums during the shooting of *The Sea Hawk*, neither of which involved her. The first occurred during the scene aboard the Spanish galleon when the captive Englishmen are being lashed into shape by the slave-master, played by David Kashner, an acknowledged expert who whipped a flower from between Dorothy Lamour's lips in *The Road to Singapore*. In *Captain Blood*, Kashner had lashed the slaves so realistically, always bringing the tip of his whip within a hair's breadth of the actors' torsos, that Errol had insisted upon his appearance in *The Sea Hawk*. Michael Curtiz, however, decided to teach him a lesson for turning up late one morning, slipping the actor a few dollars to make the scene 'a little more authentic'. When the thong bit into Errol's shoulder, he leapt from his bench, bursting his prop chains, seized the handle of the bull-whip and roared at Kashner, 'Do that again and I'll shove every inch of this all the way up your fucking arse!'

Errol's second outburst took place during the last week of shooting, when Lili Damita visited the set to tell him in front of everyone that she was pregnant. At this stage in his career, when he was at his artistic and sexual peak and able to have his pick of the Hollywood beauties, a child was the last thing Errol needed – or so Damita appears to have thought. 'She made a classic remark,' he recalled. '"Fleen, you think you've screwed every dame in Hollywood, but now I've screwed you, my friend. You will have a child!"'

Errol reacted to the news by going off to get drunk, then left Damita – and his parents, who seemed to be showing no signs of ever wanting to leave Hollywood – in order to spend a 'boys only' week on his yacht. He returned to base to work on his next film. *Santa Fe Trail*, a title which had absolutely nothing to do with the events in the movie, it told of the dissension between the abolitionist John Brown (Raymond Massey) and the US Army, which resulted in the attack on the Harper's Ferry Federal Arsenal on 16 October 1859, after which Brown was hanged for treason. Errol played the cavalry commander, Jeb Stuart, while the part of General Custer went to Ronald Reagan. There was Hollywood's usual rewriting of history: Stuart and Custer are seen graduating from the West Point Academy in 1854, whereas Custer did not graduate until seven years later, and *Stuart* comes across as the real hero simply because the actor portraying him was the biggest star in the cast. Neither was the abolitionist presented as an entirely sympathetic figure: the underlying theme running through Robert Buckner's somewhat lame screenplay was that it was all perfectly well to fight slavery, but was *violence* truly necessary?

Within days of finishing *Santa Fe Trail*, Errol, Bill Lundigan and a handful of male friends left Hollywood aboard the *Sirocco* for what would be a six-week tour of Latin America. Errol told the press that the purpose of the trip was 'to take a well-earned break and maybe spread a little goodwill in the process'.

Detractors, most notably Charles Higham, later professed that this was yet another exercise in espionage, particularly because Errol was trailed much of the time by FBI agents. This was only partly true: the FBI's chief concern was that the Flynn gang were on one of their not-so-clandestine 'chicken' hunts (the pursuit of teenage boys and girls in a part of the world where such things were more or less a part of life).

The director of the FBI was the notorious J. Edgar Hoover, who had held the position since 1924 and would retain it until his death in 1972. For years, Hoover had suspected Errol of having sex with minors and on more than one occasion had come perilously close to having him arrested. Hoover was well aware, however, that Errol knew that he himself – once denounced by Truman Capote as 'the killer fruit' – liked to dress in women's clothes and that, since 1928, he had been involved in a homosexual relationship with one Clyde Tolson, who had worked for three successive secretaries of war before joining the FBI.

Flynn supporters, on the other hand, have claimed that Errol was actually working for British Intelligence, of which there is also some proof. It may well be, of course, that with his love of danger he was killing two birds with one stone – rallying against the support for Hitler in South and Central America while having as good and illegal a time as possible in his off-duty hours. If this was true, however, only the pleasure side of his trip met with any degree of success. Aside from several semi-official engagements with various consulates and the British Red Cross, and a few radio broadcasts, Errol's 'work' here only resulted in a brief article for the *Los Angeles Examiner* which any Reuter hack could have penned and a longer, more self-absorbed piece for *Photoplay* which ultimately proved that, if anything, Errol Flynn was far too loquacious to have made a trustworthy spy:

> I did not go down there on a binge... They – Germany and Italy – are getting ready to fight US, not just the British Empire, and they want to fight us in our own back yard, South America... I know, I was there and saw the preparations, the 'tourists', the Fifth Columnists, the huge radio programmes, the saboteurs. I fought them every way I could. That's why I went!... They gave me quite a write-up. According to Virgie [Virginio Gayda, editor of *Giornal d'Italia* and fervent supporter of Mussolini] I'm the tops, the deadliest, dirtiest, conniving son of a macaw that the unspeakably cunning British Propaganda Minister has ever sent out!

Upon his return to Hollywood, Errol spent a few days supervising the work on Mulholland House, as he had baptised his new home, before starting work on a film which would receive more than its fair share of adverse criticism, largely on account of the fact that it was billed as 'a frothy and sophisticated comedy'. Viewed as a semi-serious, *Thin Man* type spoof, however, *Footsteps in the Dark* is not that bad. Errol played Francis Warren, a wealthy investment counsellor who leads a secret double life as the crime writer F. X. Pettijohn, whose best-selling novel, *Footsteps in the Dark*, has caused considerable controversy.

Much of the information for Warren's tome has been gleaned from his liaisons with the police chief, Inspector Mason (Alan Hale), and not even his wife Rita (Brenda Marshall) knows the truth about him. He is sussed, however, by a would-be client, Fissue (Noel Madison), who is later found on his yacht, having died of suspected alcohol poisoning. To humour him – and because he is over-critical of their investigatory techniques – the police ask Warren to assist them, and he finds out that the dead man had frequently visited a burlesque, where the artiste-in-residence is the sluttish stripper, Blondie White (Lee Patrick). Suspecting that Fissue has been murdered and that Blondie may hold the key to the killer's identity, Warren befriends her, assuming the guise of Lucky Tex Gilbert, a wealthy Texas rancher with a dreadful hairstyle and an even more dreadful accent. 'Gee, Blondie,' he enthuses before executing a painful-to-watch jitterbug. 'Words come outta you just as beautiful as oil comes out of a derrick.'

Out on the town with his 'lady-love', Warren is seen by one of his wife's friends, and Rita's mother subsequently hires a private detective to keep tabs on him. By this stage, Warren is convinced that *Blondie* is the killer – until she provides the police with an alibi that she was visiting her dentist (Ralph Bellamy) at the time of Fissue's death. Blondie then tells Warren that she is being menaced by her ex-husband and that she must leave town; she has already left her suitcase in a locker at the railway station and all she needs now is money. Warren is more than willing to help. 'I've gotta roll on my hip so big,' he boasts. 'A gee-raffe couldn't look over it!'

Rita, meanwhile, believes that her husband must be having an affair, and the police, having learnt that Francis Warren and F. X. Pettijohn are one and the same, suspect *him* of murder when Blondie is found dead in her apartment. By the time, however, Warren has worked out who the real killer is – Davis, the dentist, who fails in his attempt to dispose of him the way he did Fissue, by injecting him with a non-recognisable poison. The film ends with our hero sneaking out of the house to help investigate another case, only this time accompanied by his wife.

Errol's next film, *Dive Bomber*, turned out to be his swansong with Michael Curtiz. Having sworn never to have anything to do with 'that son-of-a-bitch kangaroo' after *Santa Fe Trail*, Curtiz was tempted into a reunion with Errol only by way of a fat pay cheque. America was about to enter the war and this film, shot in glorious Technicolor and full of rip-roaring action, was a bravado attempt at showing the rest of the world what the American troops were made of. Much of it was shot on location at San Diego's Naval Air Base, and aboard the aircraft-carrier *Enterprise*. But the storyline and the script were poor, and the general opinion of the critics was this was the kind of adventure movie the average American did *not* wish to see Flynn in.

On 10 May 1941, Lili Damita gave birth to a son, and the couple decided to call him Sean – one of the few things they ever agreed upon. The event brought about a brief and surprisingly peaceful reconciliation and 'the happy family' posed for the press while Errol extolled the importance of fatherhood. 'Out of this impossible snarl of two volatile people, there came something good,' he said afterwards, and though he was not present for the birth – he was at sea with Bill Lundigan and Bruce Cabot – enjoyed being a parent. However, he made it clear to Damita that despite the child, they were *still* husband and wife in name only, and within hours of the press vacating the Flynns' apartment, he was off again on his boat.

Relations between Errol and Michael Curtiz had not been quite as severe on the set of *Dive Bomber* as they had in the past: therefore, while Errol was sunning himself on the *Sirocco*, Jack Warner assumed that the pair would be willing to work together on *The Constant Nymph*, which was about to go into production with Joan Leslie. He assumed wrong: both the actor and the ebullient, ever-cursing Hungarian had sworn never to cross paths again, and had no intention of going back on their word. A few months later, the proposed film would begin shooting with French star Charles Boyer. Errol, meanwhile, was told that his next part would be that of General Custer in *They Died With Their Boots On*, and Raoul Walsh was brought in to direct.

A hard-talking, living and boozing individual despised by many of the stars he worked with – most notably Marlene Dietrich, who described him to me as 'the biggest pain in the ass I ever knew' – Raoul Walsh was worshipped by Errol, who immediately recognised a kindred spirit who inspired and encouraged his tastes in adventure and rebelliousness. As a boy, Walsh had evaded parental discipline by running away to sea, and in his youth he had worked on cattle drives. In 1909, at the age of 22, he had appeared in his first film as an extra, and six years later he had portrayed Lincoln's assassin, John Wilkes Booth, in D. W. Griffith's *Birth of a Nation*. More film roles had followed, his last being in the Somerset Maugham story, *Sadie Thompson*, which he scripted and directed in 1928. After that, he was only interested in working behind a camera, most famously directing Douglas Fairbanks' *The Thief of Baghdad*. Walsh's trademark was his famous black eyepatch, which he had started wearing after losing an eye when a jack-rabbit shattered the windscreen of his car. Because of it, Errol affectionately called him 'One-Eyed Bandit', and Walsh reciprocated by calling him 'The Baron'.

As with his previous real-life heroes – Fletcher Christian, the Earl of Essex and Jeb Stuart – Warner Brothers were more interested in giving George Armstrong Custer the characteristics of Errol Flynn than in presenting him as he really was. Thus, a reputedly dull man but brilliant cadet became a witty no-hoper with a drink problem, fond of eating raw onions, and of such little regard as far as his peers are concerned that his men are informed of his generalship before he is.

The film begins with Custer arriving at the West Point Academy in 1857 (looking remarkably mature for a lad of eighteen), accompanied by several pet dogs, wearing a uniform he has designed for himself, and not even having bothered to enrol. He is befriended by a cadet named Ned Sharp (Arthur Kennedy) who shows him to his 'quarters', actually those of a superior officer, and rewards the young man by punching him at muster, whence Sharp becomes the foe. Henceforth, Custer's sloppy, unruly behaviour and brawling find him persistently on punishment duty, and it is on one such occasion that he meets and falls in love with Elizabeth Bacon (Olivia de Havilland).

When war is declared between the North and South, Custer graduates as a lieutenant and leaves for Washington, where in a society cafe he worms his way into the affections of General Winfield Scott – a superb performance from Sydney Greenstreet – by sharing with him the establishment's last portion of his favourite creamed Bermuda onions. This meeting leads to him being appointed with the Second Cavalry, where he encounters the hated Sharp once more. 'The face I always like to shake hands with,' he says. Already the hero of several battles, he then marries Elizabeth and is relocated to Fort Lincoln, in the heart of Sioux territory. Here he comes face to face with the formidable Crazy Horse (Anthony Quinn), with whom he signs a peace treaty. Sharp, not content with selling rifles to the Indians, then plans to run a railroad through their sacred burial grounds in the Black Hills.

The showdown with Sharp is a muted scene, where Custer tells him about the basic difference between money and glory: 'You can take the glory with you when it's your time to go.' The temporarily teetotal Custer then gets him drunk, and transports him in the back of a waggon to the battlefield at Little Bighorn. Here he will make amends by dying a hero in the conflict he has supposedly helped to cause when Custer's men attempt to prevent the Sioux from retaliating after being duped. Custer's so-called 'Last Stand', which took place on 25 June 1876, was not as spectacular on celluloid as the final scene in *The Charge of the Light Brigade*, but the imagery of a futile, wholly unnecessary bloodbath – where 220 soldiers were massacred by several thousand Indians – is just as effective. It was turned into a tearjerker by Max Steiner's incorporation of 'Garry Owen' into the score, an authentic Irish drinking song which Custer himself had adopted in 1866.

Equally moving was Custer's farewell in the film to his wife, a semi-allegorical touch because Errol and Olivia de Havilland, who were never less than the best of friends, had decided to part company after eight films together. They both agreed that the time had come for Olivia to be a star in her own right, rather than 'Flynn's girlfriend'. 'We'll grow fat and happy together,' she optimistically tells him, though he fears they might never see each other again, particularly when he reads a passage from her diary, within which she has written, 'A premonition of disaster such as I have never known is weighing me down. I pray God I be not asked to walk alone.' He then tries to comfort her by saying, 'The more sadness in parting, the more joy in the reunion,' adding tenderly, 'Walking through life with you, ma'am, has been a very gracious thing.'

They Died With Their Boots On also brought Errol a personal tragedy. Among the 'crew' on his last *Sirocco* trip were two young men, Stephen Raphael and 28-year-old Jack Budlong, who had been promised parts in his future films providing they 'came' up to scratch – a pun which had been intended. Of the two, Errol had taken a particular shine to married Budlong, the heir to a $1 million estate in California, and about to become a father for the first time. 'He was very good-looking, an athlete, an excellent polo player,' Errol recalled, 'He followed me round like a puppy. I wanted to see him get places in films. He had all that the world can offer –

except fame as an actor.' Errol had kept his word and both men were hired as extras for the film. Budlong, however, was injured on 30 July during the Little Bighorn scene when he fell from his horse on to his sword. He died six days later. Errol mourned him for the rest of his life, changed his name to William Meade in his memoirs to protect his sexuality, and insisted that Raoul Walsh leave the small sequence of film in which he appeared intact, as a mark of respect.

In August 1941, while *They Died With Their Boots On* was still in production, Errol had a blazing row with Lili Damita which left not one piece of crockery intact in their kitchen, and the next day she walked out on him, taking baby Sean with her. Two weeks later, he was contacted by her lawyer and informed that she would be filing for divorce. Errol was genuinely taken aback. After five years, he had come to regard their 'impossible to live with, impossible to live without' situation as the norm, and probably had not anticipated it ever ending. The divorce was acrimonious, but not as messy as it could have been. Damita did not give Hollywood what surely would have been *the* scandal of the century by divulging details of Errol's love life, primarily because she too had slept around indiscriminately with both sexes, but she did manage to exact a settlement which in her words 'would screw him rotten for the rest of his miserable life.' She would receive a minimum payment of $1,500 a month so long as she never married again, effectively forcing her to stay single until after Errol's death.

Suffering badly from insomnia, loss of appetite and depression – though he attributed the latter condition to the exhausting schedule of *They Died With Their Boots On* and William Meade's death – in the middle of the month Errol took the *Sirocco* out to Balboa on a trip that would ultimately prove to be his worst nightmare. Errol always maintained that the best friend he *ever* had was not a human being but his dog, Arno. 'The little mutt', as he was lovingly called, had become a celebrity in his own right over the years – attending functions and premières, showing up at nightclubs and restaurants, and even sharing his master's bed on the rare occasions that Errol slept alone. En route to Balboa, Arno jumped over the side of the yacht, and a few days later his body was washed up on the shore. Errol received a call from the coastguard to collect it, but he was too distressed to do so. After arranging for Arno to be interred close to where he had been found, he later buried his collar and lead in the garden of his as yet unfinished house.

Arno's death had unexpected repercussions when a viper-tongued gossip columnist named Jimmy Fidler wrote a sarcastic piece about the event, attacking Errol for not claiming the dog's body and drawing the conclusion, '*That's* how much he cared!' Bruce Cabot, who had held a weeping Errol in his arms after learning about his dog's death, decided to take Errol to dinner at the Mocambo, knowing full well that this was one of Fidler's favourite haunts for picking up spicy stories. Here, just days before, Fidler had received a severe tongue-lashing from Tallulah Bankhead because he had attacked her for wasting so much time raising over $500,000 for the war effort when, in his opinion, America should never have entered the war in the first place. Prior to this, he had upset Errol by denouncing *Dive Bomber* as 'talentless pro-war propaganda'.

Now, as anticipated, Errol saw red. Marching up to Jimmy Fidler he told him, 'You don't deserve the dignity of a fist,' then delivered a swift slap across the face which nevertheless sent Fidler reeling across several tables. Errol was then stabbed in the ear by Mrs Fidler's oyster fork, and the hack served him with a writ. Fortunately, this amounted to nothing. Errol apologised privately to Fidler, who refused to accept it, declaring that there was nothing to be sorry for, and the two men became close friends!

It was only when Errol collapsed in the elevator of a Hollywood medical centre that he realised there was something radically wrong with him, yet even then, the emergency doctor who treated him diagnosed nothing more than 'acute nervous exhaustion'. A few weeks later, however, a specialist delivered a much more serious prognosis: on account of his 'extravagant' lifestyle – an over-surfeit of drink, drugs and cigarettes – his heart and lungs were irreparably damaged. He was told that, at best, he might live another five years, but only if he took better care of himself.

Errol shared his grim news with a handful of his closest friends, including Bruce Cabot and Raoul Walsh, adding that he was wholly unafraid of dying, and that if he did have but a few years left, he would certainly make the most of them. His consumption of cigarettes and booze increased twofold overnight, as did his appetite for sex: at the age of 32 Errol is said to have enjoyed sex three times every day, with both male and female partners. There were also reports of him unbuttoning his flies and exposing himself in front of relative strangers, and masturbating while chatting to lovers on the telephone.

At the end of 1941, however, when Errol finally moved into Mulholland House, he was suffering from chronic depression. With the Japanese attack on Pearl Harbour, America had at last entered the war, and he was desperately upset not just because he was unfit to fight but at some of the remarks being levelled at his 'cowardice' by the press. He was also becoming increasingly dependent on opium. While making *They Died With Their Boots On* he had read Thomas de Quincey's classic novel of 1822, *Confessions of an English Opium-Eater*, and, reflecting on how the drug had heightened his sexual pleasures with Ting Ling O'Connor, had subsequently decided that this might be the only way of getting him out of the doldrums. A contact on the lot had soon fixed him up with a regular supply, and when friends began commenting on his ashen features, he laughed off the effects of the drug as 'just fatigue'.

Ostensibly, Errol was swayed from this particular path of self-destruction by the unexpected arrival of an Australian chum named Freddie McEvoy. Two years older than Errol, similarly built, but nowhere near as good-looking, McEvoy had attended an English public school where his education had suffered because he had only been interested in sport and having a good time. In 1936 he had captained the British bobsled team at the Berlin Olympics, winning no medals, though they had won the World Championships in St Moritz the following year. By this time, McEvoy had earned himself a reputation as a stud, running a team of gigolos which operated along the French Riviera, servicing wealthy matrons and socialites. In 1949, he had married Beatrice Cartright, a disabled heiress 30 years his senior, a union which ended in the divorce courts soon after his reunion with Errol. McEvoy is also said to have been 'close' to his manservant, a young, French-speaking Russian defector named Alexandre Pavlenckov...whom Errol at once purloined to work as his major-domo!

'This was a bachelor house. No woman would live here with me. Not Lili, nor anyone else,' Errol said of his new home, adding with almost glib satisfaction, 'Strange people wended their way up the hill to Mulholland. Among them pimps, sports, bums, down-at-heel actors, gamblers, athletes, sightseers, process servers, phonies, queers, salesmen ... all kinds and all types, as the Lord of Nature composed them.' Yet during his first weeks here, he was in too much of a drug-induced haze to enjoy or even observe its opulence – until Freddie McEvoy realised what was going on and organised a search of every room while Errol was at the studio. His stash of opium syrettes was eventually discovered in one of the bathrooms and disposed of, which led to Errol dragging McEvoy out into the garden and attempting to thrash the living daylights out of him, only to end up battered and bruised himself.

Cured of his dope habit for the time being, Errol concentrated on his other great addiction – sex. In his sumptuous living room, shocked guests would ignore the Van Gogh and Gauguin originals and stare incredulously at the pornographic magazines stacked next to copies of *Time* and *Life*. The cocktail cabinet had a spring-loaded opening device shaped like a bull's genitals, and 'his' and 'hers' dildos could be found in the bathroom and bedrooms, along with a selection of aphrodisiac creams and potions. Errol's own bedroom had a huge circular mirror on the ceiling above the bed, although he rarely slept in it himself. 'Special' guests chez Flynn were always grateful that 'mine host' gave up his room as well as supplying them with a pretty girl or boy, depending on their taste. What they were unaware of was that the mirror was two-way, and that Errol and his buddies were monitoring their nocturnal activities in the 'jerk-off' room above.

Another early visitor to Mulholland House was John Barrymore, as witty, alert and vindictive as ever, yet physically a wreck. Barrymore always called Errol Navarre because he said he reminded him of a portrait he had once seen of Henry IV of France, and Errol always refused to believe that Barrymore was no longer The Great Profile, but a worn-out has-been. An alcoholic since the age of fourteen, he had been relegated to appearing in cheap B-movies, and most recently he had toured the United States with his fourth wife, Elaine Barrie, in *My Dear Children*, a pathetic series of performances to which audiences had flocked to witness him fluffing his lines and vomiting and urinating on the stage.

Barrymore turned up at Errol's home in the middle of the night in January 1942, following an argument with his wife. During the next three weeks – Errol called them the most frightening he had experienced since leaving New Guinea – he virtually took over the household. With a penchant for urinating anywhere but in the lavatory, Barrymore would simply open the nearest window and void his bladder, often drenching some unsuspecting passer-by. When Errol complained that this was washing all the varnish off his window-sills, he took to using the fireplace or the nearest wardrobe! Finally, unable to stand any more, Errol went to see Barrymore's wife and effected an uneasy reunion, though he later expressed some guilt over ejecting this troublesome but loveable rogue from his home.

Unable to fight in a real war, Errol teamed up with Alan Hale, Arthur Kennedy, Ronald Sinclair and Ronald Reagan for *Desperate Journey*, a *Boy's Own* style adventure with a large pinch of Enid Blyton thrown in for good measure. The antics of this particular Famous Five – an Australian, an American, a Canadian, an Englishman and a Scotsman – are scarcely credible, with the over-eponymous heroes depicted as far too gung-ho, while the Nazis are portrayed as bumbling dolts with hammy accents.

The men of the Royal Air Force's 282 Squadron, under the command of Flight Lieutenant Forbes (Errol) are dispatched to Schneidemül, close to the Polish border, to complete an exercise begun by Polish saboteurs – namely the destruction of a railway switchpoint handling German munitions trains. The bombing is a success, though their plane is brought down and only five survive, to be captured by the enemy and hauled before the sneering but wholly unconvincing Major Baumeister (Raymond Massey). The quintet escape – having first learned the secret locations of a number of Messerschmidt factories – and in the guise of Nazi soldiers, aided by Forbes' command of the German language, they board an enemy controlled train en route to occupied Holland. 'We're going to be the first invasion to hit Germany since Napoleon,' Forbes declares, bringing the response from one of his colleagues, 'Napoleon, where did you put the brandy?'

In Holland, the friends are helped by a pretty patriot, Kaethe (Nancy Coleman), walk into another Nazi trap, and become involved in a cross-country car chase which ends when Forbes' crew – now reduced to three – run out of fuel and chance upon a captured British plane with which the Germans are about to bomb the Battersea Waterworks. 'Maybe we'll get a chance to do something if they break off for lunch,' Kennedy's character says. Then, after much camp carnage, and as England swims into view through the cockpit windscreen, Forbes chirps, 'Ah, England. Now for Australia and a crack at those Japs!'

Desperate Journey, as long as it is not taken seriously, is not a bad film, and most of the scenes are expertly handled by director Raoul Walsh. The critics, however – who still knew nothing of Errol's health problems – all agreed that the film was third-rate, and that Warner Brothers should not delay in putting Errol into another of his more acceptable swashbucklers.

Errol, however, did not want to and – against his doctor's orders – he immediately began shooting *Gentleman Jim*, the fictionalised story of the boxer James John Corbett (1866–1933), widely reputed to have brought 'science' to the sport, and the first world champion under the present Marquis of Queensbury rules. A larger-than-life character who also starred in films and appeared on the vaudeville circuit, Corbett had won the world heavyweight championship in 1892 by knocking out the former bare-knuckle fighter, John Lawrence Sullivan, after 21 gruelling rounds. He subsequently lost his title five years later to Robert Fitzsimmons, though Hollywood cut Corbett's story short way before this point and supplied him with a love interest which was entirely fictitious and a vanity which was highly improbable. In this film the great prize-fighter is less concerned about bruises and broken bones than he is with his trainer messing up his hair.

Errol always maintained that Jim Corbett was one of his favourite roles, because they had so much in common: both were descended from Irish stock, both had been expelled from school for antisocial behaviour, both had had acrimonious splits from their wives. At six feet two inches and 185 lbs, Errol was slightly taller and heavier than the champion, and he was of course an accomplished boxer so refused to have a double for the fight scenes. In order to perfect Corbett's famous 'dancing footwork' and left hooks, he was guided by former welterweight champion and trainer, Mushy Callahan.

The action begins in 1887, when the young Corbett, employed as a bank clerk, attends an illegal bare-knuckle fight in his native San Francisco. The event gets him an introduction to the somewhat snooty Victoria Ware (Alexis Smith), who sponsors him to fight for the Olympic Club, run by her father, ostensibly because she cannot stand his cocky mannerisms and believes that a good hiding from his opponent might rid him of his arrogance. Corbett wins the fight in a sequence which is both exciting and authentic in its execution, cameraman Sid Hickox paying particular attention to Errol's footwork. Errol also looks superb, bare-chested and in tights which are a good deal more revealing than Robin Hood's had been. 'Mummy, why doesn't Daddy look like that in his underwear?' a child pipes, bringing the response, 'He did – *once!*'

As the plot unfolds, Corbett further alienates himself from Victoria by kissing her when she is least expecting it. 'I hope some man knocks your block off,' she tells him, though the chances of this seem unlikely when he is seen winning every contest he enters. One, against Joe Choynski, takes place on a barge in one of the sets left over from the 1941 film, *The Sea Wolf*, behind which is one of the ships from the production. Then finally comes the fight with Sullivan (Ward Bond) in New Orleans, for which the cantankerous Victoria puts up the stake money – money which she declares will be well spent just to see Corbett lose. He does not, of course, and when she witnesses the again improbable 'humbling' scene that takes place between Corbett and the defeated champion – when Sullivan not only tells him that the best man has won, but also presents him with his own championship buckle – Victoria finally admits she is in love with him. This particular piece of scripting would be much repeated in newspapers:

> JIM: Well, how do we stand?
> VICTORIA: Yes, I like you, but it wouldn't surprise me if I loved you more than you loved me.
> JIM: *Love*? *Us!*
> VICTORIA: Fine way for a gentleman to behave!

> JIM: Oh, darling. That gentleman stuff never fooled
> you, did it? I'm no gentleman!
> VICTORIA: [kisses him] In that case, I'm no lady!

Two significant events marred the shooting of *Gentleman Jim*. On 29 May 1942, John Barrymore died. Errol's great pal was 60, but on account of his lengthy trail of self-destruction looked much older, and according to his doctors it was amazing that he had lasted so long. His demise also proved that Hollywood sometimes has a decidedly short memory, for despite his former legendary stature there were few mourners at his funeral, and even his pall bearers were men he had loathed. The writer Gene Fowler was with Barrymore when he died – he later penned a definitive biography of the actor – and it was he who accompanied his body to Pierce's Funeral Home on Sunset Boulevard. Errol's friend John Decker sketched him lying in his casket, and the only mourner was an elderly prostitute from better days.

Barrymore's sad exit, however, was not his acting swansong, for several of Errol's Olympiads, now augmented by Raoul Walsh, had without Errol's knowledge decided to give Barrymore the send-off they believed he deserved. Taking Walsh's car, they drove to the funeral home, where for a suitable fee Walsh persuaded the undertaker to 'loan' them the actor's unembalmed corpse for an hour or so. They then conveyed this to Mulholland House, where they positioned him in Errol's living room – in his favourite armchair, which he had commandeered not so long before, next to the fireplace-cum toilet. Needless to say, the shock almost gave Errol apoplexy. He rushed into the garden screaming, and it took Walsh and his cronies some time to coax him back into the house. Even after they apologised for playing a prank which *had* been in the very worst taste, he never forgave them completely.

A few weeks after Barrymore's death, Errol was taken ill on the set of *Gentleman Jim*. This time it was in public, so the press were on the scene within minutes. Warner Brothers issued a statement to the effect that their star was suffering from exhaustion, brought about by the mammoth fight scene with Ward Bond, and no one found just cause to doubt this. Even when a subsequent statement declared that Errol was taking a week off from shooting, no one even began to suspect that this apparently supreme example of health, strength and physical fitness had been rushed to Los Angeles' Good Samaritan Hospital after suffering a *heart attack*, albeit a mild one.

Earlier in the year, through Marlene Dietrich, who would soon be actively involved with Central Intelligence, later the Office of Strategic Services – Errol had been introduced to the Foreign Information Service's Wallace Deuel. He had suggested that with his 'Irish' connections – Professor Flynn's popularity was such that he had recently been appointed head of Northern Ireland's Air-Raid Precautions – Errol would make 'an excellent instrument of American propaganda' should he be dispatched to Eire.

Whether Deuel's comment had been made with tongue in cheek is hard to discern, but Errol had taken him very seriously. As active service was not a possibility after his recent health scare, Flynn was keen to find other ways to become involved. He asked the head of Central Intelligence for a uniformed position so that he could travel to Dublin and persuade the Eire government to allow the United States loan of its air and navy bases. Central Intelligence responded to Errol's not unusual request by sending a copy of his letter to President Roosevelt himself. There was, however, no reply, and in the summer of 1942 Errol contacted his friend William Randolph Hearst, the newspaper magnate who had sponsored his trip to Spain. Hearst immediately offered him an assignment as a European correspondent for the International News Service, to begin at the end of October.

In the August, Errol received his naturalisation papers, and to celebrate he threw a huge party on the *Sirocco*, off Catalina Island, where the chief guests – Freddie McEvoy, Stephen Raphael and Bruce Cabot, who by this time were all living together in rented mansion on Bel Air's St Pierre Road – were told to bring as much 'fanny' of both sexes as they could muster at such short notice. The party raged on for days and only ended when .Jack Warner summoned Errol back to Hollywood to start work on a new film.

Edge of Darkness, directed by Lewis Milestone, was the first in a spate of films about the German occupation of Norway. But if Errol's name headed the credits, the acting honours were shared by his best supporting cast in years: Ann Sheridan, Ruth Gordon, Judith Anderson, Nancy Coleman and Helmut Dantine, a dashing, twenty-five-year-old Austrian who had fled to Hollywood on the eve of the war to escape Nazi persecution – only to end up playing a German pilot in *Desperate Journey* and a fully-fledged Nazi in this one.

Dantine, like Patric Knowles, soon found himself fighting off Errol's amorous advances – though had Errol been aware that the young man was Jewish, he most definitely would not have been interested – claiming that Errol was not his type. Dantine had long-since set his sights on Tyrone Power, and according to a statement given at the time by his friend Tallulah Bankhead, as Power was away fighting in the war, Dantine was 'saving himself' for his return. Errol made up for his disappointment by having a fling with a busty, eighteen-year-old actress named Blanca Rosa Welter, whom he had met on a weekend break in Mexico. She would later change her name to Linda Christian and 'get one over' on both Dantine and Errol by *marrying* Tyrone Power.

Edge of Darkness takes place in the autumn of 1942 when a Nazi patrol ship sails into a coastal village to find everyone dead: the locals, the occupying force and their *kommandant*, Koenig (Dantine) have apparently wiped each other out in an extermination battle, yet the Norwegian flag is still fluttering high above the German garrison. Henceforth, the events leading up to the rebellion are told in flashback.

Gunnar Brogge (Errol) is the head of the local fishermen's union and also the underground Resistance movement. His fiancée, Karen (Sheridan) is as fearless as he is, her father (Huston) is the community's only doctor, and her brother Johann (John Beal) is a 'quisling', or Nazi sympathiser. Gerd Bjarnesen (Anderson) is the hard-as-nails hotelier – the film's noblest performance – whose husband has been murdered by the enemy. These people form but part of the group who smuggle arms from England, under the *kommandant*'s very nose, regardless of the consequences this might have on the largely pacifist population, and despite the protestations of their pastor (Richard Fraser). 'It isn't a question of being a Nazi,' someone declares of their own leanings, 'it's a question of protecting what's yours.'

When Koenig suspects that the villagers are up to something, he confiscates their fishing vessels and grants his soldiers leave to run amock. The schoolmaster's house is commandeered and his possessions torched. Karen is raped in the church, and when her father avenges this by killing a German officer, Koenig orders a mass execution, forcing the prospective victims to dig their own graves. They are saved, however, by their compatriots. The pastor machine-guns the firing squad from the church tower, and the whole village marches on the Nazis, decimating them while Koenig flees to his quarters to commit suicide after killing his mistress (Coleman) and casting a last furtive glance at Hitler's portrait. The film then returns to whence it began, with apparently no one left alive on either side. Then, as the officers from the patrol boat are hoisting the German flag, Brogge appears and shoots them. The surviving villagers are seen walking away, while the narrator declares over the closing credits – and one must remember that at the time of the film's release, the United States had yet to augment the war – 'If there is anyone who still wonders why this war is still being fought, let him look to Norway...' For Errol, putting aside aimless pursuit of Helmut Dantine, *Edge of Darkness* was not a happy experience. Halfway through shooting he was subjected to the most harrowing ordeal of his life, one which would very nearly cost him not just his career, but his freedom and his sanity.

5

An Ideal Scapegoat

'Rape to me meant picking up a chair and hitting some young lady over the head with it and having your wicked way. I hadn't done any of these things.'

It emerged that the police had been wanting to question Errol, 'informally', for several weeks, but had been unable to locate his exact whereabouts. *Edge of Darkness* should have begun shooting on location in Monterey at the end of August 1942, but as this had been held up on account of bad weather, Errol and his friends had gone off on another of his jaunts – his last, he declared, before he embarked on the Hearst commission and at the end of September, with the production still running to schedule, the company had been able to return to the Burbank studios to film the interiors. Errol was not apprehended on the set, as has been suggested, but at Mulholland House one evening early in October, by two plain clothes officers who informed him that a seventeen-year-old girl named Betty Hansen had accused him of statutory rape.

Errol's initial reaction was to declare that he had no idea who Betty Hansen was, adding that females had a tendency to fling themselves at him, so he had never had cause to even *think* of raping anyone. The officers then explained that the operative word in this instance was 'statutory' – even if the alleged victim had been *willing* to have sex with him, the fact that she had been under the legal age of eighteen meant that he had committed an imprisonable offence. It could mean being jailed for ten years in the State of California.

Errol was then told that Betty Hansen had been picked up on a vagrancy charge and taken to the Juvenile Hall, where the custodian had gone through her personal effects and found a scrap of paper containing Errol and Bruce Cabot's telephone numbers. When questioned by the police, she claimed that she had had intercourse with Errol in the Cabot-McEvoy-Raphael mansion on 27 September. After sitting on the edge of his chair after a tennis and swimming party, she had complained of feeling unwell and Errol had taken her upstairs, removed her clothes and complimented her on her 'nice breasts and fanny', before undressing himself, keeping on just his socks and shoes, and then having sex with her twice in succession. Errol was astonished to hear this, and after some thought did remember the forthright, buck-toothed girl. His utterance, however, 'You don't mean that frowsy little blonde?', would cause him considerable strife in the not so distant future.

Errol called his lawyer, a young Irishman called Bob Ford, and the pair drove to the Juvenile Hall, where Betty Hansen accused him of his supposed crime to his face, a legal requirement in the State of California. The young woman was then taken into the interrogation room, wearing a regulation brown denim uniform – 'She was gruesome-looking,' Errol recalled – and she repeated the story she had told the police. When asked by Ford if she had put up a fight, however, she surprised him by replying, 'No. Why should I?' Errol then denied the charge and was allowed to go home, and the next morning his lawyer was contacted by the District Attorney and informed that it was highly unlikely that any further action would be taken.

This was not to be. A few days later, Errol was arrested again. This time a 'minor' named Peggy La Rue Satterlee, a hoofer from the Florentine Gardens burlesque whom Errol did know – she had been an extra in *They Died With Their Boots On* – accused him of twice having sex with her aboard the *Sirocco* in August 1941, though why it had taken her fourteen months to come forward was not clear at this point.

Almost certainly, Errol *had* had sex with Satterlee, who was later proved to have been at least eighteen, and possibly 21, at the time of the incident, but aware by now that there was some kind of conspiracy brewing up against him, he denied the charge. In his memoirs he would comment, unashamedly, 'If you meet a young lady who invites herself for a trip on your yacht, knowing in advance full well what the risks are, who the hell asks for her birth certificate, especially if she is built like Venus? And if afterwards she tells you she has had the most wonderful time, who has been hurt?'

Errol was now charged with *four* counts of statutory rape. Bail was fixed at $1,000, and he was ordered to stand before the Grand Jury on 15 October. The press had a field day, digging up all the dirt they could on Errol's so-called 'murky' past, yet scarcely scouring the surface and adopting such turgid headlines as 'ROBIN HOOD ACCUSED OF RAPE' and 'THE DIRTY DEEDS OF CAPTAIN BLOOD'.

On the eve of Errol's court appearance, police officers had to be posted outside the gates of Mulholland House to prevent female fans from getting in. Many of these yelled through this cordon of security, begging Errol to do to them what he had allegedly done to Hansen and Satterlee. Others sent him parcels containing their underwear, inviting him to sleep with it under his pillow before returning it, and he received a number of marriage proposals from middle-aged matrons. Such support – albeit fanatical – touched him, and gave him the courage to face whatever fate had in store for him. 'I wanted to shrink into the ground with shame,' he said of his entry into the courthouse. Throughout the hearing, however, he acted with supreme dignity. Betty Hansen had been briefed by her defence that, should she actually be charged with vagrancy at a later date, she could be detained at the Juvenile Hall for up to four years. She had also taken exception to Errol's describing her as 'frowsy'. She now told the court that before the incident she had had a regular job at a drugstore, but when a friend had promised that Errol Flynn would set her up with work – exactly how and doing what was not ascertained – she had not balked at the idea of meeting him. Hansen and her friend had gatecrashed a party at the Cabot-McEvoy-Raphael mansion, but had been asked to stay for dinner by Errol's stuntman pal, Buster Wiles. Hansen then amended her earlier statement to the police concerning the sex session itself, stating under oath that she had tried to fight Errol off, adding, 'But I didn't struggle *very* hard!'

Upon hearing this, and further evidence from Peggy La Rue Satterlee and Freddie McEvoy, the Grand Jury felt there was little more they could do than return a verdict of 'No True Bill'. In other words, they did not believe one word of the prosecution.

Under normal circumstances, once a Grand Jury had declared such a verdict it was unusual – though not impossible, according to the law – for the District Attorney to press for a case to be taken any further. Unfortunately for Errol, things did not quite work out this way. That same evening, after he and Bob Ford had celebrated their 'victory' with Cabot, McEvoy and Raphael, Errol received a telephone call from a well-known extortionist named in his memoirs for legal reasons only as 'Joe', a man who had been blackmailing studio chiefs for years.

Errol was told by Joe that if Jack Warner and he knew what was good for them, they would deposit a package containing $10,000 at a designated pick-up spot. Had Errol submitted to Joe's demands, the matter might have been resolved, but as he *knew* he was innocent – as apparently did the Grand Jury – he gave the caller a piece of his mind, and hung up.

Two days later, however, Errol received another visit from the police: the District Attorney *had* overruled the Grand Jury's decision, and Errol would have to stand trial. He was fingerprinted, mug-shots were taken, and he was measured for a prison uniform – so sure were the police that he would not get off. There then followed an emergency meeting between Jack Warner and Bob Ford wherein both agreed that, while Errol's own lawyer would go on offering him moral support throughout the ensuing proceedings, what he really needed was an attorney with sufficient clout to defend him against what appeared to be considerably more than a straightforward case of statutory rape.

For more than a decade the District Attorney, Buron Fitts, had ruled over a bevy of corrupt politicians and police officials, offering a protection racket to the studios for those of their stars who were threatened by scandals which would wreck their careers. Among these had been Cary Grant and Randolph Scott, Barbara Stanwyck and Robert Taylor, Tyrone Power, and Charlie Chaplin. The war had also added its incipient complication in the fact that, now 'escapism' movies were all the rage, their stars were not as controversial as they once had been.

The last straw, however, had come when Fitts, after spending an unprecedented three terms in office, had recently been defeated by John Dockwiler, known throughout Los Angeles as 'Honest John'. It was on account of Dockwiler's reputation that the paybacks had stopped, and as 'Honest John' was not quite as honest as his publicity machine had made him out to be, repercussions were inevitable and his team began looking for a means of getting even. 'They had won the hard way, and they had vengeance in their hearts,' Errol recalled. 'They said, "OK, instead of getting any preferential treatment the first guy of you lot who gets into trouble has had it. Watch." I was the first guy.'

It was Jack Warner who brought in Jerry Geisler, long renowned as the best showbusiness lawyer in California. If anyone could get Errol off the hook, whether he was guilty or not, Warner declared it would be Geisler, the man who had successfully defended Bugsy Siegel when accused of the murder of Harry Greenberg, and Busby Berkely on a drunk-driving manslaughter charge, when he had knocked down and killed three pedestrians.

The preliminary proceedings opened on 2 November, with Deputy District Attorney Thomas Cochrane defending Betty Hansen and Peggy La Rue Satterlee. Hansen was the first to take the stand. Jerry Geisler's 'researchers' had unearthed an event from her past and he was sure that this alone would get the case thrown out of court, particularly when she changed her testimony again by stating that she had stayed for dinner at the Cabot-McEvoy-Raphael house *against* her will. Cross-examining her, but not heavying her in any way, Geisler prompted her to tell the court of an argument with her sister, with whom she had formerly lived, which had resulted in her relocating to a downtown hotel recommended to her by a man she had 'met on the street'. Hansen also confessed that she had been in the habit of telling acquaintances that she was eighteen, but only so that she could work at a drugstore that did not employ minors. She also admitted to using an alias: Ronnie Hansen.

The next witness to take the stand was Peter Stackpole, a photographer from *Life* magazine who had been on the *Sirocco* in August 1941 when the alleged rape of Peggy La Rue Satterlee had occurred. Stackpole stated that at Errol's request he had taken several shots of Satterlee, including a coloured one which Errol had instructed him to be captioned $5,000. In other words, as had happened often in the past, Errol planned to find her a small part in one of his films in return for services rendered. Satterlee herself, surprisingly, was not asked to take the stand, and when Errol's turn came to face the court, all he pronounced were the words 'Not guilty'.

Four days later, in a brief summing up, the judge in this first hearing approved the District Attorney's plea, in that the matter should be referred to trial: a date was set for 23 November, with bail once more being fixed at $1,000. Jerry Geisler told his client that he had every confidence of a walk-away victory, but when this hearing was adjourned until 14 January, Errol decided that he would not be taking any uncalculated risks. He had already told Freddie McEvoy that he would never go to jail, and now his friend arranged for a two-seater plane to be on permanent standby on a tiny strip in Burbank to fly them to Mexico if the proceedings took a turn for the worse.

Meanwhile, during this uneasy 'recess', Errol agreed to appear in *Thank Your Lucky Stars*, a Warner Brothers quickie spectacular aimed at raising money for the war effort and boosting public morale. Between them, Jack Warner and the producer, David Butler, agreed that each of the twelve major names in the film should be paid $50,000, while the lesser stars and bit-part players should receive their regular rate – and that *all* of these fees should be donated to Allied charities. Only Eddie Cantor objected, telling Warner that it was 'a disgrace to humanity' to give away so much priceless talent for nothing. He very quickly changed his mind, however, when cornered in a studio bar by Errol, John Garfield and Bette Davis, none of whom could stand him on account of his tight-fisted ways.

Unlike *Stage Door Canteen*, its rival production, *Thank Your Lucky Stars* had no running storyline, just one mostly forgettable song and dance routine after another with pretty dire performances from Eddie Cantor, Joan Leslie and John Garfield. Dinah Shore fared only slightly better with the title song, and a mildly expressive 'How Sweet You Are'. Much more entertaining was the vaudeville duet from Alan Hale and Jack Carson, and an all-black revue version of 'Ice-Cold Katy Brown' led by Hattie McDaniel. The scene-stealers, however, were Bette Davis's jitterbug and her *sprechtsinger* interpretation of 'They're Either Too Young Or Too Old', and Errol's extremely good 'That's What You Jolly Well Get', especially written for the film by Arthur Schwartz and Frank Loesser. In the sketch he played a Cockney sailor, a 'wide boy' who breezes into a London pub with tall tales of his alleged wartime heroics – a familiar ruse enjoyed by the customers, who are accustomed to paying for his beer in exchange for being entertained. 'Hurrah, he's won the war,' his pals sing, hoisting him on to their shoulders and carrying him around the room, to which he responds, 'And I won the one before!' – before they throw him through the window, into the street! He then reprises the song in the finale, looking more than a little camp in his mariner's cap and vest. Miming to a tenor he announces, 'That voice is so divine, I'm sorry it isn't mine!'

Errol spent the Christmas of 1942 quietly, with a handful of male pals. Lili Damita visited, with baby Sean, but in his current mood even the presence of his son failed to cheer him up. For the time being, he declared, he was 'off women', and much of the festive season was spent playing cards, swimming and chatting with the Olympiads. And to prove to the outside world that he had no intention of misbehaving, Errol allowed the occasional reporter into Mulholland House. Many of the phallic references to his lifestyle had been temporarily moved or covered up, and there was a large notice pinned to his bedroom door which declared, 'LADIES, YOU ARE RESPECTFULLY REQUESTED TO PRODUCE YOUR BIRTH CERTIFICATE OR APPROPRIATE IDENTIFICATION BEFORE ENTERING THIS SANCTUARY.'

On 14 January 1943, over 2,000 fans jostled outside the Los Angeles Courthouse. Most of these were women, though there was a sizeable contingency from the A B C D E F – the recently founded American Boys Society for the Defence of Errol Flynn. Other admirers and interested parties had queued for two days to ensure a place in the public gallery. Errol arrived ten minutes before the proceedings were scheduled to commence. And though he later said that he had been 'churning up inside', he was able to smile at the crowd, pose for photographs and sign a few autographs. There was a cry of 'Draft dodger!', and one woman yelled out, 'You can take me to your bedroom any time you like, Errol. I sure as hell won't complain!', to which he muttered, 'You'd

better be careful what you're saying, my dear. I might take you up
on that!' However, when a reporter asked him why Jerry Geisler
had chosen a jury of which nine of its members were women, he
merely shrugged his shoulders and walked into the courthouse. A
few minutes earlier, the lawyer had replied to the same question,
'Because a woman can *see* things in another woman within
minutes, things it would take a man five *years* to work out!'

Betty Hansen was the first to take the stand. Her defence, still
Thomas Cochrane, had instructed her to wear dowdy clothes, and
no make-up. Errol had already dismissed her as 'gruesome', and
several newspapers would make the point that there must have
been something radically wrong with Errol Flynn if *this* was the
type of girl he had become attracted to.

Hansen began her testimony by repeating the story she had told
umpteen times already, only now there was a *new* twist: after
Errol had taken her up to his bedroom, and she was feeling a little
better, she had begged him to return her to the other guests, to
which he had retorted, 'You don't think I would really let you go
downstairs, do you?' He then clicked the door shut and, she
assumed, locked them in. Hansen then added that when Errol
started undressing her, she genuinely thought him to be doing so
to put her to bed on account of her indisposition. There were
guffaws of laughter from the public gallery when she followed this
statement with, 'Then the next thing he done was undress himself.
He took off everything but his shoes!' A photograph had just been
published in the *New York Times* of Errol, as Custer in *They Died
With Their Boots On*. Henceforth, the questions became
extremely personal, so much so that several female reporters
walked out of the court, later declaring that had they reported
such 'filth' many of their younger readers would have been
gravely offended.

COCHRANE: Miss Hansen, would you please tell the jury
what you were wearing when Mr Flynn took
you upstairs?

HANSEN: I had on a sports shirt, slacks, shoes and
stockings brassiere and panties. We were
lying down. Then he had an act of intercourse
with me.

COCHRANE: Do you mean that the private parts of Mr
            Flynn were inserted into *your* private parts?
HANSEN: Yes, and afterwards he told me to go to the
            bathroom. Then he told me that he would
            phone me the next night at seven...He
            crossed his heart and said he would but he
            never did.

Under Jerry Geisler's gentle but thorough cross-examination,
however, Betty Hansen's 'virginal' mien started to crumble:

GEISLER: Miss Hansen, when Mr Flynn took off your
            panties, did you *still* have no idea of what
            was going to happen? You didn't think *then*
            about sexual intercourse? And if that is so,
            when *did* you think about it?
HANSEN: When I *had* sexual intercourse with him, sir.
GEISLER: And when you left Mr Flynn that night, did
            he kiss you? Did he hold you tightly in his
            arms?
HANSEN: Oh, yes!
GEISLER: And did you kiss him back?
HANSEN: I kissed him back. Just one smack. It wasn't
            lingering.
GEISLER: Do you remember when you were first taken
            to Juvenile Hall, Miss Hansen? Did you not
            tell the officer there it would be easy to get
            money in this 'sucker' town?
HANSEN: No, sir, I certainly did not.
GEISLER: And, did you not have sexual intercourse
            with the man who introduced you to Mr
            Flynn?
HANSEN: He tried several times, but I didn't let him.

Geisler's cross-examination of Betty Hansen resumed the
following day, when once more her defence had instructed her to
dress in her shabbiest clothes. And this time the questions were
more personal:

GEISLER: Miss Hansen, did you undress in front of two
            men at Mr Flynn's house to prove that you
            were a *true* blonde?

HANSEN: No, sir, I did not.

GEISLER: And how long did the alleged sexual act last?
            Did it hurt very much?

HANSEN: About thirty minutes... and no, it didn't hurt
            much.

GEISLER: During that time, did Mr Flynn *say* anything
            to you?

HANSEN: He said I had nice breasts... and he also said
            that I had a nice fanny.

GEISLER: And, is it not true that before this alleged
            incident you were *already* being held at the
            Juvenile Hall for another reason, the fact that
            you had been involved in an act of sexual
            perversion? Did you not admit before the
            Grand Jury, *under oath*, that you had
            performed two acts of sexual perversion with
            a man? To be specific, did you not testify
            before the Grand Jury that you committed an
            act of *oral* perversion with a man in a motel
            room, and another act of oral perversion with
            a man at your residence?

HANSEN: Yes, sir. I did...

Geisler had made his point, and actually named the young man in
question – Armand Knapp, one of several studio messenger boys
to whom Hansen had apparently offered 'lip-service'. There were
gasps of astonishment from the court that an uneducated,
allegedly 'innocent' minor, a girl who clearly understood what
was meant by 'oral perversion', had had to have the term 'sexual
intercourse' explained to her.

The afternoon session on 15 January, however, opened with
Thomas Cochrane petitioning Justice Stills for a verdict of mistrial
on account of two signed affidavits in his possession which alleged
that two of the jurors – Elaine Forbes and Lorene Boehm – had
been elected only because they were 'Flynn-friendly' and had
sworn that they would never convict him, even if he *was* guilty!

The judge *did* adjourn the proceedings until the matter had been investigated, but they resumed three days later, with only Forbes stepping down of her own free will.

The first witness to take the stand on 18 January was Peggy La Rue Satterlee, of whom Errol recalled of their first meeting, 'She was a beautiful girl. Her upholstery was sensational. Her waist was a lovely moulding. She had long, dark, silky hair, and could have passed for anywhere between twenty and twenty-five.' Thomas Cochrane had now effected a sterling transformation: Satterlee was wearing flat-heeled shoes, cheap clothes, and her hair was in pigtails!

Having been 'enlightened' as to what sexual intercourse actually was – Geisler once more bringing disgusted gasps from the court with his 'inserting his private parts into your private parts' explanation, and bringing the outburst from one spectator, 'Just how *many* private parts does this guy have?' Satterlee told the court how the alleged attack had taken place in August 1941, during the *Sirocco*'s cruise to Balboa. She and her sister had been invited aboard the yacht by Errol's stuntman friend, Buster Wiles, and throughout the trip, she claimed, Errol had referred to her as 'J B' – 'Jail Bait'. On the second night of the trip, he had entered her cabin in his pyjamas. She had been wearing panties and a slip. She concluded, 'Then he got into bed with me, and I guess he completed an act of sexual intercourse.' Cochrane next asked Satterlee what Errol had done to her clothing, to which she responded, 'He pulled my underwear down, then pushed my skirt up as far as my navel. I resisted at first . . . I didn't fight or nothing. I just told him he shouldn't have been *doing* that!'

If Errol *had* had sex with this young woman against her will, she had certainly not tried too hard to avoid him during the journey home, for she next told the court how she had allowed him to take her to his cabin to look at the moon, though she could not quite remember if she had seen it or not. She added, 'He pulled me down on the bed again and took off my clothes. Then we had intercourse, and I kicked and I knocked the curtain down. I fought against him!'

In his cross-examination of Satterlee, Jerry Geisler did little to spare her feelings. Firstly, he produced one of the photographs that Peter Stackpole had taken for *Life* magazine: in it, the young woman looked ravishing, exactly Errol's type, and *exactly* as he would describe her in his memoirs. And when he asked her if this was how she usually looked, and she nodded, Geisler was pretty sure that her story would not be swallowed by the jury. He asked her why she was now looking drab, in pigtails, to which she replied flatly, 'Because sometimes I feel like it.' Then he demanded to know why, when she claimed to have put up a struggle during the second alleged rape, she had not done so the first time. Her response – 'I guess I didn't think it would be worth fighting when there were so many of Mr Flynn's friends there' – only brought titters from the gallery. Satterlee then confessed that she had neither been forced nor dragged down the stairs to Errol's cabin, but that he *had* pushed her back on to the bed when she had tried to get down, and that she had become very angry – although she was unable to recall whether she had crossed her legs or not. 'I began fighting very hard,' she remonstrated, 'though not as hard as I could because I was trying to fight and think at the same time.'

It was at this point that Jerry Geisler moved in for the kill, delivering a succession of quickfire questions – *all* answered in the affirmative – which caused such an uproar in the packed courthouse that Justice Stills threatened to expel the entire public gallery:

'Miss Saterlee, since the start of this trial have you stayed in good hotels or in the homes of policewomen?'
'Have you been treated well – taken out bowling, to shows and on trips?'
'Have you been promised a job when this trial is over?'
'Have you recently had an operation, and was not this operation a criminal act?'
'Did you ask the District Attorney's Office not to prosecute this man, or to reveal his identity?'
'And was the promise made to you that they *wouldn't* prosecute this man providing you agreed to testify in *this* case?'

It did not take very long for Satterlee to confess that in the recent past she had been involved with two men *besides* the alleged incident with Errol. The first of these, who was not named (though he has subsequently been revealed as an actor named John Dale), had got her pregnant and forced her to have an abortion. The second was Owen Cathcart Jones, a 43-year-old officer with the Canadian Air Force who had worked as a technical and sequence adviser for *Desperate Journey*. Cathcart Jones had set her up in the apartment she was now sharing with her sister: Satterlee claimed that shortly before the trial, he had asked her to marry him. There were hoots of derision from the gallery, however, and from several members of the jury, when Satterlee confessed that Cathcart Jones had taken her out on several dates to a local mortuary, where they had 'fooled around playing hide-and-seek among the stiffs'. Then she brought forth gales of laughter with her admission, 'Owen loves me so much that he calls me pet names, such as his little strumpet. That's some kind of English muffin!' This was a classic Freudian slip, for she had actually meant 'crumpet'.

Considerably more condemning, however, so far as the nature of this case was concerned, was Satterlee's admission that she was in possession of a driver's licence which effectively proved that she was *eighteen* years of age. And her obvious lies were highlighted further when Jerry Geisler asked her exactly how high up from the cabin floor Errol's bunk had been. After she had stated that it had been 'around knee-high', he produced photographic evidence to the contrary: the bunk was five feet from the floor, a long way, he concluded, for even a man of Errol's strength to haul a woman if she had been struggling.

When the time came for Errol to take the stand, Geisler addressed him no differently than he had the other witnesses, though everything does appear to have been meticulously rehearsed beforehand. He began by asking him about his draft status, which Errol replied would depend on the outcome of the trial, and about his medical classification, which he said was 4F. He was cautious not to say *why* he had been turned down for military service, claiming that he still did not know why himself. Errol then stressed that he had not had intercourse with Betty Hansen, and denied locking the two of them in his bedroom, particularly as there had been no lock on the door. This story had previously been corroborated by Freddie McEvoy, who swore under oath that at no time during the evening in question had Errol left the party room to go upstairs with Betty Hansen, or any other woman.

Errol next denied kissing Peggy La Rue Satterlee or calling her 'JB' during her trip on the *Sirocco*, or that he had 'spiked' her hot milk 'to facilitate seduction'. He further denied the two counts of statutory rape, declaring that his cabin was so constructed that it would have been impossible to see the moon through the porthole. He then added, genuinely choking back the tears, that entertainment had been the *last* thing on his mind during this particular trip: not only had he been mourning the recent death of William Meade, but en route to Balboa his beloved dog, Arno, had gone overboard. One of the crew members from his yacht had already confirmed this, and that Errol had stayed at the helm of the *Sirocco* all the way back to Hollywood.

On the morning of 5 February, the prosecution and defence began their summing up. Thomas Cochrane spoke aggressively when telling the jury exactly what sort of a person he thought Errol Flynn was – a man with impeccable manners and a polished accent which gave the *impression* of good breeding, yet an actor all the same, a man who was *paid* to do and make impressions, and without any doubt whatsoever 'a ravisher of young women'. 'You must not be misled by this man's performance in court,' Cochrane concluded. 'The *only* way of studying what kind of man Mr Flynn is, is by studying the laws he has broken. Did he have sexual relations with these *girls*, whether they wilfully submitted to him or not? The law under which we are trying Mr Flynn is designed to *protect* under-aged girls. And under such a law they *cannot* give their consent to sex attacks. This man is a sex criminal and as such of the lowest form of criminal this court has ever had to deal with. A man who preys on young girls *must* be sent to prison where he belongs!'

Jerry Geisler, too, did not mince words, as indeed was expected of an attorney whose average fee was $100,000. He had already exhibited the photograph revealing what Peggy La Rue Satterlee usually looked like, and expressed his opinion that the pigtails and dowdy clothes were but a sham. He had also shown the jury the photograph of the interior of Errol's cabin, which he now reproduced to scale on a large blackboard so that everyone could see, reiterating the fact that it would have taken a man of Herculean strength to have hoisted Satterlee on to his bunk. Geisler then announced that it was not his intention to smear the reputations of these alleged victims, adding, 'I *cannot* smear them because they smeared themselves long before *I* ever heard of them!'

Geisler then reminded the jury just *how* immoral Betty Hansen and Peggy La Rue Satterlee were – one having taken part in a (then) act of sexual perversion, and the other having secured an abortion. This was the first time the word 'abortion' had been used during the trial, causing pandemonium and several faintings in the public gallery. Errol's lawyer then stressed that Satterlee *had* been told that neither she nor the father of the aborted child would be sent to prison, and that the District Attorney *had* promised Betty Hansen that she would not be prosecuted for performing oral sex on a man, so long as they both agreed 'to testify the other way'. He concluded, 'Mr Flynn must not be sent to prison because of these girls' lies. It is your duty to return him to his proper place as one of filmdom's brightest stars...and I know in my heart that you will set him free.'

Justice Stills, in *his* summing up, instructed the jury *not* to take Errol's celebrity status into consideration while deciding their verdict, and to regard the varying testimonies of Satterlee and Hansen with extreme caution. The jury, after deliberating for four hours, could not reach a unanimous decision, and spent the night in a hotel. Errol, unable to eat or sleep – and forbidden by Jerry Geisler to touch so much as a drop of alcohol – spent much of his time chain-smoking and taking calls from well-wishers and friends. Several of these, including Buster Wiles, Freddie McEvoy and Bill Lundigan, had arranged for 'heavies' to be positioned in and around the courthouse the next morning. If Errol *was* found guilty, these would overcome any obstacles from police and security and get him to a car, which would spirit him to the air-strip and the flight to Mexico, then Venezuela, a country from which he could not be extradited back to the United States. Financial support was also promised from his fellow Olympiads, though Errol was distressed to learn that only days before, one of their members, the elderly character actor Spencer Charters who had appeared in six Flynn films, had been found dead in his fume-filled car. 'If only I had the guts to take the easy way out,' Errol told Bill Lundigan.

Errol actually appeared to be on the verge of passing out when

Justice Stills was handed the slip of paper upon which had been scribbled the verdicts for each of the four counts of statutory rape. When the words 'Not guilty' were pronounced after each one, he jumped to his feet and let out an ear-piercing 'Whoopee!' as the entire courtroom rocked with applause, cheering him as vociferously as they would any triumphant Broadway première. He then rushed to the front of the court, kissed forewoman Ruby Anderson on both cheeks, shook hands with her colleagues, signed a few autographs, and announced, clearly on the verge of tears, 'My confidence in American justice is justified. I am sincerely grateful to all those of you who've encouraged and supported me through this ordeal.'

For Peggy La Rue Satterlee and Betty Hansen, their fifteen minutes of fame were over. Deservedly shamed and hounded by the press, they returned to the obscurity from whence they came – Satterlee to her family in Applegate, California, and Hansen to her parents in Lincoln, Nebraska. From here, in 1996, Hansen added a coda to the story. Breaking her silence after more than half a century – and insisting on being filmed in a semi-darkened room because, she claimed, she was still terrified of being recognised – Hansen finally decided to 'tell the truth' to a British documentary maker for a programme in Channel Four's *Secret Lives* series. Few people were surprised that, once again, she had changed her story, for in this renewed confession, she and Peggy La Rue Satterlee had been *together* at the Cabot-McEvoy-Raphael mansion:

> We was sitting at the edge of the pool and we were frolicking. The girl and I were playing normal, having fun, and I heard him say, 'Oh, a wild cat from Nebraska!' That's what he called me, and I never cared for that. He kept looking at me, then we went up and naturally made love. What was wrong with *that*? I don't think you could say I was innocent because I had love with him, but I believe I was. It was the first love in my life and he is the first and maybe the last.

For Errol, meanwhile, this quite unnecessary ordeal really *was* over, barring any repercussions which would have to bear the test of time, and he was now free to get on with what he was best at – making movies, hell raising and making love.

6

No Sad Songs For Me

'I felt used. Used by the studio, used to make money. Used by the press
for fun. Used by society as a piece of chalk provides the world with a
dab of colour.'

Warner Brothers' biggest worry – that Errol's rape trial might
affect his success at the box office and lose them revenue – had
been over nothing. It cost *Errol* money, around $600,000 – much
less than Jerry Geisler usually charged his clients, but money
which he borrowed from Jack Warner, who had the audacity to
add five per cent interest.

Errol was universally praised for the dignity that he displayed
throughout his ordeal, and in the eyes of his admirers his esteem
was only elevated. Fans of both sexes now began fantasising
about what it must have been like to have this fabulously
packaged slab of beefcake force himself upon them, particularly
when they were able to see so much of him in the recently released
Gentleman Jim. Errol Flynn was now a *personal* hero who, unable
to fight for his country, had emerged victor from a more
formidable foe – immorality. 'Justice has prevailed,' was all that
Jerry Geisler had to say to the press, while Errol remarked with
almost boastful simplicity that his lawyer had never once asked
him if he was guilty or not.

On the negative side, however, Errol found himself lampooned
by critics and comedians: it was quite evident that his antics off

the screen were no mere rumour, that sex, boozing and brawling all went hand in glove so far as this man was concerned, though little was known as yet about his drug taking, and hardly anything at all about his homosexual dalliances. The term 'In like Flynn' became a password among the American troops – an assertion that one had 'scored' on a date or pick up – but far from annoying Errol, the phrase only amused him. Everywhere he went, women threw themselves at him, while his fan mail bordered on the lewd, some letters containing pictures of 'his' children. At a charity polo match in Fort Myers, attended by President Roosevelt, he tried to avoid a mob of screaming women, only to be grabbed by a burly young man and kissed on the lips. Complete strangers would march up to him in bars and try to pick fights. Most of the time, Errol would 'blarney' himself out of a tricky situation, but in extreme cases he would take the protagonist outside and thrash him, often ending up in court for defending himself.

Unable to work out *why* he had suddenly become a figure of international hysteria, Errol had a large, square question mark embroidered on to all of his clothes. 'My own confusion became my trademark,' he said. 'My own questioning of myself. I felt I must carry this symbolism to gratify my own curiosity or torment. Or to make people think.'

And yet, though proven innocent by 'the people', Errol had not learnt his lesson as far as young girls were concerned. Over the next fifteen years there would be many more, although the one he fell for during his trial said she was eighteen. Nora Eddington was a pretty, leggy redhead who ran the tobacconist's kiosk at the Los Angeles courthouse, and the first time Errol stopped off to buy cigarettes and peered over the counter at her 'luscious ankles', he was determined that he would have her.

Certainly, Errol would not have thought twice about chatting up *anyone*, and few women in America would have turned down Errol Flynn. This time, however, his move had been planned tactfully: the courthouse had been buzzing with reporters, and one false move with a female of indeterminate age would have spelt disaster. Errol therefore called upon the services of his 'official pimp' – his stuntman pal, Buster Wiles, who had been supplying him with girls and young men since, on account of his trial, he had been unable to go looking for his own.

Errol's instructions were explicit: Wiles was to find out all he could about Nora Eddington – her family background, details of her love life, and most importantly, if she was a virgin. A few days later, Errol learnt that Nora's mother was half-Mexican, and that her father, Jack, was a sheriff's secretary who lived in Acapulco with his second wife, Marge. And yes, Nora *was* a virgin, though this situation could soon change because she was engaged to a marine. 'We'll soon see about that!' Errol is alleged to have told his friend.

Nora was then invited to Mulholland House for afternoon tea, and Errol behaved like the perfect gentleman, even kissing her hand when she arrived. 'I had dark intents, but she was a withholding type,' he remembered later. Nora must also have been incredibly naive, or perhaps just plain stupid, *not* to have read Errol's intentions: very few young women visited his home without expecting to be seduced by *someone*.

In all his adult life Errol had never had to press any partner, male or female, into going to bed with him, a fact which made the rape allegations all the more unbelievable. And if a prospective partner *had* turned him down, for whatever reason, there had always been another on standby. In March 1943, however, there was no such thing, and Errol committed what he had been accused of – forcing himself on Nora after bingeing out on cocaine and alcohol with Bruce Cabot.

A few days after this event, and wholly unrepentant, Errol told Nora that any possible relationship between them would have to be put on hold as he had received a call-to-arms from Jack Warner, who was eager to get on with the business of making money now that his star had breezed through his ordeal with his popularity intact.

Northern Pursuit, directed by Raoul Walsh, was an uninspired choice for Errol's 'celebratory comeback'. Another anti-Nazi movie, in it he played Steve Wagner, a Canadian Mountie whose 'links' with the Fatherland lie with the fact that his parents were born there, and that he speaks the language fluently. Pretending to defect from the police force, Wagner acts as a guide for a group of Nazis who are planning to bomb an area in the Hudson Bay. Once more, the German leader was played by Helmut Dantine, who again found himself shunning Errol's advances, and his leading lady was an unconvincing Julie Bishop, whom he marries in the film. At this point in the story a crafty one-liner was incorporated into the script by Warners' publicity department: after swearing to Bishop that she is the only girl he has ever loved, he turns to the camera and cracks, 'What *am* I saying?'

In May 1943, when shooting was almost completed, Errol collapsed on the set of *Northern Pursuit* and was rushed to hospital, where an official statement declared that he was suffering from 'the recurrence of an upper respiratory ailment'. The press still did not know why he had been excused from military service, or that his tuberculosis was steadily getting worse.

After spending a week in hospital – and successfully seducing at least one of his nurses – Errol discharged himself and headed off for what he predicted would be the showdown of the century, with Jack Warner. Barging into the mogul's office without knocking, and having made no appointment, he sat down without being asked and put his feet up on Warner's desk – all sackable offences, had he been a lesser mortal. He then told Warner that unless he received a substantial pay rise – 'I'm an American citizen now, so you'd fucking well better start paying me like one!' – the new picture would not get finished! To a certain extent, Errol was not being unreasonable. He still was not in the same earnings league as contemporaries such as Robert Taylor and James Stewart, yet his films were making bigger profits than theirs, particularly in the wake of his trial. Warner therefore negotiated a new contract: not only would Errol have an increase in salary, he would receive a percentage of the box office, some script approval, and more say in the choice of his directors and co-stars.

Satisfied for the time being, Errol finished the film, and the next day set sail on the *Sirocco* for Acapulco to recuperate. The doctors had ordered him to take things easy, but as usual he was only interested in pleasing himself. 'It's my life to fuck up any way I choose,' he told Bruce Cabot. 'After all, what do I have to tie me down?' He was almost made to swallow these words when he returned home towards the end of June, for he received a call from Nora Eddington: the girl he had raped while sky-high on cocaine now informed him that she was pregnant, adding that she was so terrified of telling her father and stepmother that she had left home. When she demanded to know what *he* was going to do about the situation, however, Errol did not mince words. Although he was devoted to his son, Sean, he declared that one mistake was enough and offered to pay for an abortion. Nora, a devout Catholic, was horrified by this and – telling him that she was only *seventeen*, which appears to have been true – she pleaded with him to marry her, if only so that her baby might be born legitimate. Despite her beliefs, she even agreed to divorce him afterwards. Errol surprised her by accepting the proposition but said he would only consider the divorce part if they did not get on after the wedding.

The secret ceremony took place in August 1943 in Acapulco, where only weeks before Errol had cavorted aboard the *Sirocco* with pick-ups of both sexes. The witnesses were Jack and Marge Eddington, who knew nothing about the baby. There were no other guests, and no photographs appear to have been taken. Neither did Errol show any concern for his new bride: hours after the ceremony, he returned to Hollywood, leaving her in Mexico.

Just days later, a middle-aged couple turned up at Mulholland House, accompanied by their lawyer, claiming that Errol had picked up their daughter, Shirley Evans Hassan, in a nightclub in January 1940, as a result of which she had become pregnant. The lawyer went on to explain that Errol's 'daughter' was now almost three years old and 'the very spit of her father'. He also demanded a $1,750 a month maintenance settlement.

Whether this particular allegation *was* true has never been ascertained, though when one considers Errol's extreme promiscuity and the fact that he almost never took precautions, saying once, 'What is the point of eating one's dinner with gloves on' it is highly unlikely that he did not father any number of children on the wrong side of the blanket. He did deny having anything to do with this baby, however, when the Hassans argued that it had been conceived in the front of Shirley's car one evening when, driving along Hollywood Boulevard, he had asked her to pull over to the side of the road. Declaring that such 'acrobatics' would have been impossible for a man of his size to have performed in a cramped space, he told his major-domo, Alexandre, to give the couple whatever cash there was lying about the house – around $3,000 – and he never heard from them or their daughter again.

The Flynns' baby, a girl eventually baptised Deirdre, was born in Mexico City on 10 January 1944. Errol was present at the birth, having told reporters in Hollywood – who still did not know that he was married – that he was heading to Mexico for another vacation. Most of them came to the conclusion that *some* woman must have been involved, and aware that his movements were probably being monitored, Errol did not disappoint. He boasted that he was sleeping with Nora's flat-mate.

Errol's secret was made public, however, at the end of January when a hospital spokesman 'leaked' the news of the baby's birth to a local reporter, who after checking with the registry office sold the story to a Los Angeles tabloid. This broke just as the new family arrived back in Hollywood – Errol and his latest fling on one flight, Nora and the baby on another. Mobbed by reporters, Errol denied the whole affair, telling them, 'Where you guys are concerned, I'm *always* getting married. Sorry, sports, but it isn't true this time, either!' What he did not know was that Jack Eddington had already given *his* statement to the press.

Nora moved into Mulholland House, though only until Errol found her and the baby a place of their own. 'This was the only way I would be married to anybody,' he recalled. 'Separate house, separate lives, separate people.' Prior to this, the new addition to his family was introduced to what he referred to sarcastically as 'Tinsel Town's hoi-polloi'. This took the form of a huge party at his home to which were invited resident hacks Hedda Hopper and Louella Parsons, Bruce Cabot and his fellow Olympiads, John Decker, Tallulah Bankhead, Helmut Dantine, Ann Sheridan and a host of other Hollywood stars, and David O. Selznick. Jack Warner was sent a card specifically requesting him *not* to attend. 'He'll only want to start turning the water into wine,' Errol cracked. 'And in any case, what Warner doesn't see won't harm him.'

The press were only interested in whether the rumours that the Flynns were getting divorced after just six months of marriage were true. Errol assured them that they were, then declared halfway through the party that he had changed his mind, while Nora merely prevaricated. And fortunately for Errol's fans, who genuinely believed that he was now a family man, the press left before the naked waitresses came in with the coffee and liqueurs and before the host retired for the night. After months of persistence Errol had finally 'cracked on to' Helmut Dantine, after Tallulah Bankhead had reprimanded the dashing young Austrian. 'For God's sake, fuck with him, darling. After all, why should *you* be the odd one out?'

The Flynns did not live apart for very long, however. Tired of finding the press camped outside her door every morning, Nora took baby Deirdre to Mulholland House and told Errol that she would be staying put, unless he really did want a very messy public divorce on his hands. Errol offered a practical compromise: Nora and the youngster would stay in a guest room, until such time as he had added a new wing to the house to accommodate them. He then made it clear that he would never give up his lifestyle for her or for anyone else, and that providing she did not interfere in his affairs, she would have a far better time in Hollywood than she would living with her relatives in Mexico. Reluctantly, Nora agreed and a few days later her stepmother, Marge, arrived for what should have been a short vacation. However, not only did she accept her son-in-law's unconventional views on marriage, she agreed to stay on at Mulholland House as his housekeeper!

During the summer of 1944, Errol and Raoul Walsh made *Uncertain Glory*, co-starring Paul Lukas. Set in occupied Paris, this was perhaps his best war film so far: he played Jean Picard, a killer who evades the guillotine when the prison in which he is being held is bombed during an air-raid. Lukas played the detective who recaptures him near the Spanish border. On their way back to Paris the train within which they are travelling is diverted when a bridge is blown up by the Resistance. This gives Picard sufficient time to become involved with a local girl (Jean Sullivan), but when the Nazis take 100 villagers hostage and threaten to kill them unless the culprit owns up, Picard, who is going to be executed anyhow, becomes a modern-day Sydney Carton and dies a hero.

Soon after completing *Uncertain Glory*, Errol and John Decker – acting on another of Errol's whims – decided to go into business together, and opened the Decker-Flynn gallery on Beverly Hills Alta Roma Road. Here, the prize exhibits were Errol's Gauguin and Van Gogh from Mulholland House – both, it was later disclosed, had been smuggled out of occupied Europe from under

1935. Errol's first Hollywood film, *Captain Blood*. Shooting was fraught with temper tantrums owing to his relationship with co-star Ross Alexander.

Arguably his most celebrated role. Errol *became* Robin Hood!

With his first wife, French actress Lili Damita, who introduced him to Hollywood's closeted gay society.

This rare late-1930s picture, sold discreetly under counters, shows Errol proudly displaying his 'wares'.

With Bette Davis in *The Sisters*, 1938. The pair loathed each other, and Bette never learned the secret ingredient of the omelettes he cooked whenever he asked her round for brunch!

Aboard his yacht, *Zaca*, with F.F.F. member Howard Hill, the champion bowman who covered his 'shooting' in Robin Hood.

Hunting ducks, early 1950s, with third wife, actress Patrice Wymore.

Errol as 'The Gentleman Hobo' on The Red Skelton Show, October 1959 just days before he died. With him is his last lover, Beverly Aadland. He was 50, she 16.

the Germans' noses – and there were also works on display by lesser known post-Impressionists, as well as regular exhibitions from local contemporary artists.

The venture caused Nora Eddington to question her husband's 'deep friendship' with Decker. Indeed, some years later she told a biographer that the painter had been 'subconsciously in love' with Errol, and jealous of her for being an integral part of his life. John Decker *was* unashamedly bisexual, he almost certainly did sleep with Errol, but he could never have envied a woman who was Errol's wife in name only.

Errol's next project, another war picture, was to be *Objective Burma!*, but with a little time on his hands before shooting was scheduled to begin, he accepted an invitation to join a travelling concert party which for several weeks toured American army bases in Alaska. In effect, Errol's participation saw him doing little more than playing himself: cracking jokes about his reputation and the rape trial, reading out sweethearts' letters, and repeating the song-and-dance patter from *Thank Your Lucky Stars*. He enjoyed the experience, and came very close to accepting an offer from Marlene Dietrich to augment the OSS (Office of Strategic Services). Marlene told me, 'I called him, and he said he would have done anything to get away from the Hollywood rat-race, and that dreadful wife of his. The problem, however, was that we all had to pass a medical, and at that time Errol was in poor health. The OSS simply wouldn't have taken the risk.'

Objective Burma! is one of the few contemporary war films that can still keep audiences riveted 50 years on, and it was the only one of Errol's movies to have had an all-male cast. Although the plot is fictitious, it is entirely credible. Because it is a 'man's picture' – in other words, the heroics of the Flynn character, Major Charles Nelson, are centred around his devotion to his unit and ultimately his country, as opposed to proving himself to a female love interest – the dialogue contains no offside double entendres and there is no posing or vying for the best camera angle or hogging every scene he appears in. Because the story was so believable, *Objective Burma!* would remain one of his favourite films. 'Sometimes make believe is reality and presents reality better than life itself,' he would say of it.

The film opens with Nelson briefing his men on the perilous

mission which lies ahead of them, the destruction of a Japanese radar station in the heart of the Burmese jungle. The exact location of the station is not made known to them, for reasons of security, until they are airborne. They are accompanied and are about to be impeded, or so they think, by Mark Williams, a middle-aged, philosophising journalist (Henry Hull). And while Nelson is one of the few not to refer to a sweetheart or wife back home, something may be read into the soft spot he nurtures for the handsome young lieutenant, Sidney Jacobs (William Prince), with whom he has previously shared an adventure (!) in New Guinea, where they have been caught swimming naked. Ironically, Errol is alleged to have had a brief affair with Prince while shooting the film.

The parachuting into Burma is one of the most thrilling scenes in any war film, and like the tense jungle sequence which follows is conducted almost entirely without dialogue, complemented by Franz Waxman's atmospheric score which alternates with the natural sounds of the jungle. The enemy target is blown up with comparative ease, but when the plan to airlift Nelson's men to safety fails, they are forced to split into two sections and trek over 150 miles through the jungle. Jacobs' group are captured, tortured and butchered by the Japanese; the young man's face is not seen when he is found, dying, and he begs his friend to end his misery, which Nelson cannot do. As Jacobs dies and his own still-colonial reserve finally cracks, Williams lets rip with a hysterical outburst which would later bring cheers from American cinemagoers. It brought condemnation from the Japanese government, however, who also took exception to Errol's reference to the enemy throughout the film, and in interviews with the media, as 'monkeys':

> I've been a newspaperman for thirty years. I thought I'd seen and read about everything that one man could do to another, from the torture chambers of the Middle Ages to the gang-wars and lynchings of today. But this is different. This was done in cold blood by a people who claim to be civilised. Civilised and degenerate mortal idiots! Stinking little savages! Wipe them out, I say! Wipe them off the face of the earth!

One by one, Nelson's soldiers are killed, until just eleven of the original 40 remain. He receives orders to change direction, so that even he does not know the objective of his mission. All that matters is to obey orders, and such is the loyalty of his men that one of them says, 'I'd follow *him* down the barrel of a cannon!' There are tremendous close-up shots from cameraman James Wong Howe of men close to the edge, and almost unbearable suspense during the final showdown with the Japanese as the two sides vie to outwit one another. And in his final scene, Nelson delivers a heartfelt response to the superior who tells him, 'You have no idea how important blowing up that radar station was to us.' Digging into his pocket and producing the identity tags of his slain comrades, he says, 'Here's what it cost – a handful of Americans.'

Objective Burma! was one of the few films which realised Errol's true acting potential, and one which pricked consciences around the world. Not all of the critics approved of it, however, and it caused an international furore when it premièred in London in September 1945. Despite the fact that its technical adviser was Major Charles S. Galbraith, a British commander who had been badly wounded during the actual Burma Campaign, the British press reacted to the closing credit, rolling over footage of a fleet of American-only planes flying over the jungle, with the dedication, 'To the men of the American, British, Chinese and Indian Armies, without whose efforts Burma would still be in the hands of the Japanese'. They did not like the fact that Jack Warner had instructed the scriptwriter to place the word 'American' first, suggesting that *America* had played the most vital role in the conflict and not Britain's legendary 14th Army, dubbed 'The Forgotten Army' by Lord Mountbatten.

Errol was especially hurt by some of the comments levelled at him by David Niven, one of the first Hollywood stars to have joined up. Niven, who to be fair knew nothing of Errol's 4F status, told the press that considering Errol's fondness for brawling and his predilection for taking on absolutely anyone, he *should* have been fighting the war single-handedly. He obviously felt no loyalty towards Britain *or* his native Australia, he added, and had taken the 'yellow' way out by becoming an American citizen. Errol swore that he would never speak to Niven again.

The last straw, however, was Zec's cartoon which appeared in the *Daily Mirror*, depicting a uniformed Errol, sitting in a studio chair with his name on it, while the ghost of a British soldier is telling him, 'Excuse me, Mr Flynn. You're sitting on my grave!' Jack Warner announced that he had commissioned a prologue for the film, explaining that *Objective Burma!* told only of *one* specific incident during the campaign, and that his film was in no way an attempt by the American nation to undermine Britain's heroes or to capitalise on a tragic event by making money out of it. His actions came too late: the British Home Secretary received so many complaints from the public that the film was withdrawn after just one week.

It was while shooting *Objective Burma!* that Errol decided to sell the *Sirocco*. As much as he adored his yacht – 'More than I could any woman,' he had once remarked – he now convinced himself that by breaking the old tradition and changing a vessel's name, he had only brought bad luck upon himself. 'A mariner doesn't kill a dolphin, shoot an albatross or change the name of a boat,' he wrote in his memoirs. 'I had never been superstitious, but look what happened.'

For several months, the *Sirocco*'s new owner kept her moored at the boatyard, and occasionally Errol would drive out and look at her, caressing her lovingly and often leaving in tears. He began looking for a replacement straight away, but finding a boat which matched his specification was far from easy: most of the vessels he had in mind had been commissioned by the government and were patrolling the San Francisco coast in search of enemy submarines. He therefore decided to wait for a while, and reluctantly busied himself with his work, hopeful at least that his next film, *The Adventures of Don Juan*, would bring him as much personal satisfaction as his last.

The story of the infamous womaniser had already been filmed by Warner Brothers back in 1926 with John Barrymore in the title role, and the obvious comparisons between the two actors had been foremost in Jack Warner's mind when he commissioned a script from George Oppenheimer and Harry Kurnitz in the autumn of 1944. Errol always went into stitches every time Oppenheimer's name was brought into the conversation. In 1938, when he had enjoyed a brief spell as Robert Taylor's lover, Oppenheimer had scripted his *Three Loves Has Nancy* which, Errol quipped, could not have been a more appropriate title for the actor he hated for being so good-looking and for turning him down at a party with a snarled, 'Fuck off, Flynn. I'm no goddam faggot!'

Raoul Walsh had been hired to direct *The Adventures of Don Juan* and Max Steiner had already begun work on the score. Then, at the end of May, Jack Warner called Errol and told him that the project would have to be put on ice for the time being: the American film industry was currently in the throes of a dispute between the set designers and their trade union, and whereas most film companies were contending with rehashed sets from old movies, this would not be the case with *Don Juan*. Errol merely shrugged his shoulders, and told Warner to find him something else, adding, 'Anything but a bloody cowboy film!' When Warner replied that what the studio had in mind *was* another Western, Errol cursed him black and blue over the telephone.

Although the only non-American to enjoy any kind of success in Westerns, Errol had always detested them, declaring that no sane cinemagoer would ever take seriously a cowboy with a clipped colonial accent, and flatly refusing to even consider delivering his lines in a John Wayne drawl. The fact that Jack Warner now proposed *San Antonio* brought him dangerously close to ripping up his contract. The script was poor, the sets second-hand – even Max Steiner's score had been purloined from the earlier *Dodge City*. Even so, Errol agreed to do the film because he presumed that old side-kicks Alan Hale and Guinn 'Big Boy' Williams would be given parts. Warner informed him that Williams was filming elsewhere, and Alan Hale flatly refused to work in any production with the second male lead, S. Z. Sakall – a chubby Germanic actor, popular with the public but despised by his colleagues for persistently mangling the English language and throwing everyone off cue – and once more Errol threatened to walk out of the production. Lili Damita's rapidly increasing alimony demands, however, and Warner Brothers' $200,000 fee went a long way towards persuading him to change his mind ... and the fact that he would be working alongside an actor he had always admired, Paul 'Killer' Kelly.

Tall and mean-looking, Kelly had begun his career as a child star in 1908 and in April 1927, with over thirty films behind him, he had been jailed for the manslaughter of his mistress', actress Dorothy Mackaye's' husband. Upon his release in 1931 the pair had married, and nine years later she had been killed in a car crash. The fact that Kelly was a brawler-par-excellence who had more or less killed a man with his fists (aided somewhat by the victim's acute alcoholism) impressed Errol no end, and hoping that it might get him into a real fight with Kelly – which it did not – Errol got the scriptwriters to slightly amend one of the final scenes, as will be revealed.

San Antonio was a big budget picture directed by David Butler, a man Errol neither cared for nor respected until Errol told him, after shooting a particularly arduous scene, 'Butler, I don't give monkey's fuck for this movie!' Butler's response, 'Neither do I' earned him immediate membership of the Olympiads. Errol played cattleman Clay Hardin, who sets off for San Antonio after years of self-imposed exile across the Mexican border – his quest to prove that local bigwig Roy Stuart (Kelly) is the head of an organised cattle-rustling syndicate. Hardin has Stuart's tally-book listing the names of the ranchers he has robbed.

The townspeople are mostly Hardin supporters, but initially are too frightened of Stuart and his fiendish rival, Legare (Victor Francen) to help him. Aware that these two are planning to ambush him on the outskirts of town, Hardin 'hitches' a ride – leaping off the back of his horse and climbing through the open window – with the stagecoach conveying chanteuse Jeanne Starr (Alexis Smith) to an engagement at Stuart's saloon. In San Antonio he gives the tally-book for safe-keeping to his best friend, Charley Bell (John Litel). Then there is light relief when the whole town attends Jeanne's opening night – Smith looks stunning and sounds good, crooning 'Some Sunday Morning', though the evening ends badly when Charley Bell is murdered by Legare.

For a while, Hardin suspects Stuart of the killing, and Jeanne of being in league with him. He then discovers a witness to the event– Jeanne's lily-livered manager (Sakall), and after Stuart has dispatched Legare in a shoot-out at the ruined Alamo mission fortress, Hardin pursues his quarry across the desert, where they fight it out with their fists – Stuart being fatally injured by hitting his head against a rock, *almost* what had happened to Paul Kelly's rival back in 1927.

Errol was suffering chronic depression whilst shooting the film, and occasionally this shows up on the screen – a neurasthenia which stemmed from the combination of a pointless second marriage, a former one which was bleeding him dry in alimony payments, and an over-surfeit of drink, drugs and sex. He was also, at thirty-six, developing a paunch which he nevertheless was able to 'hold in' whilst the cameras were rolling. The rosacea blotches on his face were another matter, and had to be camouflaged by thick make-up. Jack Warner did manage to wrench from him a half-hearted promise that he would not drink on the set, and David Butler saw to it that a jug of black coffee was waiting for him each morning when he turned up for work, always looking very much the worse for wear. Alexis Smith also made a point of bringing fresh oranges to the studio when Errol's doctor informed her that the blotches on his face were caused by a lack of vitamin C. Errol would empty half a bottle of cognac into the coffee when no one was looking – and, using a hypodermic syringe, he injected each orange with a shot of vodka, a trick he had picked up from Ann Sheridan.

Errol was well aware that he should have been receiving medical treatment for his various addictions, yet he also knew that to seek such help might only result in the *true* state of his health being leaked to the press. Why he should have been frightened of this is not known, for had the truth come out he would no longer have had to worry about the 'draft-dodger' and 'coward' outbursts which seemed to follow him everywhere. Whatever his reasons, Errol decided that he would cure himself.

By this time, halfway through shooting *San Antonio*, the extra wing had been added to Mulholland House, and the Flynns were leading more or less separate lives. Some years later, in a television interview, Nora said that she had never minded her husband's one-night stands and flings, but would have objected to full-blown affairs. She concluded, 'I said to him, "If you want to make a go of this marriage, and obviously you do because we're adding the nursery and all kinds to the house, I ask just one thing of you. I'm not going to try to get you to change your ways because I know I can't, and I certainly can't be over your head every five minutes. I just don't want any of the ladies you associate with outside of this house brought to the dinner table."'

Errol's greatest fear, he later said, was mediocrity, and in both his artistic and personal life he was convinced that he was heading this way. This was and always will remain the bane of heart-throb stars, who by and large have to rely on looks and physiques as opposed to their sometimes dubious acting talents. Cary Grant, Rock Hudson, Marilyn Monroe and Judy Garland all suffered on account of this, and all were pushed close to or even over the edge at some time or other. Most recently Errol had been affected by the Seconal suicide of his old flame, Lupe Velez, who had ended it all at the age of 36, after discovering that she was pregnant. He was also upset because, since the rape trial, he had become fodder for stand-up comics' jokes. Even journalist pals such as Sheila Graham were no longer taking him seriously, and she published a piece in one of her columns about his dissatisfaction with the new film, concluding, 'Flynn does not want to be the rich man's Roy Rogers.'

Throughout his entire adult life, Errol had prided himself on his astute knowledge of narcotics. 'I'll shoot up with anything,' he once said. 'And I know I'll never become addicted because I do it only for fun.' At this 'middle' stage of his life, he was experimenting with virtually anything. Even on his 'boys-only' trips to Mexico, when doctors had prescribed vitamin shots not just to combat his recurrent malaria but to enable him 'to keep the old pecker going and coming non-stop', he had asked them to spice up the injections with a little something extra. This was never a problem in South America if one had the funds to pay for such a service and the fact that his sexual performance could only be counterbalanced by massive quantities of drugs caused Errol and his rapidly diminishing entourage untold grief.

Virtually all of Errol's friends deserted him, albeit only temporarily, during a phase of cold turkey. For several days he shut himself in his room and tried to cope without drugs altogether, only to end up screaming himself very nearly insane. Only Nora and the major-domo, Alexandre, were permitted to enter this inner sanctum and, occasionally, Freddie McEvoy, who did not help matters much by telling him, 'It's nothing to worry about, sport. You're just going barmy!' Raoul Walsh, Errol's much loved 'Uncle' *did* visit, but after seeing Errol in a pretty nasty tantrum – his intake of drugs may have been diminishing slowly, but his drinking had increased twofold – he left, declaring that he would never set foot in Mulholland House again until its owner was 'cured or in his box'.

Errol also became increasingly violent towards those who were only interested in looking after his wellbeing. He would bash his wife for no reason at all, then hours later plead with her to forgive him, claiming that he could not remember attacking her. There were fights with Bruce Cabot, Freddie McEvoy and Raoul Walsh, often over nothing at all, with both protagonists frequently ending up in hospital. All of these people begged him to enter a rehabilitation clinic, but Errol always refused, terrified of the adverse publicity this might bring. In rare moments of lucidity he even began planning his own funeral, telling Nora that it did not matter what happened to his body after his death, so long as she did not have him interred among the celebrities at Forest Lawn. 'I don't want to be buried amongst all those Jews,' he said, adding, 'Better to bury me at sea, with sharks I can trust!'

Errol's depression culminated with him actually contemplating suicide, sitting on the edge of his bed one evening for several hours with a loaded revolver in his hand. And, unable to go through with it the first time, he repeated the procedure the next evening, finally firing the gun into the darkness, jolting himself back to reality and realising what a fool he had been. What is remarkable is that both Bruce Cabot and Freddie McEvoy *saw* him with the weapon in his hand, yet neither man tried to stop him.

Errol finally came to his senses when, in September 1945, he received a telephone call from the boatyard that had bought the *Sirocco*: the proprietor had just acquired a two-masted, 118-foot schooner called the *Zaca* – the Samoan word for *peace* – and was he interested in having first refusal? Errol instantly fell in love with it, and bought it for an alleged $25,000. Originally, the boat had belonged to a family of San Francisco bankers, but during the war it had been requisitioned by the American Navy and painted regulation grey. Errol spent around $45,000 having it restored and while this was being done began work on his 31st film, *Never Say Goodbye*. The critics declared unanimously that if *this* was the best that Warner Brother could come up with, Errol might be better changing studios at once – or perhaps even giving up acting altogether. The plot was tediously routine: a divorced couple who have not stopped loving each other are brought together by their seven-year-old daughter, played by Patti Brady, a child star of whom Errol remarked, 'I loved her so much that I persistently wanted to step on the little brat's head!' Eleanor Parker played his ex-wife, as best she could given the appalling script. Indeed, the film's only redeeming features were its score by Frederick Hollander, of *The Blue Angel* fame, and Errol's rendition of the Warren-Dubin classic, 'Remember Me'.

Refusing to take a break, despite suffering severe physical *and* mental depression, Errol went straight into shooting *Escape Me Never*, a seemingly unnecessary remake of the Elisabeth Bergner/Hugh Sinclair classic of 1935. His co-star, playing the part of the waif, was the British-born Ida Lupino. Following in the footsteps of the Oscar-nominated Bergner was for her a near impossible task, though Errol did not fare too badly as the struggling musician who accepts her and her baby into his home, falls in love with and marries her, and comforts her when the baby dies. This was also the last Flynn film to feature a Korngold score, and in his final Hollywood outing the composer excelled all expectations by also writing its self-contained ballet, 'Primavera', and the song 'Love For Love'.

In February 1946, with *Escape Me Never* in the can, Errol actually *invited* his parents to visit him in Hollywood: the *Zaca* was about to embark on her maiden voyage, and Errol was intent on fulfilling one of his father's lifelong ambitions by taking him on a scientific expedition to the Galapagos Islands. He did think about asking Marelle to join them, until she publicly expressed her disgust over the 'crowing rooster' emblem emblazoned on the yacht's house-flag, which Errol had described as 'the symbol of my omnipresent hard-on'. When his mother declared that *she* would never set foot on what would soon almost certainly be transformed into a floating brothel, he shrugged his shoulders and responded, 'Suits me fine. That way I won't end up throwing her into the briny!'

And yet, though he was still openly referring to his mother as 'The Cunt', he insisted that only she should appear with him in the publicity pictures taken on the eve of the *Zaca*'s launch. The occasion was the publication of his second book, *Showdown*. Loosely autobiographical, it recounted the tale of a young Irishman's journey to the South Seas. It sold well, though largely on account of its author's celebrity status: the critics panned it almost to a man. Errol told the *Herald Tribune*, however, that he did not mind this. His fans, he declared, would make up their own minds whether his work was good or bad, as they had always done with his films. He then added that he had already begun drafting his next tome: entitled *Good Deserving Girls*. It would detail his amorous adventures in Hollywood. This admission alone had Jack Warner and Errol's lawyer reaching for the telephone at once warning him that even the title might prove tantamount to career suicide. Errol told reporters at the press launch, organised by New York's Sheridan Press, that he did not care about this, adding, 'If I had a choice I would *rather* write books with plots of my own choosing than churn out movies which nowadays are mostly rubbish, with juvenile plots which are an insult to even the lowest form of intelligence.'

The *Zaca* trip was financed by Warner Brothers, who supplied Errol with a director, Charles Gross, a cameraman, Jerry Corneya, and several crew members to add to his own. The objective, a documentary film which would go on general release at the end of the year. The venture also proved a crafty move for Errol: he was now legally entitled to claim back most of the money he had spent on the *Zaca*'s renovation as a tax loss, because according to him the boat was now officially a business acquisition!

Accompanying Errol and Theodore on the trip were Nora and John Decker – Errol's idea of 'fun' because neither could stand the mortal sight of the other – and Carl Hubbs, professor from the La Jolla headquarters of the Scripps Institute of Oceanography. Howard Hill, the archery coach from *Robin Hood*, was also asked along, and the cabin boy – Errol called him 'the maiden for my voyage' – was Wallace Beery Jnr, the seventeen-year-old son of the actor.

The first few weeks at sea were, as Errol had predicted, a nightmare. Nora and John Decker fought like cat and dog, and an unfortunate accident left Wallace Beery with a harpoon through his foot. Errol's wife then began suffering from what everyone assumed to be seasickness: she was in fact pregnant, and left the *Zaca* to return to Hollywood when the party reached Acapulco. John Decker, having heard on the shipping forecast that the sea was about to turn very rough, followed suit the next day, accompanied by Errol's father. For Theodore, the expedition had not been a waste of time, even though Errol had changed his mind about going to the Galapagos Islands. Off the coast of Mexico he had discovered three new species of herring, the first of which he named *Zaci* in honour of Errol's boat. Whether his son and daughter-in-law were honoured to have the others, *Erroli* and *Nori*, named after them, is not known.

Errol spent several days in Acapulco. As part of the deal with Warner Brothers, the *Zaca* had been requisitioned by the studio to be used in Orson Welles' *The Lady From Shanghai*, starring his then wife, Rita Hayworth. After this, Errol sailed for the Panama Canal, spending a few days in Venezuela – 'where the lads' and lasses' pussies were the tightest in the world' – before heading for Cap Haitien. Here they ran straight into the tail-end of a hurricane, a terrifying ordeal which saw the boat tossing and pitching hopelessly off course for four days with not even Errol having the slightest idea of where he was until, once the storm had subsided, he found himself drifting towards Kingston Harbour in Jamaica.

For Errol, Jamaica was *the* precognitive dream for which he said he had been searching since his halcyon days in New Guinea. He fell in love with the lush, beautiful island on sight and wrote in his memoirs, 'Now I know where the writers of the Bible had got their description of Paradise. They had come here to Jamaica, and then their words had been set down and they have been read ever since.' His arrival was the media event of the year. The locals recognised him the instant he stepped ashore, unkempt and unshaven. Entrepreneurs and socialites clamoured to be photographed with him, and boatyard owners rushed to repair the storm-damaged *Zaca* with no thought of remuneration. He stayed at the best hotel in Kingston and was invited to dine with the Governor and the British Consul, an event during which he told the press, 'I was once Governor here, hundreds of years ago!' He was referring to the closing scenes in *Captain Blood*, of course.

Within days, Errol had decided that he wanted to live in Jamaica. The morning after his arrival – having already 'sampled two of the local dishes', one of each sex – he met a young white woman named Blanche Blackwell, and it was she who escorted him on a tour of the island. Errol became so infatuated with Blanche – though later he told friends that having sex with her for the first time had been an unpleasant experience because she had been suffering with a boil on her bottom – that he asked her to marry him, casually forgetting that he already had a wife back home and that Blanche too was married. Blanche turned him down gently while they were exploring Navy Island, a tiny plot of land within the harbour at Port Antonio, which had recently been put on the open market for an estimated $100,000. Errol merely shrugged his shoulders and told Blanche that if he could not have her, he would 'marry' the island instead and adopt its 30 or so inhabitants as his new family. The papers were signed the next day.

Errol also purchased a plot of land along Jamaica's north shore which he baptised Boston Estate, around which he had constructed a bright blue fence so that visitors to Jamaica could see it as their planes were landing. Over the course of the next few years, this would rapidly expand as more and more of the capital Errol could ill afford would be ploughed into it, though he did not spend as much time there as he would have liked. Boston Estate would soon boast its own herds of sheep, cows and goats...and dozens of stray cats and dogs. Errol would make a little money from his citrus groves and copra plantation, though much of this would be swallowed up by the exorbitant running costs of the other properties he would own on the island.

Errol returned to Hollywood in time for the birth, on 12 March 1947 at St Joseph's Hospital, of his second daughter, Rory. There was another furious row with Jack Warner who during his absence had decided that his next film should be *Cry Wolf*, with Barbara Stanwyck, an actress he positively loathed because a few years previously she had submitted to studio pressure and married Robert Taylor – because the press had latched on to the fact that both of them were gay. He never took into consideration, of course, that he had allowed Jack Warner to badger him into marrying Lili Damita for exactly the same reason. Also, Errol had never forgiven Taylor for snubbing his earlier advances, or for being allowed to prove *his* manhood – seething after a *Photoplay* feature had included himself and Stanwyck in a list of 'unmarried husbands and wives' – by enlisting with the American Navy. On the first day of shooting, Errol marched up to Stanwyck and barked, 'Has Bob fucked you yet? No? *I'm* still waiting, too!'

Cry Wolf was a decidedly un-Flynn-like movie, with more than a touch of Algernon Blackwood sinisterism in its make-up. Errol played Mark Caldwell, a creepy professor who lives in an equally creepy house. The film opens with him in mourning for his nephew (Richard Basehart), who is not really dead, but being cared for in another wing of the house so that his loved ones will not discover that he is insane. What Caldwell does not know is that his nephew had entered a sham marriage so as to claim his inheritance, which Caldwell is holding, and when his widow (Stanwyck) arrives at the house and bumps into him in the garden, he goes berserk and kills himself.

Cry Wolf may have given Errol an opportunity to act a serious role which did not call for him to rely on his looks and charm, but it was only moderately successful at the box office. Considerably better received was *Escape Me Never*, which only now went on general release, inadvertently ill-timed and with a title that could not have been more appropriate. Tired of her husband's ceaseless philandering, Nora had left him, taking her children with her. Errol did not care: not only was he still seeing Helmut Dantine, he was also involved with Ida Lupino. The latter affair, however, was short-lived because Nora read in the press that he and Lupino were planning a trip to the Bahamas aboard the *Zaca*. Errol's wife did not try to prevent this from taking place, but when he returned to Mulholland House she had moved back in.

Errol's next film was *Silver River*, yet another story of the Civil War, but one more favoured by the critics than his last. 'This is a good rip-snorting Western, well stocked with fist-fights and gun brawls for them as likes 'em rough and tough,' enthused *Variety*. Attention was also drawn to the quarrel between Errol and Jack Warner concerning the gun provided by the props department, which Errol declared 'looked like a kid's toy'. Shooting was therefore held up for three days while a Los Angeles gunsmith designed him a double-action 44-40 Colt revolver, a feature of which were special grips to enable rapid cross-draws from left to right. For several years Errol would keep the weapon in a drawer next to his bed at Mulholland House.

The production was further delayed when, in the middle of June 1947, Errol's pal John Decker died of cirrhosis of the liver. When Bill Lundigan joked that Decker had consumed so much whisky during his last years that it would take the crematorium staff a week to put the fire out, Errol insisted upon watching the gruesome event through an opening in the wall. Decker's body exploded, bringing on an attack of nerves which confined Errol to his bed for days.

In *Silver River*, Errol for once portrayed the villain, an unscrupulous army officer who turns professional gambler. His co-stars were Ann Sheridan and Thomas Mitchell, and once more the production proved troublesome. When Errol turned up for the first day's shooting – blind drunk at ten in the morning – there was an almighty bust-up with director Raoul Walsh. Though one of his best friends, Walsh had started to tire of Errol's sloppy attitude towards his work and his unsociable habits. He thought nothing of snorting cocaine between takes or shooting up with anything he could lay his hands on, having sex in his dressing room with prostitutes or extras and always making a point of leaving the door open, and exposing himself, usually with a full erection, to visiting luminaries. Indeed, such was his behaviour at this time that Warner Brothers consulted with their lawyers to find some way of breaking his contract so that he would not be able to sue them.

Raoul Walsh, who had made up his mind never to work with Errol again, got away with putting his foot down about the drinking – promising him that if he lay off the booze each day until five o'clock, he would join him in getting 'rat-arsed' once the set had closed. Walsh also began collecting him from Mulholland House each morning, to make sure he reached the studio on time. Errol refused, however, to give up the sex sessions, telling Walsh what he would tell others in the future: 'I don't expend much energy these days, sport. I just sit back in my chair with my flies undone – reading the papers whilst they work on me!'

It was quite probably Jack Warner who called Nora one afternoon and invited her to the lot, anticipating that if she 'caught him out', he might think twice about humiliating anyone in the future. Nora arrived just as Errol's latest 'plaything' was leaving, and storming into his dressing room, she bawled him out for 'screwing around'. Errol quietly responded, 'I wasn't screwing, dear. The lady was *sucking*!'

7

'If It Moved, Flynn Fucked It!'

'I could have anything that money could buy. Yet I found that at the
top of the world there was nothing. I was sitting on the pinnacle, with
no mountain under me.'

In October 1947, some three years after the project had first been
conceived, and with Vincent Sherman replacing Raoul Walsh as
director, Errol began working on *Adventures of Don Juan*. Three
weeks into shooting, he marched into Jack Warner's office with
his usual expletives-peppered demand for a salary increase,
though this time Warner decided to call his bluff. 'Fine,' Errol
retorted 'I'll see you when I get back from my holidays!' That
same afternoon, he set off on the *Zaca*, taking Nora with him, and
he stayed away from Hollywood for more than a month – until
Warner contacted him and offered a new deal. Errol would only
receive a slight increase in salary, but he would be released from
his contract once a year to make a film with any major film studio
of his choosing. He agreed, and returned to the set at once.

The scenario and script of *Adventures of Don Juan* is wittier
and more camp than any of Errol's other swashbuckler films.
Indeed, Errol once referred to it as 'a two-hour piss-take',
knowing that the critics, more than ever before, would draw
obvious parallels between the actor and the character he was
portraying. Much of the camp content stemmed from the fact that
Errol and the scriptwriter, George Oppenheimer, 'spoke the same

'If It Moved, Flynn Fucked It!'

language'. Between them, they are reputed to have slept with every one of the muscular young actors who portray Don Juan's fencing students in the film, and Oppenheimer had several times 'put on shows' beneath the mirror in Errol's bedroom for the benefit of those in the 'jerk-off' room.

Don Juan's amorous exploits have taken him around the world, and this film begins with him being caught out in a lady's bedroom, somewhere near London, by an irate husband. 'I have loved you since the beginning of time,' he has told her, adding after she has reminded him that they only met the day before, '*That* was when time began!' And now, to evade capture by the husband's men, he and his faithful servant Leporello (Alan Hale) run into a group of soldiers who are waiting to escort a Spanish nobleman to London to meet the bride he has never seen, in an arranged marriage which is hoped will bring lasting peace between England and Spain. Masquerading as the Spaniard, Don Juan enters the city in a scene lifted straight out of *Elizabeth and Essex* – a Warner Brothers cost-cutting exercise – but he is recognised by his 'intended' as a former lover, though he himself has had so many women that he is unable to remember her. 'This time I won't *let* you forget me,' she tells him, as she locks the door. He is, however, surprised again, thrown into a dungeon, and subsequently turned over to de Polan, the visiting Spanish ambassador (Robert Warwick).

At this stage, the real swashbuckling begins. The friendly ambassador allows Don Juan to return to Spain, having extracted from him a promise that he will support Queen Margaret (Viveca Lindfors), who like himself is against going to war with England. In Madrid, he learns that his Lothario's reputation has preceded him, yet when he singlehandedly fights off soldiers sent by the hated Duke de Lorca (Robert Douglas) to pressgang men into military service, those who have condemned him now accept him as their hero. At the royal court, Don Juan encounters de Lorca, who secretly is plotting with the simple-minded King Philip III to send another armada to England, one which he hopes will not fail like the last one. 'Tell me, Don Juan,' he asks sarcastically, 'do you hire men to spread tales of your romantic conquests?', to which comes the equally catty response, 'No, your excellency. That's a service that's always been known to be free of charge!' De Lorca next attempts to woo our hero into supporting his cause, but when Don Juan tells him, 'I prefer to be on the side of the friends of Spain, not her enemies,' one instinctively realises that a showdown will not be far off, particularly when Don Juan discovers that de Lorca has arrested his Spanish ambassador friend and incarcerated him in a torture chamber. De Lorca takes over the palace, arrests Margaret for opposing him, and has Don Juan beaten up and sentenced to death. In this scene, when he staggers around looking quite dreadful, Errol was actually drunk, but Vincent Sherman decided not to shoot it again because it was so realistic.

All ends well, of course. Don Juan and the ambassador are rescued by two of his men disguised as monks – another idea 'borrowed' from *Robin Hood* – and he and his fencing students put on a spectacular display while saving the queen, with whom he has fallen in love. And finally he confronts de Lorca in a duel which is every bit as exciting as any other Flynn swordfight – culminating in an astonishing leap down a steep flight of steps (executed by Errol himself and not, as has been stated, by a stuntman). Flinging aside his rapier and plunging his dagger into his foe's heart, he growls, 'This sword is not for a traitor – you'll die by the knife!' Then off he goes to say goodbye to his queen, knowing that with his kind of reputation they must never become lovers. 'Where will you go?' she asks. 'Who knows,' he replies. 'Into oblivion, I suppose, where most legends go!'

This, however, is not to be. Although Don Juan has vowed to cut down on his amorous activities and head for the new university in Lisbon, where he will study and perhaps pen his memoirs, there is temptation en route to the border when a coach conveying a pretty lady (Nora Eddington!) stops to ask him directions. Following this enchanting vision, he tells the by now exasperated Leporello, 'My dear friend, there's a little bit of Don Juan in every man, but since I *am* Don Juan, there must be more of it in me!'

Adventures of Don Juan was an ordeal for all concerned with its production, though none of this shows in the finished print. *Escape Me Never* had just been released, earning such bad reviews that Errol threw a tantrum on the set, and asked Vincent Sherman to drive him home, where he spent the next two days in bed nursing a migraine. The studio doctor was summoned, and prescribed drops for blocked sinuses, and the next morning Errol returned to work, surprising everyone with his bright and breezy attitude, unusual for him first thing in a morning. What his colleagues did not know was that he had switched the contents of his bottle: each time he shoved the nozzle up his nostrils he was sniffing back a potentially lethal mixture of cocaine mixed with vodka!

Because he was also suffering from the 'shakes' through trying too drastically to cut down on his drinking, and couldn't remember lengthy pieces of dialogue, Errol's scenes had to be kept as brief as possible, then spliced together. After one mammoth 24-hour bender, he and Alan Hale were so drunk – yet, incredibly capable of pronouncing their lines without slurring them – that several property men had to crouch below shot and hold on to their legs to prevent them from falling off their horses. The make-up artist, Perc Westmore, also had a gruelling task getting Errol ready for the camera each morning: because of the drugs he was taking, the thick paste which had to be applied to his bloated face kept peeling off. This called for specialised lighting, which worked well most of the time, except in one of his love scenes with Viveca Lindfors when it is possible to observe how pitifully ravaged his features have become. Vincent Sherman, a fine director but a man who was wholly incapable of exercising the Spartan discipline that Errol needed at this time, could not prevent Errol from drinking on the set. He coped by getting as many shots of him as he could while he was sober, then as the day progressed, shooting around him.

When Jack Warner found out about this, he threatened to visit the set and sort out 'that Australian upstart reptile' once and for all. When the film was released, Warner placed a full-page advertisement in the *Hollywood Reporter* which read, 'Dear Errol. Just saw your picture and it was great – sensational! Thank you for a wonderful picture!' Errol retaliated to such obvious sarcasm by calling Warner and telling him, 'Your piece in the newspaper was much appreciated, sport. I just wiped my arse on it!'

For Warner Brothers, the enterprise was a costly one, for the production would go way beyond its $2 million budget, and not just on account of Errol's 'indispositions': a new score had to be commissioned from Max Steiner now that Korngold, the studio's original choice, had left Hollywood and George Coulouris, who had been contracted back in 1945 to play Don Juan's foe, the Duke de Lorca, was now working on another film but still entitled to be paid for this one. A finer, more sinister villain could not have been found than in Robert Douglas, an excellent actor with smouldering, almost mesmeric eyes.

Physically, Errol looked superb. By working out at home he had rid himself of his bulging midriff, and fans could not deny that he still looked drop-dead gorgeous in tights. Also, since he was *playing* the great lover, Errol rejected the studio instruction – one that he had obeyed for *Robin Hood* and *Gentleman Jim* – that 'everything' should be discreetly tucked away, particularly as his 'protuberance' as the cameraman called it, appeared considerably pronounced when he was being filmed from the side. He told Vincent Sherman, 'Since Don Juan didn't walk around with *his* cock strapped down, old boy, then neither will Flynn!'

This new, bulging Errol quickly gave way to rumours that he was phenomenally endowed, a great source of speculation over the years, which was never proved one way or the other. It was a legend that he himself loved to promote. Vincent Sherman tells of an incident which occurred during the shooting of *Don Juan*, when he entered Errol's dressing room to discuss a scene. 'He was naked but for a little towel which covered his lower extremities,' the director recalled. 'Very slowly, he removed this and I looked down, startled because he'd had Perc Westmore make him a phallic piece about sixteen inches long. Then Alan Hale walked into the dressing room, looked down, and without blinking said, "I'll take a pound and a half!"'

Sherman also spoke of Errol's 'love' of his fellow men, and his apprehension where women were concerned: 'The second or third week we were shooting *Don Juan*, he put his arm around me and said, "You little son-of-a-gun, I love working with you. I really love you!" I knew what he meant. Then he said, "I can love a man, but I can't love a woman." He didn't mean that in a homosexual sense, and yet I sometimes wondered. I think he distrusted women, maybe because they'd hurt or used him.'

During the shooting of *Don Juan*, Errol became involved with his on-screen enemy, Robert Douglas – not exclusively in a homosexual affair, but to 'augment' his sex life. He was fascinated by the slightly younger actor's pale, extraordinarily beautiful eyes, and declared that his near-perfect colonial accent sent shivers down his spine. Initially, Douglas was invited to the 'jerk-off' room at Mulholland House. Errol's bedroom underneath it now had an added feature: once the couple in the bed had finished their performance, a projector merged in with the decor above their heads would 'pep' them up again by screening a pornographic film on the the opposite wall. Once Douglas became a fully fledged member of the Flynn coterie, however, he was allowed to participate in his friend's 'other' activities. This often involved making love with women while simultaneously watching two men having sex, or masturbating each other while watching lesbians. Errol also owned films which depicted men and women having sex with animals.

'I picked up more about sex after just two hours aboard the *Zaca* with Errol Flynn than most men learn in a lifetime,' Douglas said, some years later. The actor also recounted a story of how, tired of having to prompt Errol during every single scene in *Don Juan*, Vincent Sherman decided to teach him a lesson by bawling him out in front of the entire set. 'A crowd of us tiptoed along behind Vince,' Douglas explained. 'Maybe a hundred and fifty people, all eager to see Flynn get his come-uppance. He kicked the door open, and there was Errol in his armchair – stark naked, being ridden by one woman while another stood watching, waiting for her turn. All they were wearing were their mantillas from the film. And Errol just looked up and said, "Be right with you, Uncle Vince!" Then he stretched out with one of his incredibly long legs and kicked the door shut again!'

In the summer of 1948, Errol was asked by his friend David Butler if he would make a guest appearance in *It's a Great Feeling!*, a satire on Hollywood starring Jack Carson, Doris Day in one of her first film roles, and innumerable Warner Brothers stars and personnel who played themselves. It was a movie which dated quickly and which, for a supposed comedy, had few funny moments. Carson, whom Errol regarded as a big-head on and off the screen, portrays a ham actor whose behaviour is so abominable that no one will work with him. Not only does he end up directing his own film, he drives his latest leading lady – Day, whom he has discovered working in the studio canteen – back to Wisconsin, her home town, where she weds her former sweetheart, Jeffrey Bushdinkel. During the ceremony, the couple stand with their backs to the camera, and it is only when they turn around to kiss in the closing shot that the groom is revealed to be Errol.

This paltry effort was followed a few months later by *That Forsyte Woman* for MGM, Errol's first venture with another studio since arriving in America. For him, it was a bizarre career move which could have backfired. The producer, Leon Gordon, would not allow Errol to change anything in the script, but he did allow him to choose his own role, suggesting that he should play the lovestruck young architect, Philip Bosinney. Errol plumped for Soames Forsyte, the cold, calculating 'Man Of Property' – the first book in John Galsworthy's famous Victorian trilogy which more or less formed the basis for the screenplay. 'I was sick to death of being type-cast,' he remembered. 'The world and its mother was beginning to think that I couldn't act unless I had a sword welded to my hand or unless I was sitting on a bloody horse, and I wanted to show them what I was *really* made of.'

In retrospect, Errol had chosen wisely. Though the Hollywood film does not match up to the definitive television series made by the BBC two decades later, and though his co-star Greer Garson does inadvertently upstage everyone in the production, it is by no means as dull as the critics made out at the time.

The story, told mostly in flashback, opens shortly after Philip Bosinney (Robert Young) has died in a carriage accident, when the distraught Irene Forsyte (Garson) recounts to her Uncle Jolyon (Walter Pidgeon) the events which led to her marrying Soames and why she ended up having an affair with Bosinney – stealing him from Jolyon's daughter and her closest friend (Janet Leigh).

Convinced that Irene is little more than a fortune hunter, the Forsyte clan advise Soames against marrying her, but he is head-strong and accustomed to having his way. The marriage takes place, but Irene soon realises that she has made a mistake. It takes her a while to get used to her largely obnoxious family, of which June and Jolyon, the Forsyte black sheep, are her only allies. When June falls in love with Bosinney, however, and he does not match up to the family's expectations, he and Irene are drawn inextricably closer together and fall in love. And when June finds out about their affair, she tells Soames. It is after his showdown with his young rival that Irene rushes out into the London fog, and while they are searching for her, Bosinney falls under the wheels of a coach, bringing the story up to where the film begins. Irene then divorces Soames, marries Jolyon, and goes to live with him in Paris.

While shooting *The Foreskin Saga*, as he liked to refer to it, Errol was on his very best behaviour. He refrained from drinking, and if he did take any drugs, it was discreetly. Once a year he had been given the privilege of escaping 'Jack Warner's cattle market', and he had no intention of blowing his chances of working for MGM, who were also considering him for the role of the white missionary in *King Solomon's Mines*, opposite Deborah Kerr.

Errol later admitted that the thought of meeting Greer Garson had filled him with terror. The Irish-born, redheaded star of *Goodbye Mr Chips* and *Mrs Miniver*, who specialised in the portrayal of strong-willed but sympathetic women, had been with the Birmingham Repertory Company at the same time as Errol had been treading the boards at Northampton, but though she was now just as famous as he was, the pair had never met. The film's director, Compton Bennett, who had recently triumphed with *The Seventh Veil*, was equally apprehensive about having them both on the same set, and he gave Errol a pep-talk before the actual meeting took place. Errol ignored Bennett's dos and don'ts. Striding up to Garson, he 'goosed' her and bellowed, 'Hiya, Red!' The pair became instant friends, and many pranks followed. During a scene where Soames and Irene are in a hackney carriage, Garson attached a battery-operated device to the door handle, so that Errol received an electric shock when he grasped it. Errol got his own back when she had to open her wardrobe door and reach for a dress – he was standing inside, stark naked but for his top hat!

On 8 February 1949, as *That Forsyte Woman* was nearing completion, Nora Eddington announced in the press that she had filed for divorce. The last straw had not come on account of Errol's philandering and drink-drug habits, but because she had met someone else – the crooner Dick Haymes, who had also filed for a divorce from Joanne Dru, who that same week had announced *her* engagement to the actor John Ireland. 'It's a classic case of all change partners and dance,' Errol told reporters.

'Nora's shacked up with the boy singer, and I'm off on my holidays to have a little fun!'

Mulholland House was immediately besieged by the press, particularly as Nora took several weeks to move out, but what really baffled everyone was that when she finally left, her step-mother, Marge, stayed on as Errol's housekeeper, agreeing also to look after the couple's children until their lawyers had worked out the terms of their divorce. This was not an easy process, for the wily Lili Damita had petitioned for an increase in *her* alimony payments, resulting in his having to cough up another $30,000 a year, tax-free. Errol's divorce from Nora became absolute on 7 July. Eleven days later, she married Dick Haymes.

For Errol, the break was made easier by *That Forsyte Woman* being nominated that year's British Royal Film, and Errol had been invited to the gala première in London, before King George VI and Queen Elizabeth. There would be several stops en route, each one, naturally, bringing him a new adventure – or trouble.

In New York there was a meeting with Leon Gordon, the producer of *That Forsyte Woman*. Gordon told Errol that MGM's offer to play the white explorer in *King Solomon's Mine* still stood. Alternatively, if he so wished, he could have the part of the Red Beard horse-trader in their adaptation of Rudyard Kipling's *Kim*. Originally this was to have been made in 1939, with Robert Taylor, but had been cancelled on account of the war, and a complaint from the Office of War Information, who were concerned that the Indian people would take offence at the film's central theme of white supremacy. Recently, however, the country had celebrated Independence, and the subject was not quite so touchy. Both films were to be shot largely on location – *King Solomon's Mines* in Africa, *Kim* in Northern India. Errol plumped for the Hindu role, even though it was by far the smaller of the two, because he said revisiting India would remind him of the good times he had shared there with his old crony, Herman F. Erben.

It was arranged that Errol would fly out to India as soon as he had concluded his 'business' in Europe, and when this matter was negotiated over the telephone between Leon Gordon and Jack Warner, it was decided that as Errol would be covering more air miles on behalf of MGM than Warner Brothers, MGM should foot the bill.

Meanwhile, during his brief stay in New York there was an unpleasant incident which resulted in Errol being prosecuted for actual bodily harm. He and a Warner Brothers publicist were on their way to a press shoot when their taxi was flagged down by two policemen. Probably aware of Errol's fondness for playing pranks, they forced him out of the car, frisked him and checked his driver's licence – then asked him for his autograph! Errol did not see the funny side of this, and when he called one of the policeman a 'Gestapo bastard', he was promptly arrested. The drama continued in the 8th Precinct when the same policeman prodded Errol in the ribs while escorting him to the desk. Errol turned around and stamped on his instep, a favourite trick of his if, faced with an opponent bigger than himself, he wanted to avoid a fight. Unfortunately, this only resulted in an all-out brawl and Errol, nursing several bruised ribs, was thrown into a cell.

Because Errol did not have much money on him, the Warner Brothers publicist paid his $500 bail, and he was summoned to appear in court the next morning. When he failed to turn up, he was arrested. The female judge at the subsequent hearing was not interested in listening to his excuses as to why he had not attended the original hearing, *or* why he had hit the policeman in the first place. She fined him $50 for disturbing the peace and ordered him to forfeit his bail, which would later result in the publicist suing him to get his money back! Worse still, he was made to publicly apologise to the policeman he had assaulted, though he did achieve some satisfaction when he bumped into him outside the courthouse, muttering in his ear, 'If I ever catch you alone, you yellow bastard, I'll beat your brains out!'

From New York, Errol flew to Paris, where he attended a ceremony hosted by the film magazine *Cinémonde*: he and Ingrid Bergman had been voted actor and actress of the year by its readers. The press were shocked to find him sporting a beard, which he had grown for *Kim*. He promised it would come off the moment the new film was completed, adding, 'There's absolutely no point in cultivating whiskers on one's face when they grow wild elsewhere on the body!'

Errol and Ingrid Bergman dined at Maxim's after the presentation, sharing a table with the heart-throb actor Gérard Philipe, actress Micheline Presle, and the existentialist chanteuse,

Juliette Gréco. Philipe, the finest star of his generation, had just finished work on *La Beauté du Diable*, but in spite of his mass appeal, Errol did not think him particularly good-looking, remarking, 'His ears stick out like chapel hat-pegs, and he needs a little meat on his bones. Other than that, in the sack I guess he'd be all right for practising on.' Presle he found 'beautiful but aloof', and Gréco he dismissed as 'a scruff', declaring, '*I'd* never work with either of those two in a million years!' In fact, he would eventually work with them both, and more than once.

It was at another celebrity meeting place, the Café Flore in Paris's St Germain district, that Errol met the woman he would always refer to as 'The Geek' – Iréne Ghika, a beautiful Budapest-born princess then very much a part of the city's haute-société set. Aged around twenty, Iréne was related to the Romanian royal family, and also a direct descendant of Helena Ghika, the nineteenth-century traveller and historian, one of whose books Errol had in the library at Mulholland House. Another of her recent ancestors, Prince Ghika of Moldavia, had married the notorious French courtesan-actress, Liane de Pougy. Upon hearing that de Pougy had successfully seduced *almost* as many lovers of both sexes as he had, Errol told a journalist from *Noir et Blanc*, 'Well, my dear, if *that* sort of thing runs in this lady's family, I guess The Geek and I had better get married!' Only the day before he had told the same journalist, when asked if he would ever consider marrying again, 'Isn't that a bit like asking a man who's been circumcised without anaesthetic if he'd like to go through with it again?'

In Hollywood, before the war, it had been fashionable for movie stars to marry into *la petite aristocratie*: Pola Negri, Mae Murray and Gloria Swanson had all done so, though frequently the family 'estate' had turned out to be a few acres of untenable land and a broken-down shack in some inaccessible corner of Eastern Europe. Errol wasn't going to risk this. He hired an investigator to carry out a status check on his intended and, satisfied that she truly was independently wealthy, with her own château near Budapest, he called a press conference at the Plaza Athenée Hotel and announced his engagement. Astonishingly, his first congratulatory telegram came from Marge Eddington, Nora's step-mother. Then he contacted the captain of the *Zaca*, in

Hollywood, and asked for his boat to be taken to Nice. 'In spite of The Geek's fondness for scoffing snails and raw garlic, she is a servant to my every desire,' he told reporters. 'This little lady's going to be around for a long, long time. We're going to make pictures and babies together, but more important than that, we're going to grow *old* together!'

It did not take Errol long to discover that Iréne did not have much of a sense of humour, though considering the trick he played on her, this is hardly surprising. Assuming that, as she liked eating snails she would have a similar passion for 'other crawling things', he caught several grasshoppers and bluebottles and had a confectioner coat these in chocolate, only telling her what had been inside these 'pralines' the day after she had eaten them! This trick – along with another nauseating speciality which found him masturbating into the omelette mix on the rare occasions that he fixed breakfast – would repeatedly catch out his friends over the years.

Iréne accompanied Errol to London, and she was with him when he met the King and Queen at the Odeon Marble Arch première of *That Forsyte Woman*. When the King shook hands with Errol and asked, 'Are you still having problems with Burma, Mr Flynn?' – referring to the *Objective Burma!* debacle – Errol cracked, 'Yes indeed, sir. She's pregnant!' Iréne did not find this amusing, assuming that he had given her another nickname and was referring to her.

Errol had been looking forward to seeing the sights of London, but much of his week was taken up filming some of the scenes from *Kim* at Elstree Studios, where Iréne never left his side. After completing his first take, Errol staggered into his dressing room, wiped the sweat from his face, and downed half a bottle of cognac in one go. Then he dismissed the 'script girl', telling her that he would not be requiring her 'services' for the time being. His fiancée apparently did not know what he meant by this.

From London, Errol and Iréne flew to Nice to spend a few days on the *Zaca* before leaving for India, and it was here in November 1949 that Errol discovered that his private investigator had slipped up and that his pretty princess was not quite as wealthy as he had suspected. Neither was there any château near Budapest. This, he declared he did not mind: he was already paying to keep two wives back home, and as The Geek seemed to survive on hamburgers and banana splits, she would not cost much more to keep than one of his dogs! Needless to say, the young woman took some persuading to accompany him to India after hearing *this* remark!

Errol's co-stars in *Kim* were Paul Lukas, Robert Douglas and, in the title role, thirteen-year-old Dean Stockwell, whose scenes in the film were all shot in Hollywood. When Errol and Iréne arrived in Calcutta, Douglas was already there, and the two men headed off for the nearest brothel, leaving Errol's fiancée to make her own way to her hotel. She was then informed that over the course of the next two months, Errol's time would be turned over to men-only activities: in his words, 'hunting, boozing, whoring and each-othering'. Iréne's patience was by this time wearing thin, but she had heard so much about the Flynn legend and reputation that she presumed he could not help himself. She therefore spent most of her time shopping, sightseeing or in the hotel, where Errol had insisted on separate rooms, telling inquisitive reporters, 'And that's how it's going to be until our wedding night. Don't want to end up with a bad name, do we?'

Errol's passion for playing practical jokes backfired on him in India, when he arranged a welcoming committee for Paul Lukas, who since appearing with him in *Uncertain Glory* had remained a good friend. Hiring the services of a young, large-breasted girl from the brothel he had visited with Robert Douglas, he promised her a part in the film providing she could pull off masquerading as the founder of the elderly actor's Indian fan club. Errol then loaned a uniform, at a price, from one of the airport customs officials, and paid another official to 'arrest' Lukas for illegal entry into the country. Then, while the girl was smothering her supposed idol with kisses and compliments and a burly policeman threatened him with his rifle for having a 'forged' passport, Errol stood at the back of the customs hall insulting him in mock-Hindustani... until Lukas realised that he had been had, and fell about laughing. It was only when Errol handed the second customs official a wad of banknotes for his involvement in the prank that things went wrong – Errol was accused of bribing an officer of the law, and had it not been for Paul Lukas's pleas, *he* would have been arrested!

In *Kim*, set in the Lahore of 1885, and filmed in Jaipur, Errol played Mahbub Ali, a red-bearded Afghan horse-trader doubling as a spy for the British, who are trying to stave off a Russian attack on the Khyber Pass. Kim is the son of an Irish sergeant who refuses to attend the traditional public school, preferring to earn pennies as Mahbub Ali's messenger, and to help a Holy Lama (Lukas) search for an elusive, sacred river. Robert Douglas played the head of British Secret Service. Unfortunately, it was a heavy, tedious film whose disjointed storyline and curious dialogue – laced with 'thees' and 'thous' – was lost on most cinemagoers.

In February 1950, Errol and Iréne Ghika flew from Calcutta to Rome to shoot Errol's most extraordinary and least-seen film, *Hello God*, for the actor-director William Marshall, who had appeared with him in *Santa Fe Trail*. Marshall was also the film's producer and its narrator. One of the cameramen was Paul Ivano, a former lover of Rudolph Valentino. Ivano, who had been wanting to work with Errol for many years, said at the time that it had been heartbreaking to observe how this once-beautiful idol was now 'rapidly going to seed', and that from some angles he was virtually unphotogenic.

Running at a little over one hour, this semi-documentary story tells of a young 'unknown' soldier who expresses his views on pacifism outside the gates of heaven while waiting for four pals who have been shot down at Anzio Beach. Sadly, it was never released in Britain or the United States because of legal problems. Independently made, without Warner Brothers' approval, it was later 'doctored' by Marshall, and extra scenes added without Errol's permission, *after* he had injected a great deal of cash into the production.

Because he had 'dawdled' in Europe for longer than usual, Errol found himself faced with a formidable workload when he returned to Hollywood: the completion of *Kim* and two loathed Westerns which Jack Warner decided would be filmed back to back to punish Errol for making an independent movie. *Kim* was finished with few hitches: Iréne Ghika accompanied him to the set each day, and even the bellicose Jack Warner complimented his star on his good behaviour whenever she was around.

Montana, co-starring Alexis Smith – the only reason Errol even *attempted* to fumble his way through his part – was a decidedly lacklustre production, and running at just 75 minutes effectively little more than a B-movie. For the second time in his career, Errol played an Australian, a softly spoken sheep herder who muscles in on the Montana cattle territory, managing to seduce a rich rancher (Smith) before she discovers his true vocation. The pair even get to sing together – Mack David and Jerry Livingston's 'Reckon I'm In Love'.

Errol's unusually good conduct while shooting the film might have continued had he not found out that Jack Warner had hired a private detective – masquerading as an extra – to check to see if he was still drinking and taking drugs, activities which were now listed in his contract under the heading 'PROHIBITED'. Even so, while on location in Arizona he managed to exact his revenge by complaining to the director, Ray Enright, that his dressing room was too small. When Enright half-joked that the only room bigger than the one he was occupying was the *barn*, Errol examined this and declared – within earshot of the investigator – that this would be fine, the perfect rendezvous for entertaining young ladies. He then began monitoring the movements of the investigator – and when he saw him climbing up to the loft, some twenty feet above the concrete floor of the barn, Errol waited until the man was out of sight, then removed the ladder. As it was late afternoon and almost time for everyone to retire for the day, Warner's spy was 'marooned' in the draughty loft until the next morning!

Rocky Mountain was yet *another* Civil War picture, and saw Errol cast as Lafe Barstow, a Confederate officer who finds himself at loggerheads with the Union and the Indians. Its location shots, filmed in New Mexico, were certainly more interesting and colourful than they had been for *Montana*, but the script was just as poor. Errol's love interest in the film was played by Patrice Wymore. En route to join her Union fiancé (Scott Forbes), she is rescued by Barstow from an Indian attack, while later in the plot he captures her fiancé along with his patrol. The film does not end well, however, for in the closing scenes the Confederates are all killed.

Errol had already met Patrice Wymore, a bespectacled redhead, a few months earlier at one of Marge Eddington's tea parties. 'No great shakes in the looks or upholstery department,' was how he had then described the 24-year-old singer-actress from Salina, Kansas, who though she had enjoyed some success on the cabaret circuit and the musical stage, had appeared in just one film, *Tea For Two*. She and Errol began dating during the first week of shooting, though he made it clear to her that she was not the only love in his life. What she did not know was that besides still being engaged to Iréne Ghika, he was also involved with Scott Forbes, his beefy, 30-year-old antagonist from *Rocky Mountain*. Forbes would be retained in what Errol called his 'fuckbook' for a little longer, though by August 1950 The Geek had been unceremoniously sent packing, and the press informed that he was now going to marry Patrice Wymore. 'It was the glasses that did it,' he later said. 'As soon as Pat took them off I fell for her – hook, line and scrotum!'

Errol convinced his friends – and himself – that this marriage would prove third time lucky because neither party had chased the other. Some years later he would tell a French press conference:

> Pat typified everything I'd ever longed for in a woman, or thought I'd longed for. I expected vanity, she had none. I expected lies, it took five years for her to catch me out with one. I was used to feminine wiles, but she never thought of such things. Okay, so she was square and with the two of us it was like oil meeting water. But that didn't matter. There were no tricks with Pat – just directness, sincerity and the kind of forthrightness that's incapable of being shaken by criticism. In her I'd found something to respect.

Most of Errol's friends would have been willing to swear, however, that what he *really* longed for was a housewife – a 'little lady' who would be willing to stay at home all day, fetch his pipe and slippers like a loyal servant, and above all turn a blind eye to his carousing, for here was a man who could not have stayed faithful to one person had his life depended on it.

One week after commencing his courtship with Patrice, Errol flew with her to Salina to meet her parents. Not so long before, the Wymore's had been introduced to another prospective bridegroom, Samuel Lambert, a Broadway producer twice Patrice's age, and they had reluctantly given their blessing. Errol Flynn, however, was an entirely different matter, for here was a man with quite the most dreadful reputation, about to lead their daughter up the aisle – and no doubt a merry dance afterwards. When asked by a young woman reporter at the airport if marriage would settle him down, he merely winked and quipped, 'What do *you* think?' And when asked what, if anything, he would like to have written on his tombstone, he replied, 'My motto, of course – "If it moved, Flynn fucked it!"' Perhaps if the Wymores had known that their future son-in-law had at least one boyfriend back in Hollywood, they would have persuaded their daughter not to marry him; as it was within minutes of this first meeting, they had fallen for his unquestionable charm.

This introduction to Patrice Wymore's family coincided with the publication of a lengthy, self-penned and self-glorifying study which Errol paid to have published in *Screen Guide*, under the somewhat smug heading, 'I Do What I Like'. 'I've had my share of troubles,' he begins, 'and everything I own today, including whatever freedom and peace of mind I possess, has been bought with an equal share of worry and work.'

Thenon, the piece becomes progressively maladroit, though at times it is difficult to work out if Errol is being truthful or simply trying to impress upon his future family that he really has decided to turn over a new leaf:

When I first came to Hollywood, I enjoyed whatever fame I had, but gradually it began to pall on me and from now on I want more privacy, especially in matters of my personal life. I happen to be a guy who enjoys solitude on occasion and there are times when my idea of heaven is just to be alone – and I mean *completely* alone . . .

His 'humility', too, taking into account Errol's love of exhibitionism, rankles of hypocrisy:

While I appreciate any attention I may receive in public, I must admit that crowds terrify me, and I hate the feeling I am on exhibit all the time. I want to be one of the crowd, to relax and be myself, instead of being followed and inspected by watchful and often critical eyes wherever I go.

Always the first to admit how much he loathed and tried to steer clear of such films, because he believed they had never brought out the best in his acting abilities. Errol now professed:

I think it fortunate that Warner Brothers have allowed me to make mostly historical and outdoor dramas...these are much more agreeable to my temperament than the suave dramatics of boudoirs and drawing rooms. Making romantic historical dramas, I find myself in an atmosphere I love. It's easier to combat my restlessness.

The piece did end, however, on a note of great sincerity. Indeed, it was as if Errol was writing his own epitaph already:

I have no idea to excel others – to win an Academy Award, for example. I merely desire to be creative, to leave the world something I have created – whether it be a book, a motion picture, a painting or whatever – that will add to its beauty, knowledge and understanding.

Patrice Wymore's family were disappointed that her wedding would not be taking place in her home town: Errol was scheduled to make his second independent film in France and did not wish to wait until they returned to America for fear that one of them might change their mind. There was little likelihood of this from Patrice's point of view: she was so besotted by Errol that she would have agreed to anything, and the prospect of a fairytale wedding in Monaco – which was what he had in mind – appealed to her romantic nature and more than compensated for the fact that her parents would not be present.

The new film, which between its conception and distribution would have almost as many titles as leading players before Silver Films opted for the obvious *Adventures of Captain Fabian*, had a screenplay written by Errol himself, which he had adapted from Robert Shannon's novel, *Fabulous Ann Madlock*, though there was no character of that name in it. Errol was very proud of his achievement, and pleased that William Marshall was to be its director. Marshall had also chosen two of its stars, Vincent Price and Agnes Moorehead, described by Errol as 'Hollywood's classiest dyke'. It was Errol, however, who demanded that his co-star should be Micheline Presle, the sophisticated young actress he had met at Maxim's, only to denounce as 'aloof'. He had changed his mind about never wanting to work with her after seeing her opposite Gérard Philipe in *Tous Les Chemins Mènent à Rome*. Presle took a great deal of persuading to appear in the film, however, particularly when informed that her name would be listed in the credits as 'Prelle'...so that Americans would know how to pronounce it.

Errol nurtured big plans for *Adventures of Captain Fabian*, and the film was to be shot simultaneously in English and French. Both versions were originally to be directed by Robert Florey, and in August 1950 Florey assembled the cast – barring Errol – at the Boulogne-Billancourt studios on the outskirts of Paris, for rehearsals and costume fittings. Errol had been scheduled to arrive one week after everyone else, but when he failed to turn up for the first day of shooting, he received an irate call from Robert Florey. Errol reacted by firing him, and brought in William Marshall, the director of the ill-fated *Hello God*. It was he who decided that there would only be an English-language version of the film, and that this would be dubbed for the French market. Errol decided not to argue: his tardiness had already pushed the production above budget.

Errol finally flew to Paris early in September, and work on the film began at once. Not unexpectedly, the production was a troublesome one. Although Errol was effectively the 'boss' – even joking with the crew that they would have to call him 'boss-man', as the natives had done in New Guinea – this did not mean that he was allowed to have all or indeed any of his own way with Micheline Presle, a consummate professional who abhorred his on-set drinking. She was not alone: the mostly French crew threatened to boycott the production several times because of his bad time-keeping, tantrums, and a tendency to walk off the set whenever he felt like it. By the time shooting finished in the middle of October – having been transferred to the Victorine studios, near Nice, because its allotted time in Paris had run out – Errol was informed that not one person involved with *Adventures of Captain Fabian* would ever *speak* to him again, let alone work with him.

Although Errol's name headed the credits, this was essentially Micheline Presle's film, though she is said to have been appalled by the end result: wooden sets, paltry and often incomprehensible dialogue, dreadful dubbing over the voices of the French bit-parts so that in some prints *both* voices are heard, and amateurish, jumpy editing. The story is set in the New Orleans of 1860. Presle plays Lea Marriotte, a Creole servant in the household of the obnoxious Cynthia Winthrop (Zanie Campan). Lea is arrested after the *crime passionel* slaying of a drunken footman who has tried to rape her, but she is saved from almost certain execution when Fabian, recently returned from an overseas adventure, intervenes at her trial. The judge, a relation of Cynthia's equally horrible fiancé, Georges Brissac (Vincent Price) – who has witnessed the self-defence murder but lied in court so as to avoid a scandal – is convinced by Fabian that unless *he* lets Lea go free, he will expose a number or family skeletons which will ruin the Brissacs' impeccable reputation.

Fabian too has reasons for hating the Brissacs, for they have defrauded his father. He and Lea therefore plot to bring them to heel. He dresses her in fancy clothes and buys her the local tavern, then extorts Brissac into reimbursing him. Initially, Fabian dislikes Lea telling her in a line which is pure Flynn, 'My dear, I've looked at women all over the world. All shapes, all sizes, all colours. You're no novelty to *me*!' Eventually, though, the pair do become lovers, at which point the plot takes a curious twist: while exacting her revenge on Brissac – getting him drunk so that they will be caught out by his uncle, the head of the family – he goes mad and strangles the old man. Lea then changes tactics by forcing Brissac to marry her to ensure her silence. Fabian is then implicated in the murder when the police dig up the body and find his engraved pocket-watch, which has of course been planted by the killer. He is arrested and thrown into jail, but terrified that he will still tell the truth about the first murder, Brissac plans to have him lynched before his trial, while Lea's Aunt Jezebel – played by Agnes Moorehead, who spits a lot and changes her French accent each time she appears on the screen – collects the local riff-raff to rescue him.

The final scenes of the film are quite dreadful, to say the least: the aunt is killed, and a poorly staged fight between Fabian and Brissac extends from the prison along the quayside – pausing long enough for the villain to fling a lighted torch into Fabian's ship – before the pair fall into the sea and thrash it out under the water, just as Lea arrives and the ship blows up. Pinned to the ground by a massive balk of burning timber – which rises and falls with her laboured breathing – Lea is dragged free by a man who one assumes to be Fabian, and expires in his arms. In fact, Errol was so drunk when shooting this scene that a stand-in, who was slimmer and several inches shorter, had to be used, and these closing shots caused the plot to lose what little credibility it had had in the first place.

Meanwhile, Patrice Wymore had flown into Paris at the end of September, and the ensuing scene at Orly airport had been as contrived as the plot of Errol's latest film. Errol was so drunk that he could barely stand and, presenting her with a bouquet of roses as she stepped off the plane, he told reporters, 'We're going to have lots of children, and all of them will be boys. It's always been an ambition to have all of my sons working as the crew on my boat. And seeing as Pat here is a hopeless cook, I've relegated her to First Mate!' He then attempted to sweep his fiancée up into his arms, but dropped her, and all she could do was stagger to her feet, brush the dust from her dress and walk away in disgust.

The next day, only slightly more sober Errol lunched with Jean-Charles Tacchella of *Écran-Francais*. When the journalist paused in the entrance to the restaurant to enquire about his health, he quipped, 'I feel just like a corpse. Let's go eat one!' Then he escorted him to their table, where the cutlery had been replaced by instruments borrowed from a local mortuary!

Errol told Tacchella, who later reported that he had suddenly lost his appetite, that he was hoping for a 'double-feature' wedding to take place within the week – a civil ceremony, followed by a 'full God production'. Then he abruptly changed the subject and spent the next hour talking about his adventures in New Guinea. Only at the end of the lunch did he briefly return to the subject of the impending marriage. When Tacchella asked, 'Mr Flynn, when you are married, will you settle down and refrain from your ways as a Don Juan?' Errol staggered to his feet and announced to the entire restaurant, 'My dear fellow, can you see *me* sitting next to the fire sipping tea when there's *serious* fucking to be done?'

Errol's wedding plans took some arranging. A telephone call from Prince Rainier informed him that he would be delighted to provide the civil ceremony at the Town Hall in Monte Carlo. The Catholic Church, however, issued a statement that none of its priests would conduct a blessing for a man who was twice divorced and who had lived a life of open public sin. Condemnation rapidly followed from other Church denominations.

Patrice was all for leaving France and having a simple ceremony back home in Kansas, but Errol would not hear of this. After an urgent appeal on the French radio, the problem was solved when a Paris-based Lutheran priest, Frank Guénthal, agreed to conduct the blessing because, although Errol *was* divorced, neither of his previous marriages had taken place in a church. All the same, so as not to upset his parishioners, he conducted this one well away from his patch. The couple were civilly married on 23 October 1950 by Charles Palmaro, the Mayor of Monte Carlo, and a few hours later the union was blessed at the Nice Lutheran Church, not far from the *Zaca*'s mooring at Villefranche. The chief guests were Errol's parents, Freddie McEvoy, and a representative of Prince Rainier who had to fight through the horde of 4,000 screaming fans to get into the church. Patrice wore a full-length satin and lace gown, and the four bridesmaids were extras from *Adventures of Captain Fabian* – all of whom had slept with the groom while shooting the film. And instead of the traditional wedding march, the organist played 'Drink To Me Only With Thine Eyes'.

The wedding reception took place in Nice's sumptuous Hôtel de Paris, yet even here there was high drama. As the couple were cutting the cake and the guests raising their glasses, two process servers strode into the room and handed Errol a writ which stated that he had 'lasciviously had carnal knowledge of one Mlle Danielle Dervin, aged fifteen years, to which there is sufficient photographic evidence'.

Errol did not initially deny the charge, which it was claimed had occurred the previous August aboard the *Zaca*, when the yacht had been moored on the Riviera. Had he done so, the matter might have taken some proving: like Betty Hansen and Peggy La Rue Satterlee, Danielle Dervin was a redoubtable character well known in society circles. Instead, he shrugged his shoulders and told the process servers, 'I'm sorry, sports, but I simply cannot remember. The name doesn't instantly ring any bells, but then again, I've entertained so *many* girls on my yacht!'

Errol later confessed that he had said this in jest, convinced that the writ had been a stunt pulled by one of his pals in retaliation for all the practical jokes he had played on them. Once he realised that it was not, however, he found himself facing a major dilemma: because the order had been served by a court in Monaco, he was not compelled to attend the hearing, though if he failed to do so, he risked being arrested the next time he entered the principality. And if he *did* turn up to answer for his alleged actions, because the Monagasque law did not allow bail, he could be imprisoned until his trial, the start of which could be delayed for up to three months.

Errol's mind was made up for him when, two days after his wedding, he slipped on the wet deck of the *Zaca* and fractured several vertebrae in his spine. The American Navy was visiting Nice at the time – only the day before they had fired off a sixteen gun salute in honour of the newlyweds – and they were responsible for getting him to the hospital, where for three days he drifted in and out of consciousness. He was then taken back to the *Zaca*, and ordered to stay flat on his back, on a board mattress, for a month. Then, still in considerable pain, he sailed for Monte Carlo 'to face the music'. It was a question of honour, he told the magistrate, Maître Biasset on 25 November. During his illness the European newspapers had been filled with nasty stories about him, mostly rumours spread by Danielle Dervin's family, and just as he had cleared his name before when wrongly accused of this sort of thing, he would do so again.

At the Town Hall, in the room next to the one where the Flynns had been married, the charges brought not by Danielle Dervin herself but by her parents were read out: on an unspecified date in 1949, Errol had forced their daughter into a shower compartment on the *Zaca*, pressed an electric button which had closed the door and locked them in, and raped her up against the wall. To support the accusation, the court was furnished with a photograph of Errol and the girl standing on the deck of his yacht, both fully clothed.

The Dervins concluded that although they did not wish to cause Mr and Mrs Flynn unnecessary grief in lieu of their recent marriage, their daughter's reputation had to be considered, and a one-off payment of one million francs (then around $3,000) – which they would donate to charity – would see an end to the matter. Errol dismissed the photographic evidence as 'baloney', telling the magistrate, 'Hundreds of girls, if not thousands, have posed for pictures with me aboard the *Zaca*, and so have their mothers, fathers and brothers. Are *all* of these people going to come forward and say that I *raped* them?'

Even so, Errol later said that he would have paid the money, had it not been for the Dervins' reference to the shower button. The *Zaca*'s shower rooms were scarcely big enough for one, let alone a couple attempting to make love. He then added that the incriminating photograph had not been taken aboard his yacht, but aboard that of a friend which had been moored nearby. To prove both points, he insisted that the Dervins and the magistrate should inspect the *Zaca* for themselves. At this, the hearing was adjourned until the next morning, when Danielle Dervin herself took the stand: according to Monagasque law, it was necessary that she accuse Errol to his face of his alleged crime. Like Peggy Da Rue Satterlee before her, she had been instructed by her lawyer to wear bobbysocks and pigtails.

Asked by Maître Biasset if she had fabricated her story, Danielle Dervin burst into tears and replied that in her state of confusion she had made a mistake – the rape had not taken place aboard the *Zaca*, but on the same yacht where the photograph had been taken, as Mr Flynn had rightfully pointed out. Errol was then asked to look the girl in the eye and deny raping her. This he did; laughing loudly, he pointed at Danielle Dervin, who by this time was on the verge of collapse, and bellowed, 'Who in their right mind would want to be seen in *public* with that, let alone have *sex* with it? She's ugly and she's got hairs on her legs. Credit me with at least a *little* taste, your honour!'

Errol's outburst brought the proceedings to an abrupt, hysterical halt. Both parties had been ordered not to speak to the press, and Errol kept his part of the bargain. He and Patrice returned to Nice, where they spent the afternoon sunbathing and the evening at the casino. When he learnt, however, that Danielle Dervin *had* met with the press – supplying them with a finely detailed drawing of the shower room where the alleged rape had taken place, and describing his actions as 'those of a half-crazed beast', Errol rang the Monte Carlo Chief of Police and told him that on no account would he be returning to the court until the magistrate had seen the shower room for himself. The inspection was conducted the next afternoon, and convinced that Errol had been telling the truth all the time, Maître Biasset threw the case out of court. That evening, again at the casino, a reporter asked Errol if he would be sending Mademoiselle Dervin flowers, as she had told the press he would, just to show there were no hard feelings. He replied caustically, 'Have you *seen* the girl? In my opinion, my dear fellow, a large bunch of *bananas* would be much more appropriate!'

8

Too Much . . . Too Soon

'I want to be loved but I may myself be incapable of loving . . . I hate the legend of myself as phallic representation, yet I work at it to keep it alive.'

At the end of November 1950, Errol and Patrice returned to the United States, where she was immediately offered a two-year contract with Warner Brothers. During this period her co-stars would include Kirk Douglas, though of her four films the most memorable would be the musical, *I'll See You In My Dreams*, which featured the songs of Gus Kahn. Errol's career, on the other hand, had begun to founder quite badly: over the coming decade it would have peaks and troughs, though he himself was the first to admit that his best years were well and truly behind him. It was not a question of behaviour or any diminishing of talent, but more as a result of the advent of television. A great many of his contemporaries now found themselves similarly cut off from the public as this exciting new medium drew the crowds away from theatres, cinemas and concert halls.

While Errol had been in Europe, NBC Radio had made a last-ditch attempt to attract some of the rapidly increasing advertising funds from the television network by launching *The Big Show* – a 90-minute, Sunday evening extravaganza series masterminded by Dee Engelbach, who assembled a galaxy of stars in one show. For almost a year, the idea appeared to be working. Each broadcast had a budget set at a staggering $50,000, but NBC's biggest scoop was their Mistress of Ceremonies – the formidable Tallulah Bankhead, in every possible way Errol's female counterpart.

Errol was invited to appear on *The Big Show*, and pleaded with Dee Engelbach to be given a spot in the show which was going out on Christmas Eve 1950: topping the bill was Edith Piaf. His request, however, was turned down. So many stars wanted to appear with the Little Sparrow – including Bing Crosby and Frank Sinatra – that all the names were put into a hat, and the 'winner' who earned the privilege of duetting with her on her most famous song, 'La Vie En Rose', was the opera star Robert Merrill.

Errol *did* meet Piaf after the show, and was invited to join her and her entourage at the Versailles nightclub, where after her midnight recital he stayed for supper. His own appearance on *The Big Show* took place a few weeks later, when he sang a couple of old music-hall songs and cracked a few gags. The outrageous Tallulah, who throughout the series would be reprimanded by the producer about her one-liners and what she called her 'declarations of ersatz venom', told the audience, 'And now, darlings, Mr Errol Flynn, an actor who knows exactly how to swing a weapon and one Australian who sure is big Down Under!'

The following year, 1951, dawned with Errol facing yet another financial crisis. Jack Warner had paid him the same salary for the last three years, but Errol knew that he was not in a position to demand a pay rise right now: his last few films had not done well at the box office, and for years Warner had been looking for an excuse to fire him. Yet his debts appeared to be mounting faster than his business manager, Al Blum, could pay them: lawyers were suing him for unsettled accounts, most of the cast of *Adventures of Captain Fabian* were still waiting to be paid, and although he should have been shelling out $20,000 a month in alimony to Lili Damita and Nora Eddington, over the last six months they had only received a fraction of this.

Any less extravagant man might have hauled in the reins and begun looking towards the future, but Errol did not believe that he had a future. Since receiving his 4F medical report, he had convinced himself that he would never grow old, so each day was lived to the full. To his mind, the lawyers' offices and studios would still be there long after he was gone, so why worry about them now when he could be having fun? However, to bring in a little more money he started renting out the *Zaca* to rich businessmen such as Aly Khan and the Vanderbilts...and he began baiting would-be foes in nightclubs, hoping that they might hit him so that *he* could sue them! He went to see Raoul Walsh, still a friend, and begged him to put in a good word for him with the newspaper magnate, William Randolph Hearst, who had backed his trip to Spain. Hearst was on the lookout for celebrity correspondents in the Far East – mainly to cover the Korean War, but also the border problems in Papua New Guinea which had sprung up since the island had been liberated from the Japanese. Errol was particularly interested in visiting his old stomping ground once more: he wanted to see the native women he had loved, and was certain that some of them would have borne him children. The trip was aborted, however, after a few discreet enquiries were made by the Hearst office: in this part of the world Errol was still listed as a wanted man, guilty of slave-trafficking, who would be arrested – or worse – the moment he set foot on the island. He did fly to Korea in the July, though, as part of Jack Benny's USO package which toured the Air Force bases. Again, his act consisted of a nifty soft-shoe shuffle and a song or two, and of course anecdotes about his private life, particularly his two rape trials.

During the summer of 1951, Errol was summoned to Jack Warner's office. To make up for his disappointment over not being shipped out to New Guinea, the studio had decided to set his next film, *Mara Maru*, in the Philippines. Errol was thrilled until he learnt that *their* idea of the Philippines was Newport Harbours! 'Twice as picturesque, and twice as safe,' Warner added. Errol did not see it this way, and responded, 'When I get back I hope to be pissing on your grave, you wily son of a bitch!'

Mara Maru tells the story of a salvage operation to recover an ancient jewelled crucifix. Errol played the somewhat disreputable deep-sea diver whose mission is hampered by any number of problems, not least an amorous involvement with his partner's wife. Given a decent script and a bigger budget, the film might have encouraged better box office returns. Jack Warner, however, was by this time incapable of hiding the fact that in *his* opinion, Errol was not *worth* going to a lot of trouble and expense for, and even his co-stars, Ruth Roman and Raymond Burr, were barely second-rate in this one.

Shortly after finishing the film, the Flynns sailed for Jamaica, where Errol spent a month on the rapidly increasing Boston Estate. He spent much of his time avoiding his mother, for now that they were retired, his parents were more or less a permanent fixture on the island. Residing at Boston Great House, a building which had formerly housed slaves, Marelle had set up court like some marauding warrior queen. She nagged her husband, whom Errol had put in charge of the renovations, which included the construction of a new airstrip, and persistently and publicly reminded Errol how immoral he was.

Some of Marelle's complaints were of course justified: it was not considered normal for *any* man, she declared, to expose himself in public, though Errol does not appear to have been able to stop himself whenever she was around. 'When I was a boy, my mother was always trying to hammer home the fact that genitals were dirty things,' he once said, 'so I always made a point of proving that they weren't.' Marelle also took exception to him sunbathing in the nude, but this only caused further problems: he began turning up at the dinner table without any clothes on, and always had a full erection before entering the room. When Errol announced that he had bought the Titchfield Hotel in Port Antonio – a 150-year-old wooden, two-storey white elephant – for $50,000, *Marelle* held a press conference and dictated how it would be run. The bar with its splendid view of Navy Island – from Errol's point of view, its most exquisite feature – would be closed down, the establishment would no longer 'encourage sin' by accepting unmarried couples – obviously, Marelle knew nothing of the goings-on in those rooms set aside to be shared by 'bachelor businessmen' – and there would be a resident chaplain!

Errol was furious. Declaring that he might just as well convert his acquisition into a mortuary, he gave his mother until the end of the month to leave his property. He had received a studio call from Jack Warner, and declared that he would not be responsible for his actions should she still be there when he returned.

Within minutes of arriving back at Mulholland House, however, Errol called his father and told him that he had changed his mind, explaining that life was too short for holding grudges.

At the end of October he had learnt of Freddie McEvoy's death in a boating tragedy. According to Errol, McEvoy and his third wife, the former French mannequin Claude Stéphanie, had been 'trying to earn a dishonest buck' offloading crates off illicit liquor off the West African coast when their yacht, *Kangaroo*, had run into a freak storm. Other sources maintained that they had really been dealing in drugs and illegal weapons, though nothing was ever proved. McEvoy had died heroically, attempting but failing to save his wife – whose body was never found – and Errol was considerably more devastated by his death than he would be anyone else's. The pair had shared so much: good and bad times, women and men, and the ordeal of the statutory rape trial. 'He was such a selfish fellow, not one to lay down his life for anyone,' he recalled. 'I could have understood it if he went out like a cheat, a gambler, a ne'er-do-well... but not in that gallant way.'

Against All Flags, superbly shot in Technicolor by Russell Metty, was Errol's second film as a loan-out star – this time to Universal – and besides matching his Warner Brothers salary, Errol received a share of the profits. He was also given the best co-stars he had had in some time: Maureen O'Hara and Anthony Quinn. Set in the eighteenth century, the story centres around Brian Hawke, a British naval officer spy on the trade route to the Far East. Pretending to be deserters, he and his sidekicks infiltrate a Madagascar pirate colony under the joint command of Captains Roc Brasiliano (Quinn) and Prudence 'Spitfire' Stevens (O'Hara). The latter's father has rendered the port's defences virtually impregnable.

Hoping to convince the buccaneers that he really is a deserter, Hawke succumbs to twenty lashes of the bullwhip before setting out for shore. Stripped to the waist, we see a Flynn with a slightly fuller figure than in his previous swashbucklers, but a magnificent physique nevertheless for a man of 43 who had long since pressed the self-destruct button. 'Brave men are not forgotten,' his captain tells him, bringing the response, 'Thank you, sir, but sometimes they don't live long enough to be remembered!'

The deserters are hauled before the pirates' court, where Hawke is made to prove himself by fighting and beating their toughest man. Half trusting him, they invite him to join in on a raid of a ship belonging to the fabulously wealthy Emperor of India. On

board is his pretty daughter, Princess Patma (Alice Kelley), who by
the time Hawke rescues her from her burning stateroom has been
relieved of any accoutrements which will identify her and make
her captors hold her to ransom. She falls for Hawke, only the
third man she has ever seen, but he has set his heart on Spitfire –
primarily because her temperament lives up to her name. Jealousy
then raises its head when Patma and her handmaidens are put up
for sale as prospective pirates' wives. Hawke and Spitfire bid
against one another to buy Patma – he because he knows who she
is and wants to protect her, she because she cannot bear Hawke to
have any woman but herself, despite not knowing whether she
loves or loathes him.

Hoping to clear the seas of piracy *and* save the princess, Hawke
and his friends sabotage the colony's cannons, enabling a British
man-of-war to enter the port. The ensuing heroics are reminiscent
of Errol's earlier adventure films. He fights Brasiliano, using up
every inch of the deck before plunging his blade into the mainsail
and 'riding' it back down to the deck, renting the cloth in two.
Finally, leaving his adversary mortally wounded, he collects his
'prize' from his superior – Spitfire's freedom – and sails off with
her into the sunset.

The 'sail' stunt was apparently Errol's own idea, a stunning
emulation of a scene from the 1926 Douglas Fairbanks epic, *The
Black Pirate*. The fact that this death-defying stunt was captured
in a single take – and contrary to popular belief, Errol did not use
a double – only made what happened next seem more ridiculous,
for during a routine sword fight, Errol slipped on the wet deck
and broke an ankle.

As there was no question of Errol finishing the film until the
plaster cast had been removed, shooting was put on indefinite
hold while he and Patrice retired to Mulholland House, where
they were joined by his son Sean, now almost eleven. This reunion
between father and son was short-lived, though, when Errol
received news of his mother's latest indiscretion. Some weeks
before, a call had been put through to the film set: Marelle had
found an old bell on the Boston Estate which she thought ought
to be restored and presented to the inhabitants of Navy Island as
a gesture of good will. Errol, without paying too much heed to his
mother's latest foible, had told her to go ahead, but the bill for the

'restoration' work now amounted to over $5,000...for Marelle had commissioned the construction of a new *church* to house the bell!

Errol was so angry that he decided to sort out his mother 'once and for all' and, having been told by Theodore that the new airstrip was finished, he hired a two-seater plane and a pilot to fly him to Jamaica. The flight very nearly ended in disaster: the workmen's bulldozer and trucks had been left on the runway, and smack in the middle of the tarmac was a tree which Errol's father, the conservationist, had refused to cut down! The pilot did manage to land the plane, though with extreme difficulty, and Errol cursed his father in front of the dozens of island dignitaries who were there to witness the airstrip's maiden landing.

It was during this trip to Jamaica that Errol – having attacked his mother for building a church which his estate workers had been in need of for some time – decided to spend considerably more than $5,000 clearing a patch of jungle to make way for a wholly unnecessary racecourse. An oval track, measuring 150 x 50 yards, was attached to his airstrip in such a way that its fences and stands could be easily dismantled whenever Errol's hired plane needed to land or take off. Once a year, he announced, he would hold the Errol Flynn Sweepstakes, for which he would personally put up the prize money. He even made a deal with the owners of the horses, wherein an exporter pal would take any unfit or retired animals off their hands for a good price, to be slaughtered for pet food.

The concluding scenes of *Against All Flags* were shot in June 1952, at around the time Errol signed a deal with Warner Brothers to make what he then assumed would be his last film for the studio, *The Master Of Ballantrae*. The end of Errol's long association with the company was not as acrimonious as everyone had expected. During an uncharacteristically polite, expletives-free meeting in Jack Warner's office, the wily mogul suggested to his colleagues that Errol should be allowed to buy up the remainder of his contract for a 'bargain price' of $100,000. A similar deal had been successfully negotiated with Humphrey Bogart, but Errol only laughed, demanding that the studio pay *him* $100,000 as a 'retirement' gift, in lieu of his seventeen years' loyal service. What *actually* happened is that Warner and Errol did write each other cheques for this amount, neither of which ever saw its way into a bank account. Errol's contract with the studio that had made him a household name was effectively terminated with a simple handshake and few misgivings from both parties.

Based on the novel by Robert Louis Stevenson, which Errol had first read in New Guinea, *The Master of Ballantrae* was to be shot in Europe, and the news that he would have to 'relocate' could not have come at a better time for Errol. In a meeting with his lawyers he had been made fully aware of his rapidly escalating debts. The Los Angeles County Court had served him with a writ for the $4,000 he owed in back-taxes, Lili Damita had publicly announced that she would be suing him for the $80,000 he owed her in unpaid alimony, and his son Sean's school fees had not been paid for over a year. Nora Eddington had already served him with a writ for not paying *her* alimony – his excuse for not doing so, he declared, was because he was fed up of seeing photographs in the press of his ex-wife bedecked in jewels and expensive clothes, while accompanying features insisted on how tough she was finding it trying to make ends meet. He told reporters, 'Seeing her in all that fancy clobber only brings me to the conclusion that *she* should be paying *me*!'

On top of these demands, Errol had received several writs relating to the ill-fated *Adventures of Captain Fabian*. The first, from Vincent Price, was for the $15,000 salary which Errol still owed him, though much more serious was the plagiarism suit filed by his former associate, Charles Gross, who now maintained that he had written the screenplay for the film, and not Errol. When pressed by his lawyers, however, as to what he was going to do about his debts – he had already sworn never to sell Mulholland House, his yacht, or the property in Jamaica – Errol merely shrugged his shoulders and quipped, 'Don't worry about it, sports. It'll all come out white in the wash!'

The interiors for *The Master Of Ballantrae* were filmed outside London during the late summer of 1952. Initially, Errol rented rooms at a private house in Hampstead, but after a run-in with the proprietor – following a press conference wherein a woman reporter had drawn attention to his paunch and he had retorted, 'No problem at all, my dear. I'll have fucked it off by the end of ' the week' – he and Patrice moved into a suite at the Savoy. While here, Errol received a telephone call from Helen Panther, the chairwoman of the Northampton Repertory Company, inviting him to open their annual garden party at nearby Broughton Hall. At first, Errol was wary: he had left Northampton under a dark cloud, his reputation in tatters and owing hundreds of pounds in unpaid bills. He was also convinced that the moment he set foot in the town, he would be served with any number of paternity suits. Mrs Panther was unable to vouch for the latter, but she did assure him that under British law, because five years had elapsed since they had been accrued, his debts had been wiped out.

For some reason, Patrice Wymore did not travel with Errol to Northampton, and he was accompanied by a Warner Brothers publicist and a busty Swedish model he introduced as Birgit. Two thousand fans, mostly women, crowded around the podium while he delivered his speech, swaying from side to side after downing a bottle of vodka during the drive from London. And yet few people doubted his sincerity when he announced that the best years of his life had been spent in the town. 'I had no money and nothing to eat, but I was happy,' he announced, then brought loud guffaws and howls of appreciation from his audience by concluding, 'Mind you, since then I've been to many strange places and met a lot of strange people – most of them lawyers!'

Two weeks later, much to Errol's delight, the film company moved to the first of a series of locations in the Scottish Highlands. On the day they were due to start shooting, Errol rang the director, William Keighley, and explained that he could not be there because he had to see the only doctor in Scotland capable of curing all ills – in other words, the nearest distillery! Nor did he turn up the next day, claiming that he wanted to see some of the spots associated with Stevenson. He was less fascinated with the great writer and poet than he was in the man himself and the parallels of sexuality and adventure which he said linked them spiritually. Born in Edinburgh in 1850, Stevenson – now known to have been bisexual – had spent the last four years of his life sailing the South Seas in search of his own particular image of paradise, following in the footsteps of fellow 'outsiders' Charles Warren Stoddard and Gauguin. He had succumbed to tuberculosis at 44, following a lifetime of dissipation.

Most of the critics concluded that *The Master of Ballantrae* was Errol's best film since *Don Juan*, though Stevenson's classic tale of sibling rivalry suffered ignobly at the hands of the Hollywood scriptwriters. In the novel, both the Durie brothers die, but as this was ostensibly Errol's swansong for Warner Brothers, Jack Warner had no desire to see his star 'bowing out' in such an unseemly manner.

Stevenson had described Jamie Durie, the master of Ballantrae Castle, as 'a wicked, wicked lad', a trait which Errol did not lend to his interpretation of the role. The action begins in 1745, in the midst of the Jacobite uprising. Bonnie Prince Charlie has arrived back on Scottish soil to lay claim to the English throne. The Duries, however, are so bent on protecting their estates and title, no matter who wins the conflict, that they elect – upon the toss of a coin – to support *both* sides. Therefore while Jamie stays loyal to the Stuarts, his younger brother Henry (Anthony Steel), adheres to George II. What they do not reckon upon is the jealousy of Jamie's mistress, Jessie Brown (Yvonne Furneaux), who, when she sees him kissing his fiancée, Lady Alison (Beatrice Campbell), betrays him to his enemies while giving him the impression that *Henry* is the traitor.

When Jamie's friends witness him being shot by English redcoats and falling from the cliffs into the sea, they assume that he is dead and Henry becomes the new master of Ballantrae. Jamie actually 'dies' twice, for after being dispatched by the English he returns home to die during a fight with his brother – save that when his body disappears whilst Henry is summoning help, the younger Durie is advised that it will be better for all concerned if the family believe that he has been killed by his foes. Jamie has in fact been befriended and nursed to health by an Irish rebel soldier (Roger Livesey), and when the pair end up on a smugglers' ship bound for the West Indies, Jamie's real adventure begins. The craft encounters a pirates' galleon, and after an all-out scrap hugely reminiscent of *Captain Blood*, Jamie enters into a dubious partnership with its dandified captain. He then falls for a gypsy dancer, realises the captain has double-crossed him, kills him in a duel, then sets sail for Scotland with the pirates' booty, intent on getting even with his brother.

Scotland is now occupied by the English, but an uneasy peace has been maintained at Ballantrae Castle, where a party is taking place. Assuming another identity, Jamie mingles with the guests, but he gives the game away by losing his temper with Henry, who is about to marry Alison. Henry very quickly springs to his aid, however, when a brawl erupts with the English, though when both brothers are arrested, only Jamie, the Stuart supporter, is sentenced to hang. Jessie then admits that she is the traitor – she is killed while helping him to escape his jailor – and the film ends with Jamie being reunited with his fiancée.

Parts of *The Master of Ballantrae*, notably the pirate scenes, were filmed on location near Palermo, in Sicily, for which much of the credit should be awarded to Jack Cardiff, probably best known at this time for his atmospheric camerawork on *Black Narcissus*. Jack Warner – regarded as a close friend now that he was out of Errol's hair – visited the set several times, and spent a few days with Errol and Patrice at their rented villa in the most fashionable district of Rome. He wrote in his diary, 'Henceforth, this Anschluss between the royalty of Hollywood and the royalty of Europe will form a base from which my new Italian career will be fashioned.' The environment was certainly a hot-bed of activity as far as 'floating celebrities', as Errol called them, were concerned: regular visitors at this time included Maria Callas, Anna Magnani, Marcello Mastroiani, Gina Lollobrigida, and the horrendous ex-King Farouk.

Errol was fascinated – and at the same time repelled – by Farouk, telling friends that if only he could find an actor 'with enough blubber and grease' to portray him, his story would make the most fascinating movie, particularly with Errol Flynn as its director!

Shortly after the coup in July 1952, when General Neguib seized power in Egypt, the immensely fat, 32-year-old deposed monarch had sailed for Capri, along with the three yacht loads of treasure which he had filched from his people during his reign. For a while he and his entourage – including his pretty wife, Princess Narriman – were taken in by the island's most famous resident, Gracie Fields, but when they began hogging her Canzone del Mare complex, effectively taking advantage of her hospitality by barring her from her own swimming pool and restaurant, Gracie sent Farouk packing. He relocated to Rome to take up what he declared would be a new role as international playboy, albeit that, despite having bedded an estimated 2,000 women, he had been suffering from chronic bouts of gluttony-related impotence since the age of 23. It was in an attempt to find a cure for this that Farouk consulted Errol, gatecrashing one of his all-night parties. He had, he admitted, dispensed with over $1 million on visits to hormone specialists who had prescribed any number of aphro-disiacs and supplied him with 'erection-inducing appliances', none of which had worked. Neither, he told Errol, had his immense collection of pornographic magazines and films. Errol took one look at him and offered a simple diagnosis: 'You're too fat, sport!' At this time, the six-foot Farouk weighed in at twenty stones.

Errol made the mistake of telling Farouk to drop in on him whenever he felt the urge to talk, and very soon realised why he had been ousted by Gracie Fields. Ever fearful of assassination, the ex-king travelled around with a retinue of servants and armed bodyguards who treated everyone they came into contact with like dirt. It was not very long before Errol and Patrice – who was pregnant – started to feel as though they were guests in their own home. The last straw came when Farouk's bodyguards refused to allow Errol to enter the apartment because their master was having dinner there – demolishing the contents of the huge refrigerator, including *seventeen* jars of Beluga caviar, in a single sitting! Errol waited until he had finished, then told him, point-blank, 'Bugger off, you fat bastard. I never want to see your ugly Arab's face again!'

The next morning, however, Errol called Farouk and apologised. Not that he meant it, of course: that evening he had arranged a dinner date with Orson Welles, who he was sure would be delighted to portray the degenerate monarch in his film. Errol was wrong. The great actor later said that it had been one of the most offensive requests he had ever received, and after Errol's death would be outraged upon hearing what he had written about him in his diary: 'Today I saw Orson Welles, fat and bloated as Nero with no fiddle at his hedonistic best...a man of large, perhaps great ability, able to dominate others, who is at the same time a bit of a fool.'

'Another of Gérard Philipe's cast-offs, but one with tits a man could kill for' was how Errol described another friend he made at around this time – Gina Lollobrigida, his co-star in the film that would eventually be released as *Crossed Swords*. With Philipe, La Lollo, as she was known, had just completed what would prove to be one of the most successful French movies of all time, *Fanfan La Tulipe*, a swashbuckling extravaganza which was utterly remarkable. (Even more incredible was the fact that Philipe was in the middle stage of tuberculosis at the time.) She now made it patently clear that she was not about to become another 'Flynn plaything', in response to which Errol focused his attention on his other co-star, Cesare Danova, a dashing young Italian who some years later would appear with Elvis Presley in *Viva Las Vegas*. In the film, Danova played an apprentice Lothario and adventurer who is taught the tricks of the trade by Errol's character, though according to Errol, away from the set the handsome Danova was capable of teaching even *him* a thing or two. 'The film was one long hard-on from start to finish,' he told a French reporter.

Errol made the mistake of boasting that *his* film would prove ten times more successful than the Gérard Philipe one, particularly as it would he shot in Technicolor *and* in English. His producer-pal-manager J. Barrett (Barry) Mahon also erred by allowing the images of Errol's great swashbuckling heroes to cloud his judgement. Errol was now fifteen years older, and *looked* it, and he was unable to keep up with even the oldest actors on the set. He was also plagued by any number of ailments, not least of all a bad back. Several years after Errol's death, Mahon gave a rare interview for *Film Comment*:

Errol Flynn was probably the greatest symbol of masculinity and virility developed in the modern age, the type of male that all men and boys in their hearts wished they could be. He was handsome but not pretty; big but not clumsy; intelligent without being intellectual, virile without being lecherous or overbearing. He could have gone into any profession and been successful except the one he chose. Errol didn't feel that he was successful as an actor...the roles he was cast in never gave him a chance. He drank continually because he felt he could do no more, and consequently the feeling of virility declined. Errol had this great resentment of his own industry for not accepting him for what he really wanted to be, and yet he was the personification of film glamour.

By persuading Errol to take on a role which by his own admission no longer suited him – more so, that this would be the first in a trilogy of Italian co-productions which, he declared, would resurrect his great 'swords and tights era' – Mahon was only knocking, albeit inadvertently, yet another nail into the coffin of Errol's already moribund career. And in assigning it the title *Il Maestro di Don Giovanni*, he only confused the critics *and* the public: in spite of Jack Cardiff's excellent location shots around Lauro, Southern Italy, Milton Krim's poor screenplay and amateurish direction – not to mention Errol's half-hearted heroics and a bumbling, all-Italian cast – meant that the production simply did not knit together.

Unaware that this film would prove an abject failure, Errol and Barry Mahon proceeded with their next independent project, *William Tell*. This, Errol declared, would be regarded in years to come as his best film ever. 'I was going to show the motion picture industry *and* Jack Warner how pictures *should* be made,' he later boasted. The film was also to be dedicated to his third daughter, Arnella, who had been born on Christmas Day 1952.

Again, Errol would be tempting providence. He himself had begun writing the screenplay (which was finished by John Dighton) and with Mahon fixed the budget at $860,000 – a relatively cheap exercise because the cast would consist once more of mostly unknown Italian actors. The pair then set about finding a team of Italian backers, headed by one Count Fossatoro, who immediately deposited $50,000 into a joint bank account with Mahon as, he told the press, a gesture of good faith. It was agreed that these backers would put up one half of the production costs, with the other half coming from Errol's own pocket. In January 1953, work commenced on the construction of a mock medieval village near Courmayeur, at the foot of Mont Blanc.

Errol had decided that his film would be made in Cinemascope, a revolutionary technique about to be tested on the public with *The Robe*. Barry Mahon went to see Darryl F. Zanuck at Fox Pictures and asked if he might borrow the equipment. The mogul refused and in a fit of pique Mahon threatened to sue him, but the waters were calmed by an impassioned telephone call from Errol. The equipment was handed over and transported to Italy. Errol himself auditioned the cast: when it came to selecting the younger players, he placed emphasis on looks as opposed to actual acting talents.

Errol also hired Jack Cardiff for the film – not just as photographer, but as its director. Then, finally, he cabled his friend Bruce Cabot, on holiday in Morocco. In recent years, Cabot's never-too-enterprising career had taken a nosedive but, Errol assured him, *William Tell* would catapult them both back to the top. He was sorry, he concluded, that he could only afford to pay Cabot a paltry $5,000 for playing the heavy, though he *could* guarantee that the two of them would have a whale of a time working on the film. Among the cast were 'several nubile youths and maidens specifically selected for their other talents'. Cabot caught the first flight to Rome.

William Tell began shooting in the June, and for three weeks progression was slow but sure on account of Errol's fickle health, and his and Cabot's habit of stopping mid-scene 'to exercise the lusty old steed', as the latter put it. Then, quite suddenly, the Italian producer called a set-meeting and announced that the production would have to be brought to a halt because the money had run out – Count Fossatoro, in addition to his personal contribution, had promised a $250,000 cash injection from the Italian government which had not been forthcoming, and he now demanded that *Errol* make up the deficit! Errol was devastated: he knew that to raise this kind of money he would have to sell one of his properties, or even the *Zaca*, something he would *never* do. He therefore begged his team to give him just a little more time to try and solve a financial crisis which for once was not self-imposed.

For almost. two months, shooting continued with Jack Cardiff and the Italian actors and personnel apparently so in awe of Errol – believing his pledge that they *would* be paid, eventually – that a statement was released declaring that working with such a *gentleman* was worth all the money in the world, an opinion which sadly would not endure. It was only when Count Fossatoro threatened Errol with legal action should he bring in any other backers to make up what *he* had effectively short-changed him by that the rot set in. Over the next few months there would be hurried meetings with executives from film companies around the world – including Harry Cohn of Columbia Pictures, the British producer Herbert Wilcox, and even Jack Warner, to whom Errol was not too proud to kow-tow if it meant getting him out of the mire. None of these moguls, however, would submit to refunding Count Fossatoro's investment and clear the way for other backers, primarily because the Italian was a member of the Communist Party. The 32 minutes of *William Tell* which had been edited were bought on Errol's behalf for $10,000 by a 'Cuban benefactor' who asked not to be named, and consigned to a vault in Rome. As for Fossatoro, he attempted to make up for what he had done by writing Barry Mahon a cheque for $50,000. This subsequently bounced, though the producer is said to have been delighted when told, a few years later, that the man who had duped him had died penniless.

Hot on the heels of the aborted film came the news that Errol's business manager, Al Blum, had died of cancer. This was followed by a telegram from Blum's office: just weeks before his death Blum had succeeded in balancing Errol's complicated financial accounts, and effectively his only outstanding debt was $20,000 he owed in back-taxes. Confident that he would be able to settle this without too much difficulty, Errol finalised the arrangements to return home – only to collapse and be rushed into a clinic, where doctors diagnosed hepatitis. And when Errol asked for the 'hard line' on his illness, the prognosis was not good: the young Swiss doctor informed him that there was a good chance that he would be dead within the week. After years of abuse, his liver had finally packed in. What surprised Errol's family and friends was his indifference to such grim tidings, writing in his journal, 'I'm not dead, but I'm not happy. I'm worried – worried because I *wasn't* worried when the jovial Swiss told me I had to go.' That Errol pulled through *was* a miracle, yet when he left the clinic all he could do was crack to the Italian reporters, 'It wasn't the doctors that saved my life. I made a pact with the devil years ago, and it's this – I'm not going to give that son of a bitch Jack Warner the satisfaction of outliving me! And what's more, I'm also going to beat this other business!'

The 'other business' referred to a newspaper report he had read in the clinic: according to a statement recently issued by a United States government official, an investigation had revealed that Al Blum had been stealing from him, and that subsequently he was in debt to the tune of $1 million. In Italy, Errol's creditors came down on him like vultures: he owed several months' rent on his Rome apartment, and the actors and crew from *William Tell* were now growing restless, having read in the press that some of their counterparts from *Adventures of Captain Fabian* had taken legal action against him, thus far to no avail. In all, he owed the former over $50,000 in unpaid salaries, and half as much again for their hotel expenses.

Several of Errol's society drinking partners chipped in as best they could, but when it became obvious that he could not pay his way, the bailiffs moved in, seizing his two cars, most of the furniture and ornaments from the apartment, his film equipment from Courmayeur and all of Patrice Wymore's clothes. His concierge then served him with a notice to quit, which he promptly tore up, telling the press, 'What is the world coming to, when a fellow's turfed out of his home on account of a few bills? Could things possibly get any worse than *that*?'

They could indeed. Only days later he learnt that Bruce Cabot – the man whom Errol had frequently described as 'my brother in all but name' – had, instead of taking action against the Italian film company, instructed his lawyers to issue a writ to the head of Errol Flynn Enterprises for loss of salary. When a Rome magistrate refused to hear the case because Errol's official home address was Jamaica, Cabot issued a summons through a British court for $17,000, more than thrice his salary for *William Tell*. He also threatened to expose Errol's sexuality in the British press, though had he done this, he would have been in danger of wrecking his own career for Errol later said that he would have spilled the beans on some of their early trips to Mexico. The case amounted to nothing, however.

Errol confessed that being sued by Cabot had not really bothered him, adding that it was not the first time that a buddy had bashed him or taken him to the cleaners for the sheer hell of it, while allowing the friendship to remain intact. What had *hurt*, he added, was the fact that Cabot had dined with the Flynns just *hours* before serving him with the writ. 'I could have killed the bastard,' he said. 'More's to the point, I *should* have killed him. But in the end I called him and told him that all was forgiven. Knowing what he'd done to his best buddy would haunt Cabot for years.'

As soon as he was well enough to do so, Errol returned to

Hollywood. Once again, he said, he was being forced to 'face the music' for something he had not done. Exactly how much Al Blum had fleeced him for was never made public – Errol estimated the damage to have been close to $1 million, and for once may not have been exaggerating. He himself was fortunate not to have been charged with defrauding the American government, and he was genuinely frightened. 'I had a vision of going back to where I came from,' he recalled. 'Tasmania, New Guinea, in a ball and chain, like a convict.'

However, just as Jerry Geisler had saved his neck during the rape trial, so he was rescued from total ruin by his new lawyer, Jud Golenbock, an astute man whose financial wizardry had saved several major Hollywood careers. Golenbock's theory was simple: it was a question of the client deciding which of his personal possessions were dispensable, and whether or not to declare himself bankrupt if selling even these could not get him out of the red. This was a theory, initially, that Errol would have nothing to do with, particularly when he read his mother's statement in the press, declaring that *she* had no pity for her son because almost all of his troubles were self-inflicted. He was still renting out the *Zaca* to whoever could afford the extortionate fees, and had no intention of selling it. 'I would sooner sell my wife,' he told one reporter, admitting for the first time that he and Patrice were experiencing matrimonial difficulties. He also refused $75,000 for his Gauguin, telling the prospective buyer, 'I'm not a charity case. If you *want* to buy my painting, then for God's sake pay me what it's worth!' A few weeks later, it was sold for $100,000, and Errol threw in a few objets d'art.

Errol also sold, at a loss, the Titchfield Hotel, telling reporters, 'I often wonder why I bought this Christ-bitten hovel in the first place. With its old-as-Adam English residents who keep everyone awake on a night with the thud-thud of their dropping dead, who needs the place?' The establishment's 'cordon bleu' kitchen had been infested with cockroaches when Errol had taken over – a few had wound up in his famous chocolates – and it was still crawling with them when he put it on the market. Its manager had refrained from calling in the pest controllers because the feisty cook had maintained that cockroaches were invaluable for keeping the cupboards clean!

The money raised from these various sales went some way towards placating Errol's creditors, though there was not enough left in the kitty to pay the $840,000 he owed Lili Damita and Nora Eddington in alimony. Not that this bothered him, for they were told, via his solicitor, 'If you're *so* hard up, why not do like all the other housewives and find yourselves a job. I'm going to Europe to earn *my* crust and know only too well that a little hard work never really harmed anyone!'

Errol had been invited to England by Herbert Wilcox to appear in *Lilacs in the Spring* opposite Wilcox's wife, Anna Neagle. The film was an adaptation by Harold Purcell of Neagle's recent stage success, *The Glorious Days*, the epitomy of all that was mushy, old-fashioned and camp. Its opening scenes are in black and white: Wilcox always had a problem convincing the viewer when he was about to witness a flashback, and hoped that the ensuing burst into colour might help. Knocked out during a World War Two air-raid, the singer Lillian Grey takes a historical backflip and is resurrected as Nell Gwyn, then Queen Victoria – both the subjects of earlier Wilcox-Neagle vehicles far better than this one. Then, later in the plot Lillian suffers a blackout and imagines that she is her own mother, Carole Beaumont, at the time she was courting John Beaumont (Errol), the song-and-dance man she married. The story then unwinds of how the couple separated when John refused to accompany his wife to America at the outset of her great Hollywood career, shortly after World War One, and how they became reconciled after *his* success with the advent of the Talkies. Errol and Anna Neagle had two musical interludes which were scored by Gracie Fields' former musical director, Harry Parr-Davies – a tango which Wilcox later cut from the film and a nifty soft-shoe shuffle which Errol performed well, to the music of 'Lily Of Laguna'. He later said that this had been a doddle because all he had done was repeat some of his footwork from *Gentleman Jim*!

Errol found the Wilcoxes 'more than a *little* fuddy-duddy'. On account of their impeccable morals they were highly esteemed by the British public, and as such demanded that anyone *privileged* to be working with them at least had to aspire towards their high standards. All the same, he later said that he had found them tremendous fun to be with. He was paid just $25,000 for making the film, a drop in the ocean when compared to what he was accustomed to earning, but he was more than willing to swallow his pride because Herbert Wilcox had promised to 'help resurrect' *William Tell*. *Lilacs in the Spring* would prove a big success in Britain, primarily because Anna Neagle was given top billing. In the United States, however, with its title changed to *Let's Make Up* and with Errol's name heading the credits, it was a flop.

On 2 July 1954, Errol was again invited to Northampton, this time to a garden party within the town's Franklin's Gardens in aid of the Little Theatre Fund. And this time the organisers *insisted* upon Errol being accompanied by his wife. Errol's reaction to this, although he pretended to be joking, was to tell Dorothy Fenwick of the Theatre Guild, 'Seeing as you're dictating the conditions, my dear, would you be kind enough to bear the cost to get me there?'

In his memoirs, Errol wrote that *he* had chartered a plane to convey him from Croydon airport to the aerodrome at Sywell, just outside the town. What *actually* happened was that the Theatre Guild paid for the four-seater Consul aircraft, for which they were later reimbursed by Barry Mahon, who accompanied the Flynns along with Herbert Wilcox's press agent. The party was met at Sywell by Dorothy Fenwick and the actress Freda Jackson, who later told the press that Errol had changed so alarmingly since she had last seen him twenty years before, in fact – that she had hardly recognised the 'old gent' who stepped off the aircraft. 'I had wonderful memories of a slim, beautiful young man with sparkling eyes and a dashing smile,' she said. 'But now, though the smile was still there, he looked haggard, bleary-eyed, almost a walking corpse. Thank God, then, that he still possessed his ready wit!' Jackson was referring to Errol's speech, during which he cracked, 'I've just been told that there's a new statue here called "Woman With A Fish". When I was in Northampton, I never bothered with the fish!'

From Northampton, Errol travelled to Blackpool to visit the resort's famous illuminations and to appear on the television variety show, *Holiday Time Saturday Night*. This was a live broadcast, and earlier he had met fans on the beach and joined them for a paddle in the sea. Retaining the holiday spirit, he walked on to the set with his trousers rolled up to his knees, carrying his shoes and socks in one hand and a glass in the other.

After the broadcast – by this time, his glass had been replenished innumerable times – he went of to judge a beauty contest at the Tower Ballroom, still barefoot having lost his shoes.

With Herbert Wilcox still promising to finance the aborted *William Tell*, Errol agreed to appear in another film opposite Anna Neagle – again, for a fee of $25,000, but this time on a take-it-or-leave-it basis – but while plans for this were being finalised, he stayed on in England to play Edward the Black Prince in what would be his final swashbuckler. *The Dark Avenger* – released in America under the somewhat misleading title, *The Warriors*, so that audiences there would not mistake it for a horror movie! – was an above-average film, lavishly shot in Technicolor *and* CinemaScope on location in Hertfordshire, which was sadly released at the wrong time. MGM's hugely successful *Ivanhoe*, starring Robert Taylor, had just been released.

The cast was a superlative one: Peter Finch, Michael Hordern, Noel Willman and Rupert Davies, with Joanne Dru playing Joan of Kent, whom Edward married in 1361. Initially, Errol was reluctant to work with the woman who had been the first wife of the detested Dick Haymes, always referred to by him as 'Nora's boy crooner'. They did, however, get along very well.

Set at the end of the Hundred Years War, the film opens in Northern France in 1359, with Edward III (Michael Hordern) demanding a truce from the defeated French, of whom only the all-powerful – albeit fictitious – Count de Ville (Finch) refuses to submit to English rule. Returning to England, the king leaves his son – de Ville's sworn enemy – in charge of Aquitaine, and over the course of the next hour or so much of the action concerns the enmity between the two men, and the younger Edward's attempts at rescuing the pretty widow, Joan, after she is captured by de Ville. There is also Hollywood's seemingly essential rewriting of history when we are told how Edward came about his famous nickname: in a roadside inn near de Ville's castle, he and his henchman steal a suit of black armour which happens to be hanging on the wall and happens to fit Edward's imposing frame perfectly. This, added to other oversights such as the ages of the actors when compared to those of the characters they are playing – Michael Hordern was two years *younger* than his screen son, and at 45, though physically befitting the part, Errol was facially unconvincing as the 29-year-old prince – caused many critics to scoff when the film was released in America.

As a swashbuckler, too, there is considerable evidence that Errol was way past his prime: the balconies and staircases he leaps from are closer to ground level (though he was also suffering from vertigo at the time) and, still plagued by the back injury sustained shortly after his marriage to Patrice Wymore, his movements are a little stiff. This, of course, could have been rectified had he agreed to using the stuntman provided to cover him in the heavy action sequences, particularly in the fight scenes where his face was covered by a visor and no one would have known the difference. In spite of this, however, the ultimate showdown between the two warring factions – on the leftover set of the aforementioned *Ivanhoe*, to Cedric Thorpe Davie's pounding score – was superb, with Errol dispatching the villain not with a sword this time, but an axe.

Errol's second film for Herbert Wilcox, *King's Rhapsody*, based on the Ruritanian musical play by Ivor Novello, was in comparison almost a non-event, mostly on account of Anna Neagle's dreadful singing, considered *so* bad by United Artists that by the time the film was released in America, all of her numbers had been cut. Neagle, however, was not the only contributor towards its almost inevitable failure: despite the colourful Barcelona and Majorca locations, and the costumes, the dialogue was old-fashioned to the point of absurdity. Patrice Wymore's own vocalising left much to be desired, the flashbacks had to be observed for several minutes to determine if they *were* flashbacks or merely confused continuity of the already confusing plot, and Martita Hunt's grossly overbearing Queen Mother with her neo-Edith Evans mannerisms had cinemagoers cringing in the few places the film was screened.

Basically, the storyline centres around the near-alcoholic King Richard of the fictitious Laurentia, and his mistress, Marta Kariloss (Neagle), a relationship which is brought to a temporary halt by Richard's mother when she arranges for him to be married by proxy to the young woman known as 'The Snow Princess' – Cristiane of Norseland (Wymore). 'Some day my heart will awake,' Cristiane warbles, before turning a few cartwheels, perfectly content with the idea because she is already a fan of the 'young' man, having filled a scrapbook with his pictures. The wedding takes place, but when Richard refuses to give up his mistress, Marta leaves, and he ends up falling in love with his wife, who bears him a heir. He himself is then forced to abdicate following a government coup. 'I hope my hand is steady,' he says, as he is handed the document, 'I should hate posterity to say how drunk he must have been when he signed it!' He then bids farewell to his family and goes into exile, bumping into Marta several years later in Paris. It is she who persuades him to return to Laurentia to attend his son's coronation, and to be reunited with his wife.

After a short break aboard the *Zaca* in Majorca, the Flynns then flew to Rio de Janeiro: Errol had never seen the carnival, and as Patrice was still nursing their baby daughter he assumed that he would be able to get away with having a little fun. The local newspapers reported two incidents: one where, blind drunk, he chased a Japanese tourist up a tree and tried to pull her panties down, and another where he was caught in a compromising position with a 19-year-old youth in a hotel room. This latter indiscretion he attempted to laugh off, claiming that he had merely been teaching the young man some of the tricks of his trade as 'an ex-Don Juan'. He was, however, sufficiently worried over what the press *might* have made of the event to return to Majorca the very next day.

In November 1954, Errol returned to England to work on his first television series, *The Errol Flynn Theatre*, an enterprise set up by the producer Norman Williams and the French-Canadian financier Marcel Leduc to rival similar ones spearheaded by Alfred Hitchcock, Dick Powell and Douglas Fairbanks. He filmed the prologues to all 39 half-hour episodes and appeared in six. The first, *The Mirror* also starred Patrice Wymore.

The series, however, was not as successful as everyone involved had anticipated, and the sojourn in England was marred by illness: Errol succumbed to an attack of malaria halfway through filming, and the day after leaving his sickbed he suffered a fall, cracking one of the already damaged vertebrae in his spine. 'I'm starting to fall apart,' he told a reporter, seriously. 'Might as well go ahead and start digging that six-by-two flower-plot right now!' What he did not know was that – temporarily, at least – his career was about to take an *upward* spiral.

9

Je Suis Comme Je Suis . . .

'I generally deny that I was ever a good actor, but I have turned in a
half-dozen good performances.'

It was in Majorca during the summer of 1955, when physically
and spiritually he was at an all-time low, that Errol received a call
from Universal's Albert J. Cohen, asking him if he would be
interested in starring in a film called *Istanbul*. Errol agreed at
once: he had never visited Turkey, and the *Zaca*'s crew were put
on standby. It was only after he had signed the contract that Errol
was informed that this particular Istanbul had been reconstructed
on a Hollywood backlot.

The film, little more than a rehash of *Singapore*, made in 1947
with Ava Gardner, fared little better than Errol's last effort for
Herbert Wilcox. In it he played an American adventurer – with the
usual clipped British accent – who buys a valuable diamond bracelet
from a shady dealer, after which he finds himself pursued by both
crooks and customs officials. Having hidden the jewellery in his hotel
room before being deported, he returns several years later to yet
more drama, accompanied by an amnesiac wife (Cornell Borchers)
who is also a bigamist! Most of the critics agreed that the film's only
redeemable scenes were those featuring Nat King Cole, especially
when he sang his smash hit, 'When I Fall In Love'.

In October 1955, Errol's debts finally caught up with him when
the Los Angeles County Court ordered him to forfeit Mulholland

House, the sale of which, the judge decided, would raise enough cash to pay off most of his creditors. Over the years Errol had transformed parts of his home into shrines for sex, and few prospective buyers were interested in paying an alleged $800,000 for a building which had phallic imagery in virtually every room. On top of this, there was the house's so-called 'murky' past to be taken into consideration: the press were not slow in reminding the public that someone, in the not-too-distant future, would be the owner of 'arguably the hottest cat-house in California', and that no amount of paint or restoration would alter the fact that this 'Bluebeard's castle' had been witness to some very perverted goings-on over the last two decades. Needless to say, there were no takers, and having been forced to drop the asking price, the court eventually handed the house over to Lili Damita in exchange for the alimony that Errol owed her.

Lili Damita was not, however, allowed to keep Errol's personal effects: these were auctioned, and the money passed on to his creditors – $20,000 alone to the actors and crew of *Adventures of Captain Fabin* – so that he was out of the red for the first time in years. Even so, Errol would have an inordinately tough time ahead of him: although Damita had given him free use of the tiny duplex they had shared at the Garden of Alla – more for the sake of his children, she said, than out of pity for him – her renewed alimony suit was so worded that unless he paid her $25,000 a year *and* deposited a minimum of $50,000 into a trust fund for Sean, he would go to jail. Nora Eddington then sued him for $5,000 for the non-support of his two daughters by her.

Errol's financial problems put an unquestionable strain on his marriage, though unlike his final months with Lili Damita and Nora Eddington, there were few rows – just lengthy periods of crippling silence. It was Errol's doctor who suggested that they should put a suitable distance between themselves and Hollywood, for a few weeks at least, and during the summer of 1956, taking fifteen-year-old Sean with them, the Flynns flew to Majorca, to join the *Zaca* for a cruise of the Mediterranean. For Sean's sake – Errol suspected that the boy would only go running back to Lili Damita, who had predicted that this third marriage would flounder by the end of the year, with the news that she had been right all along – he and Patrice slept in the same bed throughout the trip.

En route to the Cape Verde Islands, Errol moored the yacht off the Spanish coast, and in the middle of the night, when everyone was asleep, two men and two women climbed aboard and barged into the Flynns' stateroom, claiming that they had been invited to an all night party which clearly was not taking place. One of these had a camera, and snapped Errol as he was getting out of bed – stark naked and, in his words, in all his valour and no armour – which caused him to spin out of control, smacking one of the men in the mouth and knocking out most of his teeth. Naturally these unwelcome visitors quickly fled, and within a few hours Errol had pushed the incident to the back of his mind, aided by a bottle of cognac. By morning, however, his hand had swollen to twice its normal size, and when a Spanish doctor diagnosed blood-poisoning he was flown to a hospital in Gibraltar, where he suddenly took a turn for the worse. Tests substantiated that he had contracted an unidentified virus from the man's teeth, and for four days he lay in a coma, during which time surgeons seriously contemplated amputating his arm. Fortunately, the antibiotics he was prescribed prevented this from happening, though the side-effects from these – mixed with the lethal cocktail of vodka, cocaine and whatever other drugs could be smuggled to his bedside – kept him in hospital for another month.

For six months, Errol recuperated aboard the *Zaca* in Majorca, and it was under considerable duress – this time, he said, *solely* for the money – that he returned to work at the beginning of 1957. He had signed a one-off deal with United Artists to appear in an oddity entitled *The Big Boodle*. This was filmed on location in Cuba, a troubled country of which Errol was inordinately fond: since 1952, and for the second time, it had been in the grip of the right-wing dictator, Fulgencio Batista, though when Errol and the film crew arrived there it was widely rumoured that he would be finally brought to heel by Fidel Castro, who after two failures was planning a third coup against him.

Soon afterwards, Errol and Castro would become acquainted with each other, but for the time being Errol was only interested in getting the film over with and collecting his pay cheque. On the first day of shooting, he attempted to seduce one of his co-stars, the 23-year-old Liverpool-born actress, Gia Scala, whom he had admired in her film debut two years previously, *All That Heaven*

Allows, with Rock Hudson and Jane Wyman. When she knocked him back in the most brutal manner – branding him 'flabby, balding and geriatric' – he unsuccessfully tried to get her fired from the film, and throughout shooting the pair were permanently at each other's throats. Shortly after completing *The Big Boodle*, Scala, already addicted to tranquillisers, would be arrested on London's Waterloo Bridge for loitering, having gone there in the first instance to kill herself...bringing the acid comment from Errol, 'What a pity I wasn't there, to give her just a *little* push!' And in 1972, following a fifteen-year trail of self-destruction, Gia Scala would finally end it all with a lethal mixture of alcohol and barbiturates.

In *The Big Boodle*, Errol played a has-been casino croupier who unwittingly collects a forged banknote from a customer, only to be suspected of knowing where the plates are hidden. In order to clear his name, he turns amateur detective, sparking off a series of chases wherein the film's definitive attraction emerges as Cuba itself as we are taken on a colourful excursion of Havana's nightlife. The camera steers well clear of those spots favoured by Errol and the two young extras from the film who served as his guides during his stay on the island, and who shared his appreciation of Havana's red-light district with its gangsters, live sex shows and mixed brothels.

When Darryl F. Zanuck of 20th Century Fox saw the rushes for *Istanbul* and the pre-publicity photographs for *The Big Boodle*, he called Errol and offered him a part in *The Sun Also Rises*, a production whose pedigree was second to none. Based on the novel by Ernest Hemingway, its screenplay was by Peter Viertel, whose mother Salka had scripted several of Garbo's masterpieces. It was to be directed by the veteran Henry King, whose illustrious career stretched as far back as the silent epics of Richard Barthelmess and Lillian Gish, and with a budget of around $5 million it would prove by far the most expensive film Errol had ever appeared in. Also, he was starring opposite Tyrone Power, for whom he was still carrying a torch, though by this time Power was no longer amorously interested in him. His other co-stars were Ava Gardner, Mel Ferrer, Eddie Albert and Juliette Gréco.

Zanuck, however, who had neither spoken to nor met Errol until this time, did have some reservations about asking him to do the film. He was not sure how Errol would react to his character being described as 'a washed-up drunk' but Errol put him at his ease by telling him, 'But it's true, sport. That's *exactly* what I am!' Next, Zanuck had the invidious task of informing him that for the first time *ever*, he would not be the film's lead – Power's, Gardner's and even Ferrer's names would appear above his in the credits. Errol was not so sure about this. However, when Zanuck argued that his last few films had been anything but successful, that this one would be advertised as 'Flynn's comeback movie', and that in his opinion he would run away with all the accolades, Errol signed the contract.

Zanuck's prediction was spot-on. Errol was the star of *The Sun Also Rises*, an otherwise dreadfully boring, over-long saga whose main fault lay with the fact that its major characters were played by actors a generation *older* than Hemingway had created them.

Jake Barnes (Power) is the Paris-based newspaperman whose injuries sustained during the war have left him impotent. Initially, he is only interested in Georgette (Gréco), a pretty but stand-offish chanteuse, and in drinking with his morose literary pal, Robert Cohn (Ferrer). When old flame Lady Brett Ashley (Gardner) appears on the scene, however, Georgette is unceremoniously dumped and the trio, accompanied by another crony from days past (Albert), head for the fiesta at Pamplona, where they meet up with Brett's fiancé, Mike Campbell. Errol does not make an appearance until 50 minutes into the film, though henceforth his every gesture and turn of phrase is recompense for the tedium one has endured thus far. 'A bunch of bloody fireworks, all fizzled. That's us,' he observes, watching the colourful display and turning a blind, permanently drunken eye to easy-lay Brett's voracious advances on a local bullfighter, which leads to the friends scrapping among themselves. Brett ends up where she started during the war, driving off in a taxi with Jake to whatever fate has in store for the two of them.

In the same year, 1957, Errol, aided by the actress Dorothy Dandridge, spearheaded a campaign to close down the scandal magazine, *Confidential*, which over the last four years had threatened and frequently ended innumerable Hollywood careers with its tawdry exposés of the stars' personal lives. Gossip columns had of course been the bane of the film world for decades, but *Confidential* – in an attempt to live up to its motto, 'Tells the Facts and Names the Names' – had always managed to go one step further than the likes of Hedda Hopper, Louella Parsons and Elsa Maxwell by not always checking the authenticity of its stories before printing them and usually accompanying them with only the most unflattering pictures. It was also selling an incredible four million copies per issue.

What Errol and his colleagues loathed were the unorthodox and often unlawful methods employed by the magazine's editor, Robert Harrison, to acquire his exclusives: prostitutes and rent boys, depending on the victim's sexual preferences, were paid huge sums of money to lure them into bed, while a tiny machine hidden somewhere in the room recorded their explosive post-coital small-talk. And in special cases, Harrison would provide his 'detectives' with highly sophisticated infra-red cameras.

Errol's friend and sometime one-night stand, Rory Calhoun, was not merely outed as a homosexual: *Confidential* published a mug-shot from the Salt Lake City Police's files, along with the headline, 'But For the Grace of God Still a Convict!' Another photograph depicted another acquaintance, Dan Dailey, dressed in women's clothes. Cary Grant, arrested after being caught having sex with a sailor in a public lavatory, had managed to 'buy back' his story as had Rock Hudson, whose boyfriend had sold an exclusive to the magazine for $10,000. In this instance, Hudson's management had sacrificed one of their less-important clients, feeding Harrison 'an alternative queer story'. . . again, the unfortunate victim had been Rory Calhoun. Lana Turner, upon reading that she and Ava Gardner had allegedly shared a lover, had actually hired a hitman to kill Harrison – a mission which failed when the bullets hit a tree while he was out hunting – but the crunch had come in February 1957 when Dorothy Dandridge had filed a suit for $2 million after Harrison had divulged her reputed 'antics' in a wood with a group of naturists. He had also accused Maureen O'Hara of gross indecency with a man in the back row of a cinema, and Errol of 'certain indiscretions' with a call-girl.

Harrison, by this time the most despised man in Hollywood, had been the first to tell the world about the two-way mirror at Mulholland House, in a feature which had amused rather than angered Errol. He had suggested, jokingly, that maybe Harrison ought to spend an hour or so entertaining the devotees of the jerk-off room. However, when Harrison printed the story that he had left Patrice on their wedding night to entertain the call-girl – it did not matter that *Confidential* had got the location wrong, stating Hollywood instead of Monte Carlo – Errol saw red and served Harrison with a lawsuit for $1 million.

Errol, of course, did not need any lawyer to prove that he had been nowhere near Hollywood at the time of the alleged event; similarly, Maureen O'Hara had passport evidence stating that she had been out of the country. However, between them they hired the most expensive defence in Hollywood, simply to screw Harrison for every cent they could and end his reign of terror. And because of their actions, hot on the heels of the Dandridge writ, dozens of Hollywood stars now found the courage to do what they should have done in the first place and sued. Indeed, *Confidential* received so many writs over the next week that the film capital's public relations officer, a no-nonsense individual named Robert Murphy, warned the District Attorney that unless the matter was hushed up, all the major film studios would withdraw their financial support from the forthcoming Republican campaign.

For as long as anyone could remember – and Errol's statutory rape trial had been a supreme example of what could happen whenever hush money was *not* handed over – bribery had been rife to sanitise and protect Hollywood's elite, but this time the District Attorney had decided to do things by the book. Justice Irving Saypol, the man appointed to oversee the proceedings, which opened on 2 August, called upon the magazine to honour its motto and not only name names but *supply* the facts. In other words, they had to make available their files for public scrutiny. Upon this, there was a mass exodus from Hollywood of anyone, from the major stars down to the extras and studio personnel, who might have had something to hide, no matter how inconsequential. The event heralded by the press as 'The Trial of a Hundred Stars' amounted to little more than a large number of out-of-court settlements, none of them remotely close to the original amounts, though collectively enough to force Harrison out of business. Errol himself received a cheque for $15,000 on the actual steps of the courthouse, no great amount, but enough to keep the wolves from his door for the time being.

At around the time the courts were doing battle with *Confidential*, Warner Brothers turned towards one subject that Robert Harrison would have given his eye-teeth to expose, had the magazine been in circulation during his lifetime: 'The Great Profile' himself, John Barrymore. Jack Warner had purchased the screen rights for *Too Much, Too Soon*, the controversial autobiography of Diana, Barrymore's daughter from his second marriage to Blanche Thomas, aka the poet, Michael Strange. In 1957, the unashamedly promiscuous Diana had been found dead in her New York home, aged 38. Suicide was the official verdict, though Errol had been unable to stop himself quipping, 'The fair lady fucked herself to death. What a way to go!'

Jack Warner flatly refused to consider any other actor for the role of the screen's most infamous drunk until he had discussed it with Errol, who signed the contract at once. Warner was however deeply disturbed by the alarming change in Errol's appearance in the five years since their last meeting. He wrote in his memoirs, *My First Hundred Years in Hollywood*:

> The once strong and handsome face was puffy and grey, the dancing shimmer was gone from his eyes, and there was no longer a spring in his step. He was playing the part of a drunken actor and didn't need any method system to get him in the mood. He *was* drunk. *Too much too soon.* The words should have been carved on a tombstone at the time, for he was one of the living dead.

Errol played such a convincing drunk in the film *and* remembered his lines that one journalist who visited the lot was convinced that he could only have been sober to get everything right on the first take. When he told Errol, however, that he was going to inform his readers that Flynn had finally stopped drinking, he was warned, 'Be careful, sport. That is libel of the very *worst* kind!'

Like many subsequent 'offspring biographers', Diana Barrymore had an axe to grind as far as her father was concerned: therefore she was much less interested in chronicling the life of the great thespian than she was in blaming him for her own hedonistic life, a catalogue of broken marriages, love affairs, petty crime, suicide attempts and alcoholism. Errol, for his part, was having none of this, and would not portray Barrymore as the 'burlesque and sad clown' that he had become towards the end of life:

> When I started to try to get Jack into focus, I wanted to delve into his inner self, not to imitate him – that was too easy. I wanted to show a man with a heart, a man eaten up inside – as I knew him to be in those final days when I was close to him – a man full of regrets and all ready to die, but one last thing to live for, the love of his daughter, Diana, his desire to get back her love.

Because the events depicted in the film were contemporary and most of the leading characters still alive, the scriptwriters had to change several names or eradicate certain of their unpleasant habits. Diana's first husband, the actor Bramwell Fletcher, now became Vincent Bryant (Efrem Zimbalist Jnr). Tennis player husband number two, John Howard (Ray Danton) was not quite the vicious sadist he was in real life, and her last husband, actor Robert Wilcox (Edward Kemmer), a hopeless drunk on and off the stage, was now revealed to be a *reformed* alcoholic.

During the shooting of *Too Much, Too Soon*, Errol wandered over to an adjacent lot, where they were filming *Marjorie Morningstar*, the famous tale of the wealthy Jewish girl who rebels against the edicts of her religion by having an affair with a man many years her senior. The stars were Natalie Wood and Gene Kelly, neither of whom Errol could stand, though what he was really interested in was getting to know the dancers – most of them in their teens, and all of them attractive. By this time, Errol had publicly admitted that his marriage to Patrice Wymore was over – not that it would have made the slightest difference to his carousing had she still been around.

Over the course of the next two weeks there were innumerable one-night stands or behind-the-sets encounters, but the two which appealed to him the most were a seventeen-year-old youth named Jack, and Beverly Aadland, an articulate, leggy, fifteen-year-old blonde. The young girl was being chaperoned everywhere by her mother, a strict woman who never let her daughter out of her sight for a moment, especially when there was a known lecher like Errol Flynn around. However, declaring that he could have Jack any time he wanted, Errol pursued Beverly Aadland with all the reckless abandon of a sex-starved man of half his age. The end result of this *chasse à l'enfant* was not only infinitely more rewarding than either of them could have possibly anticipated, but it proved probably the most tender, sincere relationship Errol had experienced since the one with Ross Alexander, twenty years before. 'Beverly's the one who's going to help me by being around when I pop off,' he said at the time, a prediction which sadly would come true.

Upon saying this, however, too much should not be read into Errol's relationship with Beverly Aadland. Errol was the first to admit to his extreme promiscuity, and despised long-term affairs, so it is *very* unlikely that Beverly would have lasted any longer than his other largely superfluous, in-name-only wives. Neither, according to his surviving close friends, would she have become the fourth Mrs Flynn: Beverly was only *fifteen* when she met Errol (though some sources claim she was one year younger), and once she attained legal status, she almost certainly would have been quickly dispensed with, like all the others. Also, 'just in case', Errol retained his relationship with Jack.

Initially, of course, Errol had to be cautious whenever he was with his 'Wood Nymph', as he called her. Quite unexpectedly, his career had begun an eleventh-hour ascendancy, and he dared not risk media criticism by publicly flaunting yet another under-aged lover. Also, Hollywood's moral watchdogs had been scrutinising his movements in the fifteen years since his rape trial, though Errol no longer had to worry about Florence Aadland, since blinding her with his charm: Beverly's mother did not mind the pair being lovers, as long as their affair was kept low-key and they slept in separate rooms, though *this* particular arrangement would not last long.

In January 1958, Errol accepted the role of Edward Rochester – a ridiculous exercise in miscasting if ever there was one – in *The Master of Thornfield*, a stage adaptation of *Jane Eyre* by Huntington Hartford, the supermarket tycoon with whom the Flynns had stayed several times since the loss of Mulholland House. Matters could have been worse, for before signing the $100,000 contract which included a movie option on the play, Errol had tried to insist that Beverly be engaged as his leading lady. Subsequently the part of Jane had gone to Hartford's wife, Marjorie Steele.

Errol's acting debut on the legitimate American stage was the most ghastly mistake. He had never been capable of remembering lengthy pieces of dialogue at the best of times, though his excuse for this was that he took after his idol, Barrymore, whose famous words were now repeated when, at his first rehearsal, he told Hartford, 'With all those beautiful phrases from the classics crowding my brain, why should I bother even *trying* to remember all this Hollywood shit?' Like the Great Profile, therefore, in *his* last tour with a play, Errol had 'idiot' cards and pages from the script hidden among the props, along with tumblers of vodka. Admitting that he had never been so bored in his life, he stumbled through six weeks of provincial try-outs in preparation for the play's Broadway première at the Belasco Theatre. 'I had more fun in the Northampton Rep's production of *Jack and the Beanstalk*,' he told the press.

In Cincinnati, fate came to Errol's rescue when he received a call from Darryl F. Zanuck, inviting him to do another film for 20th Century Fox. *The Roots Of Heaven* was based on the best-selling novel by Romain Gary: John Huston would direct, and Juliette Gréco had already signed the contract to play the leading lady. Zanuck told him that shooting was scheduled to begin during the summer.

Errol deliberated for a little while: some years before he had got into a nasty brawl with Huston which had put them both into hospital for several days, and Gréco is alleged to have taken no little offence at his denouncing her as 'scruffy-looking'. When he learnt, however, that his other co-stars were to be William Holden, Paul Lukas, and Orson Welles (still not speaking to him following the Farouk debacle, but a huge box-office draw with whom any actor would have felt privileged to work), and when Zanuck told him that the film would be shot on location in Paris and Africa, he decided that it was too good an opportunity to miss. Therefore, when the curtain came down in Cincinnati, he called Huntington Hartford and told him exactly what he could do with *The Master of Thornfield*.

A few days after his walk-out, Errol escorted Beverly Aadland to the Boston Estate in Jamaica, where she was to stay while he was working on *The Roots of Heaven*. She had to spend part of the time with his parents, where she was referred to by Marelle as 'my son's latest jail-fodder', though a few weeks later the Flynns returned to England, leaving Beverly to be cared for by the staff at the Titchfield Hotel.

Within hours of settling in at his hotel at Fort Archambault, in French Equatorial Africa, Errol went down with a fever, brought on by the sudden intense heat, cocaine, and the several bottles of vodka he had quaffed on the plane. Even so, his deplorable state of health did not prevent him from making a pass at Juliette Gréco, then as now more famous for her *chansons* than her films, but a tremendously gifted actress all the same. Errol had learnt one of her most famous numbers by heart – Jacques Prévert's 'Je Suis Comme Je Suis'. Its opening lines, 'I am what I am, I was made that way', summed him up perfectly. Gréco, however, was not interested, so he turned his attentions towards Darryl F. Zanuck's son-in-law, whom he describes in his memoirs as 'a most wonderful-looking young man in the prime of youth and good shape'. Errol moved out of his hotel room and the pair shared a hut in the fenced-off actors' camp, and as had happened in the early days with Bruce Cabot, were not averse to sharing a bed when there were no other takers.

Fraternising with the locals had been forbidden by John Huston, because the region was reputed to be rife with venereal disease. Errol got around this problem by hiring a French quack doctor who not only supplied him with his essential drugs – at exorbitant prices – but bedmates for him and his friend. Huston later spoke of how he would hear what sounded like cats miaowing – the youngsters' signal for the doctor to secrete them into the actors' camp, where they would be medically examined and given an 'anti-pox' injection before being escorted to Errol's quarters.

Errol was delighted that owing to a contractual hitch with Paramount, William Holden had been replaced by the then lesser-known Trevor Howard. Holden, Hollywood's self-styled 'golden boy', had been given top billing, with Errol as his support. Now, however, Errol's name would head the credits, although his part was smaller than the Howard one, and he was awarded an appropriate increase in salary – the first time this had happened without his having to walk out halfway through a production. He was especially thrilled to be working with Howard, whose own reputation as a hellraiser was already widely known. It was Howard, one of the few men who could drink Errol under the table, who organised the 'provisions' truck which followed them around Africa – its cargo consisting of 50 *crates* of vodka and whisky!

In *The Roots of Heaven*, Errol played Major Forsythe, his third 'authentic' drunk. His earlier performance in *The Sisters*, he declared, had not counted because he had only been play-acting! In the Romain Gary novel, Forsythe is the brainwashed American soldier who has supported the Communists during the Korean War. In the film, however, he is a British Nazi sympathiser who deserts and joins a motley bunch of adventurers led by Morel (Howard), a man whose mission in life is to save elephants from extinction.

John Huston later declared that his only film with Errol Flynn had been 'an avoidable 140 degrees nightmare' – not on account of the usual histrionics, but because of location problems which would not have occurred, had Darryl F. Zanuck allowed him to have his way and shoot the jungle scenes on home ground. Of the company, which including the cast and professional extras numbering around 200, more than half succumbed to some malady or other. Eddie Albert fell victim to sunstroke, became delirious and almost died. Malaria presented the real threat: Darryl F. Zanuck's son-in-law became so ill that he had to be airlifted to a hospital near Paris which specialised in tropical ailments, and an Italian extra died. Amazingly, Errol remained malaria-free during this overseas trip, attributing his good luck to 'a several-pints-a-day ration of Smirnoff and fruit juice'. 'It was in some ways the most astonishing period of my life,' he said afterwards. 'Yet perhaps I had some preparation for all this. I had been through the New Guinea jungles, worse even than French Equatorial Africa, so probably I had a gearing for this that the others didn't.' In August 1958, en route to New York, Errol stopped off in London. His parents now owned a house in St Albans, and he had arranged to spend a few days with them. His big mistake was to have Beverly Aadland meet him at the airport, for if he had earlier told American reporters that the Wood

Nymph was his secretary – 'and quite a versatile little secretary, at that!' – he now openly admitted to the British press that they were 'more than friends'. They shared a suite at the Savoy, and Errol then announced that he was negotiating to purchase the screen rights for Nabokov's as yet unpublished but already hotly disputed novel, *Lolita*, which he said would have himself playing the male lead, and Beverly as the fourteen-year old nymphette. This time it was his *father* who put his foot down: Theodore declared that he would not have his son 'cavorting with a child' under *his* roof, or even be seen in public with him until he had come to his senses.

Nonplussed, Errol returned to the Savoy and steeled himself for what he assumed would be another unpleasant confrontation. David Niven was in town, and after a great deal of arm-twisting Errol had agreed to have lunch with him at a restaurant in Soho. The pair had not spoken since Niven's attack on him after *Objective Burma!*, thirteen years before, but now they embraced warmly and put all the animosity behind them. 'The face was puffy and blotchy and the hand that had once held the bow of Robin Hood could not have put the arrow through the Taj Mahal at ten paces,' Niven observed, 'but there was an internal calm and genuineness about him that I'd never seen before.' Niven wrote in his memoirs that Errol had even asked *him* to forgive him for being such a heel – for not offering his condolences after Niven's wife had been killed in an accident.

A few days later, Errol and Beverly flew on to New York, where they stayed in separate suites at the Park Lane Hotel: she with her mother, Florence, and Errol with his 'valet', Jack, the young dancer from *Marjorie Morningstar*. Some months before he had negotiated a deal with Putnam Publishing, receiving a $100,000 advance, to write his autobiography. His theory was that if the Errol Flynn story *had* to be told, then it might as well come from the horse's mouth in a tell-all tome which would prevent tacky rags such as *Confidential* from cashing in on exclusives which were not even close to the truth. His revelations, he declared with smug satisfaction, would rock Hollywood on its foundations.

For years, Errol had been recording his thoughts, opinions and reminiscences in his journal, and these formed the outline of *My Wicked, Wicked Ways*. For a time, too, it had seemed that Errol would go against the showbusiness tradition of employing a ghost-writer: always an early riser, each morning he would dash off a minimum ten pages, most of which, according to Putnam's editor, Howard Cady, needed little editing save for the removal of expletives and libellous comments. Now, however, Cady was forced to take stock of a tragic situation: for the screen's most famous swashbuckler, time was swiftly running out. Indeed, Errol had recently told one journalist that he was *expecting* to die during his next trip to Jamaica with Beverly.

Cady therefore arranged for Errol to meet the man who would ghost the book which Errol boasted 'would make the most virulent *Confidential* exposé look like something out of a Disney cartoon'. Earl Conrad was an established novelist, journalist and historian of around Errol's age, who vicariously described him as 'a choice representative of the human species' and 'the congenital seeker after monogamy who could live only promiscuously'.

The meeting took place in Errol's suite at New York's Park Lane Hotel. 'His face looked yellowish, haggard and bloated,' Conrad remembered some years later, explaining how Errol himself had answered the door before returning to his lovemaking with Beverly, whom he later introduced as his secretary. In his account of the twelve months he spent with the actor, *Errol Flynn: A Memoir*, Conrad would put the girl's age at around fifteen, later declare that she had only been *fourteen* the first time she had slept with Errol, and refer to her as 'Dhondi'. In Errol's autobiography she is not mentioned at all: Errol, who was perfectly willing to cast caution to the wind during the closing stages of his life, was still terrified of being involved in another statutory rape scandal. Conrad also made the mistake of informing his readers that Beverly was not very bright. On the contrary, she was an articulate young woman with a ready sense of humour, and an IQ of 140.

The next day Errol, Beverly and Conrad left for the Titchfield Hotel in Port Antonio, where the ghost-writer was supplied with a court stenographer and a typist, and Errol with 96 bottles of vodka which, he declared, would see him through the first few chapters of the book. Conrad had expected Errol's confessions to be candid, but he obviously was not prepared for their first interview, when Errol expressed his opinion about his mother, 'The Cunt'. 'I didn't know what he was talking about – sex, or something else,' Conrad observed, admitting that when the penny finally dropped he was extremely shocked, though he soon began sympathising with him:

> Migod, I have never heard any man call his mother *that* ... [then] figuring that I had to identify with the man and try to see things the way he saw them. I talked about his mother but referred to her in the same way. 'What did the cunt do then?' 'How did the cunt behave in that situation?' I was in with Flynn. It seemed he rather enjoyed hearing an outsider call his mother by that unmotherly identification.

Conrad came to the conclusion, as had others when dissecting the lives of similarly 'doomed' stars such as Montgomery Clift, Maria Callas and Judy Garland, that *all* of Errol's problems as an adult could be traced back to his mother. He had passed through life fighting and hating the world as he had inwardly fought and hated his mother. Even so, he had recognised and admired the *physical* beauty of the world as he had acknowledged this quality in Marelle. 'There is an odd expression: the apple does not fall far from the limb,' Conrad observed.

Marelle, however, was not the only one with little good to say about Errol at this time. According to Earl Conrad, both the Flynns had been eager to provide him with recollections of their son's Australian childhood, but now Marelle refused to have anything to do with the book, and all Theodore had to say was, 'Our current opinions of Errol would burn up any paper on which they were written.'

Conrad was also shocked by Errol's behaviour while the pair were working on the book: as unfaithful to Beverly as he had been to everyone else in his life, he employed several pimps who supplied him with under-aged native girls. They would be lined up below the porch where he and Conrad were sitting, and Errol would point at the one which took his fancy. 'The chosen one would be called upstairs and perhaps not be with him for more than five or ten minutes,' Conrad recalled, adding that Errol had also seduced the Titchfield Hotel's busty new secretary, an event he had described as 'like being lashed between two tugboats going down a white river full throttle'. Conrad spoke too of Errol's brief but increasingly more frequent visits to Havana, though he did not divulge what he was doing there *extant* of becoming increasingly more involved in Cuba's mounting political crisis – namely, visiting brothels which specialised in young men.

Conrad later criticised Errol for the way he treated the locals who milled around the Titchfield Hotel and Boston Estate, pandering to his every need. He always spoke to them in pidgin English, itself quite unnecessary, and the workers on his estate, fruit-pickers mostly, were so badly paid that they often had to steal from him in order to survive, and were constantly on the verge of revolt. For years, Errol had been promising them a pension scheme, yet he seemed to derive such pleasure out of seeing them bow and scrape whenever he appeared on the scene. To reward them *too* much, he said, and to offer them better living conditions, would only have taken away their subservience. In any case, he added, there was always the chance that some of the families on his estate might benefit financially by loaning him their sons or daughters for the occasional game of 'bury the banana'.

On one occasion, Conrad recalled, he and Errol had been out in the street when a girl of around thirteen had passed by with her mother. Errol had called out, 'Lift up!', and the youngster had raised her shirt and shown him her budding breasts. On another, Errol had informed his Jamaican lawyer that as he had decided to build a new $100,000 home at Castle Comfort, a few miles along the coast – and as his parents were now spending more of their time in England – Boston House would have to be sold and its staff, some of whom had been with him for over ten years, would have to leave. According to Conrad, when asked what would happen to these people, Errol had responded, 'That's their problem.'

Earl Conrad also appeared to be obsessed with Errol's penis, a subject which would take up *four* pages in *Errol Flynn- A Memoir*. Conrad jokingly suggested that Errol's infamous appendage be photographed and put on the cover of his book, to which he responded, 'Well, perhaps one day I'll press it into a bit of cement in front of Grauman's!' Whether Errol actually undid his flies and took out his 'micturitor' while *this* interview was taking place, just to prove to Conrad that it was 'unremarkable... if not short, certainly not much longer than that', is a matter for some conjecture. Historical reports have invariably ascertained that the great sexual 'exhibitors' – Valentino, Gary Cooper, Onassis, Barrymore *and* Flynn – *only* did so because this part of their anatomy was so famously Herculean.

Errol got on surprisingly well with his ghost-writer, despite the fact that he had originally asked Putnam to supply him with a younger man or woman. Had Putnam agreed to this, and the writer gone along with Errol's wishes, the ensuing autobiography would have been interrupted by the inevitable 'dalliances' and taken much longer to complete, and may not even have seen the light of day considering its subject's fragile state of health.

Conrad was by all accounts something of a dour individual with not much concept of humour, at least as far as Errol was concerned For this reason, Errol decided to 'give him a good frigging' – his term for playing pretty nasty jokes on those he considered ready to be called close friends. Conrad already knew about the incident with Paul Lukas some years before, and about the chocolate grasshoppers, so Errol figured that Conrad's 'frigging' would have to be special. The prank very nearly backfired, and did little to endear Conrad towards him: borrowing a motor-boat, Errol took Conrad and Beverly on a trip along the coast to check on the construction of the new house at Castle Comfort. Directing the boat towards that part of the ocean where the tide was at its most perilous, Errol derived enormous pleasure from upturning it and allowing his two terrified passengers to almost drown – so that he could save their lives at the very last minute! 'I wondered whether I would get pneumonia or heart failure,' Conrad wrote, explaining how Errol had expected him to be *grateful*, telling him, 'I only do things like that with and to people I like. There's no fun in unsettling a stranger!'

In November 1958, Errol received word that Patrice Wymore had finally consulted her lawyer about divorcing him, with a settlement expected to be somewhere in the region of $500,000. Errol's wife was particularly infuriated because she had had absolutely no contact with him for over six months. Soon after hearing this, he was told that Hartford Huntington was threatening to sue him for the $400,000 he had lost by his walking out of *The Master of Thornfield*. This act had already resulted in

Ralph Bellamy, his co-star from *Dive Bomber*, successfully petitioning to have his name struck off the American Equity list for gross misconduct, effectively prohibiting Errol from ever appearing on the legitimate stage again. And if the afore-mentioned were not enough, a process server with the Internal Revenue served Errol with a writ for the $200,000 they claimed he owed in unpaid taxes.

Coinciding with these demands, the newspapers chronicled the latest crisis in Errol's life: Boston House, the home provided by him for his parents on Jamaica – for which he is alleged to have charged them rent – burned down mysteriously, destroying Theodore Flynn's collection of rare books on marine biology. What is more, only weeks later Errol collected on the insurance, which happened to be *just* enough to complete the building programme at Castle Comfort. According to Earl Conrad, however, there *was* no mystery, for Errol confessed to him that he had 'sent a man around with a can of kerosene'. Conrad always maintained that he was never sure if Errol *had* destroyed his house, or whether he had tried to claim 'fun credit' for it. 'Either was possible with him,' he concluded.

Shortly after this episode, Errol suffered a near-fatal attack of food poisoning, but refused to have hospital treatment. His sister, Rosemary, had flown in from Washington and as they rarely met – primarily because they did not get on, though their encounters were far less problematic than those with Marelle – Errol wanted to spend as much time with her as possible, so convinced was he that they would never see each other again. Before Rosemary left, however, he did agree to go into a hospital in Kingston for tests and a check-up. Again, doctors were asked for the hard line. Again, the news was grim: considering the state of his liver, it was a miracle that he had lasted this long, and he would be lucky if he held out until the end of the year. And yet, when Earl Conrad asked him if he had any regrets, all he could say was, 'Just the one, sport – that I never learned to play the piano.'

10

For The Day's Growing Short . . .

'I have no fear of the Hereafter because I believe there is no such thing. Why be afraid of something I have no control over?'

As 1959 dawned, Errol began taking an active interest in the potentially explosive political situation in Cuba, and claiming that he had received a personal invitation from Fidel Castro – nothing has ever been proved, either way – once again in his 'official' capacity as a newspaper correspondent he set off for Havana, accompanied by Beverly. Earl Conrad had left Jamaica for New York, where he and Putnam's editor were going through the first draft of *My Wicked, Wicked Ways* – all 300,000 words of it – and trimming it for public consumption.

The pair arrived on the island just as the military campaign to oust the hated Batista was coming to a head and because of the obvious danger, Beverly was installed in Havana's Commodore Hotel while Errol, with his predilection for perilous adventure, augmented Castro's rebel forces. The two high points of the visit, he later said, were catching a bullet in his leg and witnessing Castro's swearing in as Prime Minister in the February, following Batista's flight to the Dominican Republic.

As a Castro sympathiser, Errol was expected to attend the executions of several Batista adherents. This affected him profoundly. 'I have witnessed many gruesome sights in my life, but none more so than a human facing a firing squad,' he wrote back to Earl Conrad, adding that in his distress he had vomited over one of the soldier's boots. Later, at the risk of being arrested by Castro, he interviewed one of the American executioners – a man named Luke Beryll. Errol's intention was to photograph Beryll 'doing his job' so that he could publish the pictures upon his return to New York and hopefully shock Americans with the revelation that one of their own could be party to such atrocities, but Beryll would not allow this. He *did*, with incredible nerve, criticise Beryll's actions to his face, declaring that if a man *had* to be condemned to death on account of his political beliefs, then he should at least be permitted to choose how he should die. His own suggestions, however, in the list he forwarded to Conrad, were equally brutal and often ridiculous: cyanide pills or poisoned caviar to be inserted into the rectum; lethal doses of morphine; being flung out of a helicopter and dashed against rocks, or into a cage with a sex-starved gorilla; drowning with a half-ton weight attached to one's feet.

Errol was invited to Castro's headquarters courtesy of a piece he had written for the *Havana Post*: Castro presented him with a black kerchief bearing his insignia, and introduced him to his brother and deputy, Raul, though he was more impressed if not infatuated by their next-in-command – the dashing young Argentinian, Che Guevara, who had seen some of his films but could not identify Robin Hood or Don Juan in this bloated man sitting opposite him at the dinner table. Errol offered to prove that the 'essential bits and pieces' were still in good working order and suggested that they spend an evening in Havana at his favourite 'house of integrity'. Guevara, although very much the ladies' man, is said to have been appalled.

Errol next focused his attention on Castro's female soldiers – the first time, he declared, that he had ever fancied anyone in uniform. None of them, however, were *allowed* to be interested in him: under the Castro regime, any 'rebel girl' found to be having a relationship was either forced to marry the man, or to suffer the consequences of a court-martial. Errol decided to cut his losses and make a film about them instead.

The semi-documentary, *Cuban Rebel Girls*, with Errol playing himself and Beverly Aadland taking the lead as the lover of one of Castro's soldiers, was without any doubt the worst film Errol ever made: a truly pathetic swansong to a mighty career. The locations for this self-scripted, self-produced piece of nonsense, which the director Barry Mahon later dismissed as 'clap-trap', were Cuba's sugar-cane fields and the Sierra Maestra Mountains, though most of Beverly's scenes were shot in New York. *Cuban Rebel Girls* was, the critics agreed unanimously, a film which should not have been made at all: it tells us little about the Cuban crisis, and serves only to remind us how ill, old and haggard the screen's greatest adventurer had allowed himself to become.

On 20 June 1959, Errol celebrated his 50th birthday with Beverly at Castle Comfort, and from here he launched his final public attack on his mother. After all these years he had located his birth certificate – though one wonders how he had completed his American nationalisation papers and any number of passport applications without it – and observed that his parents had married just five months before his birth. He positively revelled in being able to remind this elderly 'pillar of the Church and fount of wisdom' that she had narrowly missed giving birth to a bastard – if not, he added, then he had come into the world 'desperately premature'. He told Earl Conrad, 'I have Mother nailed to the mast at last and she's going to have a tough time getting out of this one – but no doubt she will, being a woman of infinite plausibility resource.'

On the same day, Patrice Wymore was questioned by reporters in Hollywood wanting to know if the rumours about her filing for divorce were true. This met with a pronounced, 'No way!' And when asked if she was still in contact with her husband, she tried to laugh it off, saying, 'I haven't even had a card from him in months. But you know Daddyo – if he sends a telegram he gets writers' cramp!'

In the July, Errol and Beverly flew to New York, where – having convinced himself that he was suffering from cancer of the throat – he spent several days undergoing tests at the Presbyterian Hospital on 168th Street. Needless to say, these tests proved negative, and upon his discharge he rested up for several weeks in his suite at the Shoreham Hotel, going through the galley proofs of his autobiography with Earl Conrad and Howard Cady. Because he was now *convinced* that he would be dead before the book was published, Errol wanted to have his will printed in the appendix. Neither Cady nor Conrad would agree to this: in the unsigned document, originally written on toilet paper and addressing his lawyer as 'Dear Jew', Errol had referred to his wives as 'mothers of kids', his children as 'darling brats', and his mother as 'an old bitch who still annoys the hell out of me'. Cady in particular took exception to the coda, which admitted that the still under-aged Beverly Aadland *was* his lover and bequeathed her $500,000, and to the lengthy postscript which declared that *anyone* attending his funeral should automatically be cut out of his will. It concluded: 'I absolutely hate the idea of well-loved people being subjected to the maudlin, sloppy bullshit "Love ya, Flynn" of some priest or minister spouting off hurriedly over my grave and wanting to get home to lunch.' The actual terms of the will, however, were never known: soon afterwards the document disappeared, forcing most of Errol's family and friends – Conrad included – to come to the conclusion that it had been little more than another of his pranks.

Once the corrected proofs of *My Wicked, Wicked Ways* had been dispatched to the printers, Errol called Nora Eddington – the only one of his wives with whom he was still on speaking terms – and arranged for her to meet him at Los Angeles airport, insisting that she bring their daughters Deirdre and Rory with her. Errol was certain he would never see them again, and Nora later told of how shocked she had been, watching him having to be assisted down the steps of the plane, then walking with a cane (though he had been using this for some time, more as a prop for sophistication than as an actual aid). And yet he was able to make light of his lamentable state, telling her, 'Don't worry about me, Ma. I've lived twice.'

Errol's visit to Hollywood was twofold: he had agreed to star in a thirty-minute television drama, *The Golden Shanty*, in which he played a con-man peddler who travels the Wild West in a supply waggon. Shot over a three-day period, this was a distressing experience for everyone concerned: not only was Errol unable to remember even the most basic lines, he was virtually incapable of moving about the set, and had to be helped on and off his waggon. At one stage, he burst into tears and told the director, Arthur Hiller, that he could not take any more.

A few days later, Errol gatecrashed a party where one of the guests was Olivia de Havilland. Creeping up behind her to surprise her, he placed his hands over her eyes and said, 'Guess who?' His former leading lady later confessed that she had not recognised him. Shortly afterwards, he threw a party at Hollywood's Frascate Grill for Beverly's seventeenth birthday, but telling the press that it was her 22nd and that he had documentary evidence on his person to prove this, which of course was not forthcoming. Guests were astonished to see Errol arrive with Beverly and Nora Eddington, though walking obviously caused him some stress: he spent much of the evening seated at his table while 'The Wood Nymph', looking lovelier than ever, fussed over him. The party ended on a sour note, however, when a furious row broke out between the two women, for no apparent reason, and Errol started insulting just about everybody in the room. The next day, he sent out his profound apologies, claiming that his outburst had been due to a mix-up in the pills his doctor had prescribed for indigestion.

Early in October, Errol made his last professional appearance, in a comedy sketch on the *Red Skelton Show*. Again, he portrayed the loveable rogue – a gentleman hobo who strides on to the stage, wearing a toff's jacket and medals, and carrying a knapsack from which he produces a familiar-looking circular object. 'Picture frame?' Skelton asks, to which he replied, raising his eyes skywards, 'That actually is a *porthole*. Memories, memories!'

Two days after the Skelton show, Errol announced that he had negotiated an alleged $100,000 deal to sell the *Zaca* to a Canadian businessman named George Caldough and before setting off for Vancouver with Beverly he told the press that he was only selling his most prized possession because he wanted the money for his divorce settlement with Patrice Wymore. None of those close to him believed this. It was as if, now that he had come to terms with facing the inevitable, he had finally begun putting his affairs in order, and as the *Zaca* was considerably more important to him than any revenue it would bring, he wanted to ensure that *it* fell into the right hands. He did not care what happened to his *money* after his death.

During the afternoon of 14 October 1959, their business concluded, Errol and Beverly were being driven to Vancouver airport by George Caldough when Errol suddenly developed excruciating pains in his back. Caldough, believing Errol's assumption that his old injury was playing him up again, immediately conveyed him to the house of a doctor friend, Grant A. Gould.

Gould, after administering a shot of morphine, advised Errol to lie on a flat, hard surface – the usual treatment for patients with slipped disc – and suggested his bedroom floor. Errol refused to do this. Gould and his wife were in the middle of a party, and he did not wish to miss out on the fun. For two hours he recounted Flynn stories: his adventures in New Guinea, his admiration of John Barrymore, the blues with Jack Warner and Marelle. Then he announced that he *would* like to rest for a while, and the doctor escorted him upstairs. Outside his door, clutching at his chest, he collapsed, and while Mrs Gould was summoning an ambulance, Gould struggled to get him on to the bed and attempted to revive him, while Beverly screamed hysterically for him to wake up.

Twenty minutes later, a surgeon from the hospital emergency room announced that Errol had suffered a massive heart attack, and that he had been unable to save him.

Epilogue

Although the official cause of Errol's death *was* a heart attack, after reading the autopsy report the coroner did not know where to begin when delivering his verdict: 30 years of chain-smoking, alcohol and narcotics abuse, acute hepatitis and venereal disease, numerous falls, the ever-present tuberculosis and the frequent bouts of malaria had turned Errol into an old, old man way before his time. It was, the coroner concluded, truly a miracle that he had reached 50.

He was widely mourned, of course, though his most fervent wish – to be buried at Castle Comfort – was denied him. Nora Eddington and Beverly Aadland had both promised this, and Errol had showed Earl Conrad the spot where his final resting place should be, under the branches of a spreading oak in the local churchyard. None of these people, however, were legally entitled to have the last say. Errol's last-known will was dated April 1954, so it was left to Patrice Wymore to make the funeral arrangements. This got off to a bad start when her husband's body was conveyed from Vancouver to Hollywood, in a *packing crate*, escorted by his stuntman pal, Buster Wiles, who is alleged to have prised open the lid during the journey and slipped in a couple of bottles of Errol's favourite vodka.

A weeping Patrice Wymore told the press, 'I loved Errol, and in my heart I always will. He was unchangeable and had to be taken as he was. Too often with some men that first excitement and romance fades, but with Errol it never did.' Wymore had obviously forgotten that she had not seen her husband in two years, and her 'love' for him did not extend to carrying out his last wishes. She arranged for him to be interred in the *last* place he had wanted – 'amongst the Jews of Forest Lawn' – offering the lame excuse, 'That's what Errol's Hollywood peers would have wanted.' A poignant though not entirely sincere eulogy was read out by Jack Warner, whose funeral Errol had desperately wanted to attend, and Dennis Morgan, the star of *It's a Great Feeling*, sang 'Home Is The Sailor'. The pallbearers were Mickey Rooney, Guinn 'Big Boy' Williams, Jack Oakie, Raoul Walsh, the restaurateur Mike Romanoff, and Errol's lawyer, Jud Golenbock. Some of his friends regarded the latter two's presence as yet another act of spite from Patrice Wymore, of whom Errol had demanded, anti-Semitic to the end, 'I don't want to be buried near Jews, and I don't want any Israelites carrying me to my six-by-two, either.' To add insult to injury, Errol's wife draped his casket with yellow roses – the flowers he had hated the most because, he once said, they represented cowardice – and did not even commission a headstone. Until his daughters rectified the situation, as late as 1979, Errol would lie in an unmarked grave. Lili Damita and Nora Eddington were so disgusted by Wymore's actions – the former actually said that if she met her, she would strangle her with her bare hands – that they did not even attend the funeral. Beverly also stayed away, fearful of a backlash from the press.

Errol's revenge on many of those whom he believed had wronged him – wives, lovers, colleagues and so-called friends – came from beyond the grave with the publication of *My Wicked, Wicked Ways*. When a spokesman from his publishers, Putnam, read out the names of these during a radio programme, many acquaintances were genuinely hurt to learn that Errol had not seen fit to mention them...though they would very soon come to appreciate their omission when many of those he *had* opened up about began protesting about the manner in which he had done so. Putnam very quickly received writs from Michael Curtiz, Lupe Velez's family, Jack Warner, Lili Damita *and* Errol's mother, among others, demanding that certain offensive passages be removed from subsequent reprints of the book. Even so, the tamed down *My Wicked, Wicked Ways* was pretty hot stuff for 1960, and it remains quite possibly the most entertaining show business autobiography ever written. It is certainly the most literate.

Errol's estate – including his various properties, jewellery and art collection, and an 800-strong herd of cattle on Jamaica – was estimated at over $2 million, though it is said he had spent *five* times this amount during his quarter-century in films. Nora Eddington told the press that she was certain that Errol had signed a will *since* the one of 1954, but it was never found. Similarly, Beverly Aadland told Errol's lawyers that he had signed another will during their trip to Cuba, leaving everything to her, but as this was never located, the bulk of his estate went to his three wives and Beverly did not get a cent. Indeed, her 'meddling' in his affairs resulted in her being investigated by the Los Angeles Police, who were interested in determining if, in having an open relationship with a man while under the age of consent, she had been guilty of any moral crime. No charges were made.

The lawsuits, the claims on Errol's estate from his creditors, and the squabbles among his relatives would continue until 1963 when, aside from the bequests to Damita, Eddington, his children, parents and the $100,000 he owed Huntington Hartford, everything would go to Patrice Wymore. A few years before his death, upon hearing that his son was going steady for the first time, Errol had sent Sean $100 to buy whichever the young man considered the most appropriate – condoms or flowers. Now, besides a $25,000 bequest, Sean was left a $5,000 bonus. Errol had told him he would be getting this, adding, 'I want you to use it to fuck your way around the world.' So far as is known, Sean followed the instruction, like Errol enjoying a succession of lovers of both sexes, but wisely never marrying.

Sean Flynn made a valiant attempt to follow in his father's footsteps, and visually showed promise. Well over six feet tall, handsome and with a superb physique, it was impossible to assume that he would not succeed. In 1962 he came across as dashing enough in the Italian-produced *The Son of Captain Blood*, and five years later appeared in *Cinq Gars Pour Singapore*. Sadly, he lacked the talent and charisma that had made Errol so unique, and his acting career quickly fizzled out. Eventually he joined the staff of *Time-Life* as a photographer to cover the Vietnam War. On 6 April 1970 he was reported missing, presumed dead, though for more than a decade Lili Damita refused to believe this, keeping on his apartment and regularly having his clothes laundered, ready for his return.

Two of Errol's daughters, Rory and Arnella, enjoyed successful careers as models, and Deirdre became a Hollywood stunt-woman. Two of his wives remarried. Lili Damita, whose divorce settlement declared that she would receive alimony from Errol only so long as she remained single, married the Iowa millionaire Allen Loomis in 1962. Three years later, Nora Eddington married a rich businessman named Richard Black, and dropped the name 'Flynn' from her impressive array of surnames. Beverly Aadland married three times. Errol's parents died in 1968 – Theodore of a stroke, Marelle after being knocked down by a car near Brighton.

Since Errol's death, both Patrice Wymore and Nora Eddington have stringently denied the two most contentious aspects of his life: that he acted as a Nazi spy during the Spanish Civil War, and that he enjoyed having sex with men, the latter something that Lili Damita never denied and often encouraged. Wymore exploded at a press conference in 1980: 'Errol, *gay*? Don't you think I would have noticed after being with him for seven *years*?' Nora Eddington made a similar observation in a television documentary, and both of them were publicly supported by a journalist, J. V. Cottom, who claimed that Errol had been confiding in him since 1946 and added that he had last spoken to his 'great friend' just days before his death. Cottom, *Ciné-Revue*'s Hollywood correspondent, concluded both lamely and ridiculously:

> Errol wasn't at all bisexual. I asked Patrice, and she *said* he wasn't. As for being a spy, how can a man who drank at least one bottle of vodka a day and never missed a date with a young girl find *time* to work as a traitor? And how could a regime as powerful as the Third Reich *trust* a man known to be suffering from premature ejaculation?

Lili Damita scoffed at these people in a French radio interview shortly before her death in 1994, saying, 'That woman [Wymore] was talking out of the top of her head, as was her predecessor. Errol hardly ever lived with Nora Eddington, and Patrice Wymore couldn't stop boasting that she hadn't seen him for years. They knew absolutely nothing about Errol's love interests, what went off on his yachts and inside that big house, and they *certainly* knew nothing about what he did or didn't do in Spain because they weren't even there!'

The retainers, stooges, spongers, hangers-on and lovers far too numerous to mention are most of them gone. Errol's third daughter, Arnella, achieved considerable success as a model, and after years of globetrotting settled in Jamaica. Then on, her life fell apart as she entered a downward spiral of drink and drugs – her mother cut off her allowance, and to finance her habit she resorted to selling vegetables from a roadside stall. In September 1998 she was found dead, aged 45. Her son, Luke, to fashion photographer Carl Stoecker, was heralded one of the world's sexiest bachelors by *People* magazine in 2003. The hard-drinking Nora Eddington died of kidney disease in April 2001, aged 77.

Errol will eternally be remembered as essentially a good man, one who achieved goals most of us only dream of – a man who lived for life with all its complexities, culpabilities, set-backs and kicks in the teeth. We, his admirers, should never regret what Errol was or some of the questionable things he did – only the sad fact that he died so young.

There were many epitaphs, few of them heartfelt and genuine or worthy of mention. Kay Francis, on the other hand, could just as well have been summing him up whilst speaking of her lost love in *Another Dawn* –

'Some men don't turn back. His luck held out. He died clean and young before anything could grow old or dim. He was always ahead of life and finally lost it in the sunset, before it could catch up with him and make him pay for all the beauty and glamour and laughter it gave him. He died *owing* life…

Appendix I

Errol Flynn: Stage Plays

1. NORTHAMPTON OPERA HOUSE (unless stated otherwise)
The regular players with the Northampton Repertory Company
during Errol Flynn's stay in the town were: Julian Clay, Freda
Jackson, John Stobart, Peter Rosser, Oswald Dale Roberts,
Donald Gordon, Dorothy Galbraith, Veronica Rose, Elizabeth
Inglis, Zillah Grey, Nora Gandy, Doris Littell and Kenneth
Grinling, several of whom doubled as administration staff. Robert
Young was the producer.

ONCE IN A LIFETIME   June 1933
Queen's Theatre, London: 6 perfs
Northampton: 4 perfs
Cora Goffin was the star. Flynn was a non-speaking extra. There
are no other details.

THE THIRTEENTH CHAIR   18 December 1933
12 perfs
Written by Bayard Veiller. Flynn played Edward Wales.

JACK AND THE BEANSTALK   27 December 1933
10 perfs
Written by Margaret Carter. Flynn played Prince Donzil.

SWEET LAVENDER   1 January 1934
                                          12 perfs
Written by Sir Arthur Wing Pinero. Flynn played Geoffrey
Wedderburn.

BULLDOG DRUMMOND   8 January 1934
                                          12 perfs
Written by Cyril 'Sapper' McNeile. Flynn played Marcovitch.

THE DOLL'S HOUSE   15 January 1934
                                          12 perfs
Written by Henrik Ibsen. Flynn played Nils Krogstad.

ON THE SPOT   22 January 1934
                                          12 perfs
Written by Edgar Wallace. Flynn played Mike Feeney.

PYGMALION   29 January 1934
                                          12 perfs
Written by George Bernard Shaw. Flynn played 2nd Bystander.

THE CRIME AT BLOSSOMS   5 February 1934
Written by Mordaunt Shairp. Flynn played the charabanc driver.

YELLOW SANDS   12 February 1934
Written by Eden & Adelaide Philpotts, Flynn played Joe Varwell.

THE GRAIN OF MUSTARD SEED   19 February 1934
Written by Harold Marsh Harwood. Flynn played Mr
Cornthwaite.

SEVEN KEYS TO BALDPATE INN   26 February 1934
                                          12 perfs
Written by George M. Cohan. Flynn played Thomas Hayden.

OTHELLO   5 March 1934
                                          12 perfs
Written by Shakespeare. Flynn played First Senator and Lodovico.

THE GREEN BAY TREE   12 perfs
Written by Mordaunt Shairp. Flynn played the tramp.

THE FAKE   19 March 1934
                                                         12 perfs
Written by Frederick Lonsdale. Flynn played Geoffrey Sands.

THE FARMER'S WIFE   26 March 1934
                                                         24 perfs
Written by Eden Philpotts. Flynn played George Smerdon.

THE WIND AND THE RAIN   9 April 1934
                                                         12 perfs
Written by Merton Hodge. Flynn played John Williams.

SHEPPEY   16 April 1934
                                                         12 perfs
Written by Somerset Maugham. Flynn played a reporter.

THE SOUL OF NICHOLAS SNYDERS   23 April 1934
                                                         12 perfs
Written by Jerome K. Jerome. Flynn played Jan.

THE DEVIL'S DISCIPLE   30 April 1934
                                                         12 perfs
Written by George Bernard Shaw. Flynn played Reverend
Anderson.

CONFLICT   14 May 1934
                                                         12 perfs
Written by Miles Malleson. Flynn played Tom Smith.

PADDY, THE NEXT BEST THING!   21 May 1934
                                                         12 perfs
Written by Gertrude Page. Flynn played Doctor Adair.

9:45   28 May 1934
                                                         10 perfs
Written by Owen Davis & Sewell Collins. Flynn played James
Everett.

2. *6th MALVERN FESTIVAL.*

In July/August 1935, Flynn appeared in three plays: *Dr Faustus*, by Christopher Marlowe, *A Man's House*, by John Drinkwater and *The Moon in the Yellow River* by Dennis Johnston. It is not known how many performances he took part in.

Appendix II

Errol Flynn: Films

IN THE WAKE OF THE BOUNTY   Expeditionary Films, 1933
Writer-director: Charles Chauvel. Photography: Tasman Higgins.
Music: Lionel Hart. Narrated by Arthur Greenaway. 70 mins.
Fletcher Christian: ERROL FLYNN. Captain Bligh: MAYNE
LYNTON. With John Warwick, Victor Gourier, Patricia Penman.

I ADORE YOU   Harold French Productions, 1934
Writer-director: Harold French. Choreography: Ralph Reader.
Music: Carroll Gibbons & Savoy Hotel Orpheans. 70 mins.
Flynn played a dancing extra. With Harold French, Margot
Grahame.

MURDER AT MONTE CARLO
                        Warner Brothers First National, 1935
Director: Ralph Ince. Screenplay: Michael Barringer. Photo-
graphy: , Basil Emmott. Art director: G. H. Ward. Based on the
novel by Tom Van Dyke. 70 mins.
Dyter: ERROL FLYNN. Gillian: EVE GRAY. Dr Becker: PAUL
GRAETZ. With Brian Buchel, Ellis Irving, Molly Lamont,
Lawrence Hanray, Henry Victor, Peter Gawthorne, Gabriel Toyne,
James Dale, Ernest Sefton, Henry Longhurst.

THE CASE OF THE CURIOUS BRIDE
                        Warner Brothers First National, 1935

Director: Michael Curtiz. Screenplay: Tom Reed. Photography: David Abel. Music: Bernhard Kaun. Art directors: Carl Jules Weyl/Anton Grot. Gowns: John Orry-Kerry. Based on the novel by Erle Stanley Gardner. 80 mins.

Flynn played Gregory Moxley. With Warren William, Claire Dodd, Margaret Lindsay, Allen Jenkins, Donald Woods, Winifred Shaw, Olin Howland, Thomas Jackson, Philip Reed, Barton MacLane, Mayo Methot, Warren Hymer, Charles Richman, Robert Glecker, James Donlan, Paul Hurst, Henry Kolker, George Humbert.

DON'T BET ON BLONDES   Warner Brothers, 1935

Director: Robert Florey. Screenplay: Isabel Dawn/Boyce DeGaw. Photography: William Rees. Music: Leo F. Forbstein. Art director: Esdras Hartley. 60 mins.

Flynn played David Van Dusen. With Warren William, Claire Dodd, Guy Kibbee, William Gargan, Clay Clement, Vince Barnett, Spencer Charters, Hobart Cavanaugh, Walter Byron, Mary Treen, Jack Norton, Eddie Shubert, Herman Bing, Maude Eburne.

CAPTAIN BLOOD   Warner Brothers First National, 1935

Director: Michael Curtiz. Screenplay: Casey Robinson. Music: Erich Wolfgang Korngold. Photography: Hal Mohr/Ernest Haller. Costumes: Milo Anderson. Art director: Anton Grot. Special effects: Fred Jackman. Orchestrations: Hugo Friedhofer/Ray Heindorf. 119 mins.

Peter Blood: ERROL FLYNN. Colonel Bishop: LIONEL ATWILL. Arabella Bishop: OLIVIA DE HAVILLAND. Jeremy Pitt: ROSS ALEXANDER. Captain Levasseur: BASIL RATHBONE. Lord Willoughby: HENRY STEPHENSON.With Guy Kibbee, Donald Meek, Robert Barrat, Pedro de Cordoba, Jessie Ralph, Hobart Cavanaugh, Forrester Harvey, Leonard Mudie, Mary Forbes, Frank McGlynn Sr, Holmes Herbert, David Torrence, J. Carrol Nash, George Hassell, Harry Cording, Ivan Simpson, Stuart Casey, Denis d'Auburn, E. E. Clive, Colin Kenny, Vernon Steele, Maude Leslie.

PIRATE PARTY ON CATALINA ISLAND
                    Warner Brothers First National, 1936
Producer: Louis Lewyn. Writer: Alexander Van Dorn. Music:

Charles 'Buddy' Rogers. Two reels.
With Errol Flynn, Cary Grant, Lili Damita, Lee Tracy, Chester
Morris, Marion Davies, John Gilbert, Virginia Bruce.

THE CHARGE OF THE LIGHT BRIGADE

Warner Brothers, 1936
Director: Michael Curtiz. Screenplay: Michel Jacoby. Music: Max
Steiner. Photography: Sol Polito. Art director: John Hughes.
Costumes: Milo Anderson. Special effects: Fred Jackman/H. F.
Koenekamp. Orchestrations: Hugo Friedhofer. Director of horse
action: B. Reeves Eason. 115 mins.
Mjr Geoffrey Vickers: ERROL FLYNN. Capt. Perry Vickers:
PATRIC KNOWLES. Colonel Campbell: DONALD CRISP. Elsa
Campbell: OLIVIA DE HAVILLAND. Captain Randall: DAVID
NIVEN. Sir Charles Macefield: HENRY STEPHENSON. Sir
Benjamin Warrenton: NIGEL BRUCE. With J. Carrol Nash,
Scotty Beckett, Robert Barrat, Colin Kenny, C. Henry Gordon,
Spring Byington, G. P. Hartley Jr, E. E. Clive, Walter Holbrook,
Charles Sedgwick, Lumsden Hare, Princess Baigum, George
Regas, Gordon Hart, Helen Sanborn, Holmes Herbert, Boyd
Irwin, Reginald Sheffield, Brandon Hurst, Georges Renavent,
Charles Croker King.

GREEN LIGHT

Warner Brothers, 1937
Director: Frank Borzage. Screenplay: Milton Krims. Photography:
Byron Haskin. Music: Max Steiner. Art director: Max Parker.
Costumes: John Orry-Kerry. Based on the novel by Lloyd C.
Douglas. 85 mins.
Dr Newell Paige: ERROL FLYNN. Phyllis Dexter: ANITA
LOUISE. Dean Harcourt: Sir CEDRIC HARDWICKE. Francis
Ogilvie: MARGARET LINDSAY. With Henry O'Neill, Walter
Abel, Spring Byington, Henry Kolker, Erin O'Brien-Moore,
Russell Simpson, Pierre Watkin, Granville Bates, Myrtle Stedman,
St Luke's Choristers.

THE PRINCE AND THE PAUPER

Warner Brothers, 1937
Director: William Keighley. Screenplay: Laird Doyle.
Photography: Sol Polito. Music: Erich Wolfgang Korngold. Art
director: Robert Haas. Costumes: Milo Anderson. Orchestrations:

Hugo Friedhofer/Milan Roder. Based on the novel by Mark Twain. 120 mins.

Miles Hendon: ERROL FLYNN. Duke of Norfolk: HENRY STEPHENSON. John Canty: BARTON MacLANE. Earl of Hertford: CLAUDE RAINS. Tom Canty: BILLY MAUCH. Prince Edward: BOBBY MAUCH. Captain of the Guards: ALAN HALE. Henry VIII: MONTAGUE LOVE. First Lord: ERIC PORTMAN. With Mary Field, Murray Kinnell, Lionel Pape, Helen Valkis, Halliwell Hobbes, Leonard Willey, Phyllis Barry, Ivan Simpson, Fritz Leiber, Lester Matthews, Elspeth Dudgeon, Forrester Harvey, Robert Adair, Harry Cording, Robert Evans, Robert Warwick, Ian MacLaren, Ann Howard, Gwendolyn Jones, Harry Beresford, Lionel Braham, Lionel Belmore, Ian Wolfe, St Luke's Choristers.

ANOTHER DAWN   Warner Brothers, 1937

Director: William Dieterle. Screenplay: Laird Doyle. Photography: Tony Gaudio. Music: Erich Wolfgang Korngold. Art Director: Robert Haas. Costumes: John Orry-Kerry. Orchestrations: Hugo Friedhofer/ Milan Roder. 73 mins.

Capt Denny Roark: ERROL FLYNN. Julia Ashton: KAY FRANCIS. Colonel Wister: IAN HUNTER. Grace Roark: FRIEDA INESCOURT. Wilkins: HERBERT MUNDIN. With Billy Bevan, Richard Powell, G. P. Huntley Jr, Charles Austin, Clyde Cook, Kenneth Hunter, Eily Malyon, Mary Forbes, Ben Welden, Spencer Teakle, David Clyde, Reginald Sheffield, Charles Irwin, Martin Garralaga, George Regas, Edward Dew, R. M. Simpson, Jack Richardson.

THE PERFECT SPECIMEN   Warner Brothers, 1937

Director: Michael Curtiz. Screenplay: Norman Reilly Raine/ Lawrence Riley/Brewster Morse/Fritz Falkenstein. Photography: Charles Rosher. Music: Heinz Roemheld. Art director: Robert Haas. Costumes: Howard Shoup. Based on *Cosmopolitan* story by Samuel Hopkins Adams. 97 mins.

Gerald Beresford Wicks: ERROL FLYNN. Mona Carter: JOAN BLONDELL. Mr Grattan: EDWARD EVERETT HORTON. Leona Wicks: MAY ROBSON. Pinky: ALLEN JENKINS. With Hugh Herbert, Dick Foran, Beverly Roberts, Dennie Moore,

James Burke, Hugh O'Connell, Harry Davenport, Tim Henning, Granville Bates, Spencer Charters.

THE ADVENTURES OF ROBIN HOOD Warner Brothers, 1938
Director: Michael Curtiz. Screenplay: Norman Reilly Raine/Seton I. Miller. Photography: Sol Polito/Tony Gaudio. Music: Erich Wolfgang Korngold. Art director: Carl Jules Weyl. Costumes: Milo Anderson. Orchestrations: Hugo Friedhofer/Milan Roder. Archery supervisor: Howard Hill. Fencing Master: Fred Cavens. Based upon the ancient Robin Hood ballads and legends. 102 mins.
Robin of Loxley: ERROL FLYNN. Maid Marian: OLIVIA DE HAVILLAND. Sir Guy of Gisbourne: BASIL RATHBONE. Will Scarlet: PATRIC KNOWLES. Little John: ALAN HALE. Friar Tuck: EUGENE PALLETTE. Prince John: CLAUDE RAINS. King Richard: IAN HUNTER. Sheriff of Nottingham: MELVILLE COOPER. With Una O'Connor, Herbert Mundin, Montagu Love, Leonard Willey, Kenneth Hunter, Robert Noble, Robert Warwick, Colin Kenny, Harry Cording, Lester Matthews, Howard Hill, Ivan Simpson.

FOUR'S A CROWD   Warner Brothers, 1938
Director: Michael Curtiz. Screenplay: Casey Robinson/Sig Herzig. Photography: Ernest Haller. Music: Heinz Roemheld/Ray Heindorf. Art director: Max Parker. Gowns: John Orry-Kerry. Based on a story by Wallace Sullivan. 91 mins.
Robert Kensington Lansford: ERROL FLYNN. Lorri Dillingwell: OLIVIA DE HAVILLAND. Patterson Buckley: PATRIC KNOWLES. Jean Christy: ROSALIND RUSSELL. John P. Dillingwell: WALTER CONNELLY. With Hugh Herbert, Franklin Pangborn, Melville Cooper, Herman Bing, Joseph Crehan, Margaret Hamilton, Joe Cunningham, Dennie Moore, Gloria Blondell, Carole Landis, Reine Riano, Charles Trowbridge, Spencer Charters.

THE SISTERS   Warner Brothers, 1938
Director: Anatole Litvak. Screenplay: Milton Krims. Photography: Tony Gaudlo. Music: Max Steiner. Art director: Carl Jules Weyl. Gowns: John Orry-Kerry. Based on the novel by Myron Brinig. 99 mins.

Frank Medlin: ERROL FLYNN. Louise Elliott: BETTE DAVIS. William Benson: IAN HUNTER. Rose Elliott: BEULAH BONDI. Grace Elliott: JANE BRYAN. Norman French: PATRIC KNOWLES. With Anita Louise, Alan Hale, Donald Crisp, Dick Foran, Henry Travers, Lee Patrick, Laura Hope Crews, Janet Shaw, Harry Davenport, Ruth Gardland, Paul Harvey, John Warburton, Mayo Methot, Irving Bacon, Susan Hayward, Arthur Hoyt, Stanley Fields.

THE DAWN PATROL Warner Brothers, 1938
Director: Edmund Goulding. Screenplay: Seton I. Miller/Dan Totheroh. Music: Max Steiner. Art director: John Hughes. Photography: Tony Gaudlo. Special effects: Edwin A. DuPar. Orchestrations: Hugo Friedhofer. Based on the story, *Flight Commander*, by Howard Hawks and John Monk Saunders. 103 mins.
Captain Courtney: ERROL FLYNN. Lieutenant Scott: DAVID NIVEN. Major Brand: BASIL RATHBONE. Phipps: DONALD CRISP. Bott: BARRY FITZGERALD. With Melville Cooper, Carl Esmond, Peter Willes, Morton Lowry, James Burke, Michael Brooke, Stuart Hall, Herbert Evans, Sidney Bracy.

DODGE CITY Warner Brothers, 1939
Director: Michael Curtiz. Screenplay: Robert Buckner. Photography: Sol Polito. Music: Max Steiner. Art director: Ted Smith. Costumes: Milo Anderson. Special effects: Byron Haskin/Rex Wimpy. Orchestrations: Hugo Friedhofer. 104 mins.
Wade Hatton: ERROL FLYNN. Abbie Irving: OLIVIA DE HAVILLAND. Ruby Gilman: ANN SHERIDAN. Jeff Surrett: BRUCE CABOT. Rusty Hart: ALAN HALE. With Frank McHugh, John Litel, Victor Jory, William Lundigan, Gloria Holden, Henry Travers, Henry O'Neill, Bobs Watson, Guinn 'Big Boy' Williams, Douglas Fowley, Charles Halton, Georgia Caine, Ward Bond, Monte Blue, Cora Witherspoon, Russell Simpson, Joseph Crehan, Nat Carr, Clem Bevans, Thurston Hall, Chester Clute.

THE PRIVATE LIVES OF ELIZABETH AND ESSEX
Warner Brothers, 1940
Director: Michael Curtiz. Screenplay: Norman Reilly Raine/Aeneas MacKenzie. Photography: Sol Polito. Music: Erich

Wolfgang Korngold. Art director: Anton Grot. Costumes: John Orry-Kelly. Orchestrations: Hugo Friedhofer/Milan Roder. Special effects: Byron Haskin/H. F. Koenekamp. Based on the play *Elizabeth the Queen* by Maxwell Anderson. 106 mins.
Robert, Earl of Essex: ERROL FLYNN. Queen Elizabeth I: BETTE DAVIS. Lady Penelope Gray: OLIVIA DE HAVILLAND. Sir Walter Raleigh: VINCENT PRICE. Francis Bacon: DONALD CRISP. Sir Robert Cecil: HENRY DANIELL. With Alan Hale, Henry Stephenson, James Stephenson, Ralph Forbes, Nanette Fabares [Fabray], Robert Warwick, Leo G. Carroll.

VIRGINIA CITY   Warner Brothers, 1940
Director: Michael Curtiz. Screenplay: Robert Buckner. Photography: Sol Polito. Music: Max Steiner. Art director: Ted Smith. Special effects: Byron Haskin/H. F. Koenekamp. Orchestrations: Hugo Friedhofer. 121 mins.
Kerry Bradford: ERROL FLYNN, Julia Hayne: MIRIAM HOPKINS. Vance Irby: RANDOLPH SCOTT. John Murrell: HUMPHREY BOGART. With Guinn 'Big-Boy' Williams, Frank McHugh, John Litel, Douglass Dumbrille, Dickie Jones, Moroni Olsen, Russell Simpson, Frank Wilcox, Russell Hicks, Victor Kilian, Charles Middleton, Monte Montague, Charles Halton, George Regas, Paul Fix, Thurston Hall, Charles Trowbridge, Howard Hickman, Ward Bond, Harry Cording, Sam McDaniel, Trevor Bardette, Tom Dugan, Spencer Charters, George Reeves.

THE SEA HAWK   Warner Brothers, 1940
Director: Michael Curtiz. Screenplay: Howard Koch/Seton I. Miller. Photography: Sol Polito. Music: Erich Wolfgang Korngold. Costumes: John Orry-Kelly. Special effects: Byron Haskin/H. F. Koenekamp. Art director: Anton Grot. Orchestrations: Hugo Friedhofer/Milan Roder/ Ray Heindorf/Simon Bucharoff. Fencing master: Fred Cavens. 126 mins.
Capt. Geoffrey Thorpe: ERROL FLYNN. Queen Elizabeth: FLORA ROBSON. Dona Maria: BRENDA MARSHALL. Don José Alvarez de Cordoba: CLAUDE RAINS. Carl Pitt: ALAN HALE. Lord Wolfingham: HENRY DANIELL, With Donald Crisp, Una O'Connor, Gilbert Roland, James Stephenson, J. M. Kerrigan, William Lundigan, Julien Mitchell, Montagu Love,

David Bruce, Clifford Brooke, Clyde Cook, Fritz Leiber, Francis McDonald, Ellis Irving, Pedro de Cordoba, Ian Keith, Jack LaRue, Halliwell Hobbes, Alec Craig, Edgar Buchanan, Victor Varconi, Harry Cording, Robert Warwick, Frank Wilcox, Herbert Anderson, Charles Irwin, Frank Lackteen.

SANTA FE TRAIL   Warner Brothers, 1940

Director: Michael Curtiz. Screenplay: Robert Buckner. Photography: Sol Polito. Music: Max Steiner. Art director: John Hughes. Special effects: Byron Haskin/H. F. Koenekamp. Orchestrations: Hugo Friedhofer. 110 mins.

Jeb Stuart: ERROL FLYNN. Kit Carson Halliday: OLIVIA DE HAVILLAND. John Brown: RAYMOND MASSEY. George Armstrong Custer: RONALD REAGAN. Tex Bell: ALAN HALE. With William Lundigan, Van Heflin, Guinn 'Big Boy' Williams, Gene Reynolds, Henry O'Neill, Alan Baxter, Moroni Olsen, John Litel, David Bruce, Hobart Cavanagh, Charles D. Brown, Joseph Sawyer, Frank Wilcox, Ward Bond, Russell Simpson, Charles Middleton, Erville Alderson, Spencer Charters, Suzanne Carnahan (Susan Peters), William Marshall, George Haywood, William Lucas, Russell Hicks.

FOOTSTEPS IN THE DARK   Warner Brothers, 1941

Director: Lloyd Bacon. Screenplay: Lester Cole/John Wexley. Photography: Ernest Haller. Music: Frederick Hollander. Art director: Max Parker. Gowns: Howard Shoup. Special effects: Rex Wimpy. Based on the play, *Blondie White*, by Ladislaus Fodor. 96 mins.

Francis Warren: ERROL FLYNN. Rita Warren: BRENDA MARSHALL. Dr Davis: RALPH BELLAMY. Inspector Mason: ALAN HALE. With Lee Patrick, Allen Jenkins, Lucille Watson, William Frawley, Roscoe Karns, Grant Mitchell, Maris Wrixon, Noel Madison, Jack LaRue, Turhan Bey, Frank Faylen, Garry Owen, Sarah Edwards, Frank Wilcox, Harry Hayden, Olaf Hytten, John Dilson, Creighton Hale.

DIVE BOMBER   Warner Brothers, 1941

Director: Michael Curtiz. Screenplay: Frank Wead/Robert Buckner. Photography: Bert Glennon/Winton C. Hock. Music: Max Steiner. Art director: Robert Haas. Special effects: Byron

Haskin/Rex Wimpy. Orchestrations: Hugo Friedhofer. Medical/
Technical advisers: S. H. Warner, Commander USN/J. R. Poppen,
Captain MC, USN. 133 mins.
Lt Douglas Lee: ERROL FLYNN. Commander Joe Blake: FRED
MacMURRAY. Dr Lance Rogers: RALPH BELLAMY. Linda
Fisher: ALEXIS SMITH. With Robert Armstrong, Regis Toomey,
Allen Jenkins, Craig Stevens, Herbert Anderson, Moroni Olsen,
Dennie Moore, Louis Jean Heydt, Cliff Nazarro, Ann Doran,
Addison Richards, Russell Hicks, Howard Hickman. Pilots:
William Hopper, Charles Drake, Gig Young, Larry Williams,
Garland Smith, Tom Skinner, Tom Seidel, James Anderson,
Gaylord Pendleton, Lyle Moraine, Garrett Craig, Stanley Smith,
David Newell, Alan Hale Jr, Sol Gorss, Don Turner.

THEY DIED WITH THEIR BOOTS ON   Warner Brothers, 1942
Director: Raoul Walsh. Screenplay: Wally Kline/Aeneas
MacKenzie. Photography: Bert Glennon. Music: Max Steiner. Art
director: John Hughes. Gowns: Milo Anderson. 140 mins.
George Armstrong Custer: ERROL FLYNN. Elizabeth Bacon
Custer: OLIVIA DE HAVILLAND. Ned Sharp: ARTHUR
KENNEDY. California Joe: CHARLEY GRAPEWIN. Samuel
Bacon: GENE LOCKHART. Crazy Horse: ANTHONY QUINN.
With Stanley Ridges, John Litel, Walter Hampden, Sydney
Greenstreet, Regis Toomey, Hattie McDaniel, G. P. Huntley Jr,
Frank Wilcox, Minor Watson, Joseph Sawyer, Joseph Crehan,
Irving Bacon, Selmer Jackson, Eddie Acuff, George Eldredge,
Spencer Charters, Hobart Bosworth, Russell Hicks, Hugh
Sothern, John Ridgely, Gig Young, Anna Q. Nilsson, Aileen
Pringle, Frank Ferguson.

DESPERATE JOURNEY   Warner Brothers, 1942
Director: Raoul Walsh. Screenplay: Arthur T. Horman.
Photography: Bert Glennon. Music: Max Steiner. Art director:
Carl Jules Weyl. Gowns: Milo Anderson. Special effects: Edwin
DuPar. Orchestrations: Hugo Friedhofer. RAF Technical adviser:
S/LO Cathart Jones. 107 mins.
Flight Lt Terence Forbes: ERROL FLYNN. Flying Officer Johnny
Hammond: RONALD REAGAN. Kaethe Brahms: NANCY
COLEMAN. Major Otto Baumeister: RAYMOND MASSEY.

Flight Sgt Kirk Edwards: ALAN HALE. Flying Officer Jed Forrest: ARTHUR KENNEDY. With Ronald Sinclair, Albert Basserman, Sig Rumann, Patrick O'Moore, Felix Basch, Ilka Gruning, Elsa Basserman, Charles Irwin, Richard Fraser, Robert O. Davis, Henry Victor, Bruce Lester, Lester Matthews, Kurt Katch, Helmut Dantine, Hans Schumm, Barry Bernard.

GENTLEMAN JIM Warner Brothers, 1942
Director: Raoul Walsh. Screenplay: Vincent Lawrence/Horace McCoy. Photography: Sid Hickox. Music: Heinz Roemheld. Art director: Ted Smith. Gowns: Milo Anderson. Montages: Don Siegel/James Leicester. Fight advisers: Ed Cochrane/Mushy Callahan. Based on the James J. Corbett, autobiography, *The Roar of the Crowd*. 104 mins.
James J. Corbett: ERROL FLYNN. Victoria Ware: ALEXIS SMITH. Walter Lowrie: JACK CARSON. Pat Corbett: ALAN HALE. With William Frawley, John Loder, Minor Watson, Ward Bond, Madeleine LeBeau, Arthur Shields, Rhys Williams, Dorothy Vaughan, James Flavin, Art Foster, Pat Flaherty, Wallis Clark, Marilyn Phillips, Edwin Stanley, Henry O'Hara, Harry Crocker, Frank Mayo, Carl Harbaugh, Fred Kelsey, Sammy Stein, Charles Wilson, Jean Del Val, William B. Davidson, Mike Mazurki.

EDGE OF DARKNESS Warner Brothers, 1943
Director: Lewis Milestone. Screenplay: Robert Rossen. Photography: Sid Hickox. Music: Franz Waxman. Art director: Robert Haas. Gowns: John Orry-Kelly. Special effects: Lawrence Butler/Willard Van Enger, Orchestrations: Leonid Raab. Based on the novel by William Woods. 120 mins.
Gunnar Brogge: ERROL FLYNN. Karen Stensgard: ANN SHERIDAN. Dr Martin Stensgard: WALTER HUSTON. Katja: NANCY COLEMAN. Captain Koenig: HELMUT DANTINE. Gerd Bjarnesen: JUDITH ANDERSON. Anna Stensgard: RUTH GORDON. With John Beal, Morris Carnovsky, Charles Dingle, Roman Bohnen, Richard Fraser, Art Smith, Tom Fadden, Tonio Selwart, Henry Brandon, Helene Thimig, Frank Wilcox, Francis Pierlot, Monte Blue, Lottie Williams, Dorothy Tree, Virginia Christine, Henry Rowland, Kurt Katch, Kurt Kreuger, Peter Van Eyck.

THANK YOUR LUCKY STARS   Warner Brothers, 1943
Director: David Butler. Screenplay: Norman Panama/Melvin Frank/ James V. Kern. Songs: Arthur Schwartz/Frank Loesser, arranged by Dudley Chambers. Photography: Arthur Edeson. Art directors: Anton Grot/Leo K. Kuter. Gowns: Milo Anderson. Dance numbers staged by LeRoy Prinz.
Pat Dixon: JOAN LESLIE. Tom Randolph: DENNIS MORGAN. Playing themselves: HUMPHREY BOGART, EDDIE CANTOR, BETTE DAVIS, OLIVIA DE HAVILLAND, ERROL FLYNN, JOHN GARFIELD, IDA LUPINO, ANN SHERIDAN, DINAH SHORE. ALEXIS SMITH, JACK CARSON, GEORGE TOBIAS, ALAN HALE. With Edward Everett Horton, S. Z. Sakall, Ruth Donnelly, Hattie McDaniel, Don Wilson, Willie Best, Henry Armetta, Richard Lane, Joyce Reynolds, Paul Harvey, James Burke, Bert Gordon, Mike Mazurki, Frank Faylen. Errol Flynn performed 'That's What You Jolly Well Get' supported by Freddie McEvoy, Monte Blue, Ted Billings, Buster Wiles, Bobby Hale, Art Foster, Fred Relsey, Elmer Ballard, Howard Davies, Tudor Williams, Alan Cook, Will Stanton, Charles Irwin, David Thursby, Henry Iblings, Earl Hunsaker, Hubert Head, Dudley Kuzelle.

NORTHERN PURSUIT   Warner Brothers, 1943
Director: Raoul Walsh, Screenplay: Frank Gruber/Alvah Bessie. Photography: Sid Hickox. Music: Adolph Deutsch. Art director: Leo K. Kuter. Gowns: Leah Rhodes. Orchestrations: Jerome Moross. Special effects: E. Roy Davidson. Based on the story, *Five Thousand Trojan Horses*, by Leslie T. White. 94 mins.
Steve Wagner: ERROL FLYNN. Laura McBain: JULIE BISHOP. Colonel Hugo von Keller: HELMUT DANTINE. Ernst: GENE LOCKHART. Jim Austen: JOHN RIDGELY. With Tom Tully, Bernard Nedell, Warren Douglas, Alec Craig, Monte Blue, Tom Fadden, Rose Higgins, Richard Alden, John Royce, Joe Herrera, Carl Harbaugh, Russell Hicks, Lester Matthews, John Forsythe, Charles Judels, James Milllcan, Robert Hutton.

UNCERTAIN GLORY   Warner Brothers, 1944
Director: Raoul Walsh. Screenplay: Laszlo Vadnay/Max Brand. Photography: Sid Hickox. Music: Adolph Deutsch. Art director: Robert Haas. Special effects: E. Roy Davidson. Orchestrations:

Jerome Moross. Technical adviser: Paul Coze. 102 mins.
Jean Picard: ERROL FLYNN. Marcel Bonet: PAUL LUKAS.
Marianne: JEAN SULLIVAN. Mme Maret: LUCILLE WATSON.
With Faye Emerson, Douglass Dumbrille, James Flavin, Dennis
Hoey, Sheldon Leonard, Odette Myrtil, Francis Pierlot, Wallis Clark,
Victor Killian, Albert Van Antwerp, Ivan Triesault, Art Smith, Carl
Harbaugh, Mary Servoss, Charles La Torre, Pedro de Cordoba,
Bobby Walberg, Felix Basch, Erskine Sanford, Joel Friedkin.

OBJECTIVE BURMA!   Warner Brothers, 1945
Director: Raoul Walsh. Screenplay: Ranald MacDougall/Lester
Cole. Photography: James Wong Howe. Music: Franz Waxman.
Art director: Ted Smith. Special effects: Edwin DuPar.
Orchestrations: Leonid Raab. Technical adviser: Major Charles S.
Galbraith, US Army Parachute Troops. 142 mins.
Major Nelson: ERROL FLYNN. With James Brown, William
Prince, Henry Hull, George Tobias, Warner Anderson, John Alvin,
Stephen Richards [Mark Stevens], Richard Erdman, Anthony
Caruso, Hugh Beaumont, Joel Allen, John Whitney, Buddy Yarus
[George Tyne], Frank Tang, Rodd Redwing, William Hudson,
Asit Koomar, John Sheridan, Erville Anderson, Lester Matthews.

SAN ANTONIO   Warner Brothers, 1945
Director: David Butler. Screenplay: Alan LeMay/W. R. Burnett.
Photography: Bert Glennon. Art director: Ted Smith. Music: Max
Steiner. Wardrobe: Milo Anderson. Special effects: Willard Van
Enger. Orchestrations: Hugo Friedhofer. Dance director: LeRoy
Prinz. 111 mins.
Clay Hardin: ERROL FLYNN. Jeanne Starr: ALEXIS SMITH.
With S. Z. Sakall, Victor Francen, Florence Bates, John Litel, Paul
Kelly, Robert Shayne, John Alvin, Monte Blue, Robert Barrat,
Tom Tyler, Pedro de Cordoba, Chris-Pin Martin, Charles Stevens,
Dan White, Poodles Hanneford, Doodles Weaver, Ray Spiker, Al
Hill, Bill Steele, Harry Cording, Chalky Williams, Wallis Clark,
Allen E. Smith, Dan Seymour, Howard Hill, Arnold Kent.

NEVER SAY GOODBYE   Warner Brothers, 1946
Director: James V Kern. Screenplay: I. A. L. Diamond/James V.
Kern. Photography: Arthur Edeson. Music: Frederick Hollander.

Art director: Anton Grot. Wardrobe: Leah Rhodes. Special effects: William McGann/Willard Van Enger. Orchestrations: Leonid Raab. 97 mins.
Phil Gayley: ERROL FLYNN. Ellen Gayley: ELEANOR PARKER. With Patti Brady, Lucille Watson, S. Z. Sakall, Forrest Tucker, Donald Woods, Peggy Knudsen, Tom D'Andrea, Hattie McDaniel, Charles Coleman, Tom Tyler, Arthur Shields, Monte Blue.

CRY WOLF   Warner Brothers, 1947
Director: Peter Godfrey. Screenplay: Catherine Turney. Music: Franz Waxman. Photography: Carl Guthrie. Art director: Carl Jules Weyl. Wardrobe: Travilla/Edith Head. Special effects: William McGann/Robert Burks. Orchestrations: Leonid Raab. Based on the novel by Marjorie Carleton. 83 mins.
Mark Caldwell: ERROL FLYNN. Sandra Marshall: BARBARA STANWYCK. Julie Desmarest: GERALDINE BROOKS. James Desmarest: RICHARD BASEHART. Senator Caldwell: JEROME COWAN. With John Ridgely, Patricia White, Rory Mallinson, Helene Thimig, Paul Stanton, Barry Bernard, John Elliot, Lisa Golm, Jack Mower, Paul Panzer, Creighton Hale.

ESCAPE ME NEVER   Warner Brothers, 1947
Director: Peter Godfrey. Screenplay: Thames Williamson. Photography: Sol Polito. Music: Eric Wolfgang Korngold. Ballet sequences: LeRoy Prinz. Art director: Carl Jules Weyl. Special effects: Willard Van Enger. Harry Barndollar. Ballet costumes: Travilla, Orchestrations: Hugo Friedhofer/Ray Heindorf. Based on Margaret Kennedy's novel *The Fool of the Family* and the play, *Escape Me Never.* 104 mins.
Sebastian Dubrok: ERROL FLYNN. Gemma Smith: IDA LUPINO. Fenella MacLean: ELEANOR PARKER. Caryl Dubrok: GIG YOUNG. With Reginald Denny, Isobel Elsom, Albert Basserman, Ludwig Stossel, Anthony Caruso, Milada Mladova, George Zoritch, Helene Thimig, Doris Lloyd, Frank Puglia, Frank Reicher, Ivan Triessault.

SILVER RIVER   Warner Brothers, 1948
Director: Raoul Walsh. Screenplay: Stephen Longstreet/Harriet

Frank Jr. Photography: Sid Hickox. Music: Max Steiner. Costumes: Travilla/Marjorie Best. Art director: Ted Smith. Special effects: William McGann/Edwin Du Par. Orchestrations: Murray Cutter. War Sequence Technical Adviser: Col J. G. Taylor, US Army. 110 mins.

Mike McComb: ERROL FLYNN. Georgia Moore: ANN SHERIDAN. John Plato Beck: THOMAS MITCHELL. Stanley Moore: BRUCE BENNETT. With Barton MacLane, Tom D'Andrea, Monte Blue, Jonathan Hale, Alan Bridge, Art Baker, Arthur Space, Joseph Crehan.

ADVENTURES OF DON JUAN   Warner Brothers, 1949
Director: Vincent Sherman. Screenplay: George Oppenheimer/ Harry Kurnitz/Herbert Dalmas. Photography: Elwood Bredell. Music: Max Steinert. Art director: Edward Carrere. Costumes: Marjorie Best/ Leah Rhodes/Travilla. Special effects: William McGann/John Crouse. Orchestrations: Murray Cutter. Fence master: Fred Cavens. 110 mins.

Don Juan de Marana: ERROL FLYNN. Queen Margaret: VIVECA LINDFORS. Duke de Lorca: ROBERT DOUGLAS. Leporello: ALAN HALE. With Romney Brent, Ann Rutherford, Robert Warwick, Jerry Austin, Mary Stuart, Douglas Kennedy, Jeanne Shepherd, Helen Westcott, Aubrey Mather, Fortunio Bonanova, Una O'Connor, Raymond Burr, G. P. Huntley Jr, David Leonard, Leon Belasco, Pedro de Cordoba, David Bruce, Monte Blue, Barbara Bates, Harry Lewis, Nora Eddington.

IT'S A GREAT FEELING!   Warner Brothers, 1949
Director: David Butler. Screenplay: Melville Shevelson/Jack Rose/ I. A. L. Diamond. Photography: Wilfrid M. Cline. Songs: Jules Styne & Sammy Cahn. Art director: Stanley Fleischer. Costumes: Milo Anderson. Orchestrations: Leo Shuken/Sydney Cutner. 85 mins.

Themselves: DENNIS MORGAN, DORIS DAY, JACK CARSON, GARY COOPER, JOAN CRAWFORD, DAVID BUTLER, SYDNEY GREENSTREET, DANNY KAYE, JANE WYMAN, PATRICIA NEAL, ELEANOR PARKER, RONALD REAGAN, KING VIDOR, MICHAEL CURTIZ, RAOUL WALSH, EDWARD G. ROBINSON. With minor stars: Bill Goodwin, Irving Bacon, Claire Carleton, Harlan Warde, Jacqueline DeWitt.

Errol Flynn appears in the last 30 seconds of the film as Doris Day's boyfriend, Jeffrey Bushdinkell.

THAT FORSYTE WOMAN   Metro-Goldwyn-Mayer, 1949
Director: Compton Bennett. Screenplay: Jan Lustig/James B. Williams/Ivan Tors/Arthur Wimperis. Photography: Joseph Ruttenberg. Music: Bronislau Kaper. Art directors: Cedric Gibbons/Daniel B. Cathcart. Costumes: Walter Plunkett/Valles. Based on John Galsworthy's novel, *The Man of Property*, Book One of *The Forsyte Saga*. 114 mins.
Soames Forsyte: ERROL FLYNN. Iréne Forsyte: GREER GARSON. Young Jolyon Forsyte: WALTER PIDGEON. Philip Bosinney: ROBERT YOUNG. Old Jolyon Forsyte: HARRY DAVENPORT. June Forsyte: JANET LEIGH. With Aubrey Mather, Gerald Oliver Smith, Lumsden Hare, Stanley Logan, Halliwell Hobbes, Matt Moore, Florence Auer, Phyllis Morris, Andre Charlot, Marjorie Eaton, Evelyn Beresford, Richard Lupino, Wilson Wood, Constance Cavendish, Isabel Randolph, Reginald Sheffield, Frank·Baker, Billy Bevan.

MONTANA   Warner Brothers, 1950
Director: Ray Enright. Screenplay: James R. Webb/Borden Chase/Charles O'Neal. Photography: Karl Freund. Music: David Buttolph. Art director: Charles H. Clarke. Costumes: Marjorie Best/Milo Anderson. Orchestrations: Leo Shuken/Sidney Cutner. Song: 'Reckon I'm In Love' by Mack David/Al Hoffman/Jerry Livingston. 76 mins. ·
Morgan Lane: ERROL FLYNN. Maria Singleton: ALEXIS SMITH. Poppa Schultz: S. Z. SAKALL. With Douglas Kennedy, James Brown, Ian MacDonald, Charles Irwin, Paul E. Burns, Tudor Owen, Lester Matthews, Nacho Galindo, Lane Chandler, Monte Blue, Billy Vincent, Warre Jackson.

ROCKY MOUNTAIN   Warner Brothers, 1950
Director: William Keighley. Screenplay: Winston Miller/Alan LeMay. Photography: Ted McCord. Music: Max Steiner. Art director: Stanley Fleischer. Wardrobe: Marjorie Best. Orchestrations: Murray Cutter. 83 mins.
Lafe Barstow: ERROL FLYNN. Johanna Carter: PATRICE

WYMORE. Lieutenant Rickey: SCOTT FORBES. Pap Dennison: GUINN 'BIG BOY' WILLIAMS. With Dick Jones, Howard Petrie, Slim Pickens, Chubby Johnson, Sheb Wooley, Buzz Henry, Peter Coe, Rush Williams, Steve Dunhill, Alex Sharp, Yakima Canutt, Nakai Snez.

KIM   Metro-Goldwyn-Mayer, 1951
Director: Victor Saville. Screenplay: Leon Gordon/Helen Deutsch/ Richard Schayer. Photography: William V. Skall. Music: Andre Previn. Art directors: Cedric Gibbons/Hans Peters. Costumes: Valles. Special effects: A. Arnold Gillespie/Warren Newcombe. Technical adviser: I. A. Hafesjee. Based on the novel by Rudyard Kipling. 113 mins.
Mahbub Ali, the Red Beard: ERROL FLYNN. Kim: DEAN STOCKWELL. Lama: PAUL LUKAS. Colonel Creighton: ROBERT DOUGLAS. With Thomas Gomez, Cecil Kellaway, Arnold Moss, Reginald Owen, Laurette Luez, Roman Toporow, Ivan Triesault, Richard Hale, Hayden Rorke, Walter Kingsford, Frank Lackteen, Jeanette Nolan.

HELLO GOD (alternative title: **The Man Who Cried**)
                    William Marshall Productions, 1951
Director/Screenplay/Narrator: William Marshall. Photography: Paul Ivano/Henry Freulich/Leo Barboni. Sound: Victor Appel. 64 mins.
The Man on Anzio Beach: ERROL FLYNN. Little Italian Girl: SHERRY JACKSON. With Joe Muzzuca, Armando Formica. Released Europe only.

ADVENTURES OF CAPTAIN FABIAN
                    Silver Films/Republic, 1951
Director: William Marshall. Screenplay: Errol Flynn. Photography: Marcel Grignon. Music: Rene Cloërec. Costumes: Valles. Sets: Max Douy/Eugene Lourie. Technical adviser: Marc Maurette. Based on the novel *Fabulous Ann Madlock*, by Robert Shannon. 100 mins.
Michael Fabian: ERROL FLYNN. Lea Marriotte: MICHELINE PRESLE. Georges Brissac: VINCENT PRICE. Aunt Jezebel: AGNES MOOREHEAD. Henri Brissac: VICTOR FRANCEN. With Jim Gerald, Helena Manson, Howard Vernon, Roger Blin,

Valentine Camax, Marcel Journet, Zanie Campan, Georges Flâteau, Reggie Nalder, Gilles Quéant, Charles Fawcett, Aubrey Bower.

MARA MARU   Warner Brothers, 1952
Director: Gordon Douglas. Screenplay: N. Richard Nash. Photography: Robert Burks. Music: Max Steiner. Art director: Stanley Fleischer. Costumes: Milo Anderson. Special effects: H. F. Koenekamp. Orchestrations: Murray Cutter. 98 mins.
Gregory Mason: ERROL FLYNN. Stella Callahan: RUTH ROMAN. Brock Benedict: RAYMOND BURR. With Paul Picerni, Richard Webb, Georges Renavent, Dan Seymour, Robert Cabal, Henry Marco, Nestor Paiva, Howard Chuman, Michael Ross.

AGAINST ALL FLAGS   Universal–International, 1952
Director: George Sherman. Screenplay: Aeneas MacKenzie/Joseph Hoffman. Photography: Russell Metty/David S. Horsley. Music: Hans J. Salter. Art directors: Bernard Herzbrun/Alexander Golitzen. Sets: Russell A. Gausman/Oliver Emert. Costumes: Edward Stevenson. 83 mins.
Brian Hawke: ERROL FLYNN. Spitfire Stevens: MAUREEN O'HARA. Roc Brasiliano: ANTHONY QUINN. Princess Patma: ALICE KELLEY. With Mildred Natwick, Robert Warwick, Harry Cording, John Alserson, Phil Tully, Lester Matthews, Tudor Owen, Maurice Marsac, James Craven, James Fairfax, Michael Ross, Bill Radovich, Paul Newlan.

CRUISE OF THE ZACA   Warner Brothers, 1952
Director & Narrator: Errol Flynn. Supervisor: Gordon Hollingshead. Script: Owen Crump. Music: Howard Jackson. Sound: Charles David Forrest. 20 mins.
This documentary of one of Errol Flynn's sea voyages was made in 1948, and filmed on 16mm Kodachrome. Legal hitches prevented its release until 1952, notably Flynn's divorce from Nora Eddington.

DEEP SEA FISHING   Warner Brothers, 1952
Supervisor: Howard Hill. Narrator: Bob Edge. 10 mins. Filmed in 16mm Kodachrome and extracted from *Cruise of the Zaca*.

Though Errol appears in this badly produced curiosity, his Warner Brothers contract prevented his name from being mentioned in both the credits and the narration.

THE MASTER OF BALLANTRAE   Warner Brothers, 1953
Director: William Keighley. Screenplay: Herb Meadow. Photography: Jack Cardiff. Music: William Alwyn, conducted by Muir Matheson. Art director: Ralph Brinton. Costumes: Margaret Furse. Fence master: Patrick Crean. Based on the novel by Robert Louis Stevenson. 89 mins.
Jamie Durrisdeer: ERROL FLYNN. Col Francis Burke: ROGER LIVESEY. Henry Durrisdeer: ANTHONY STEEL. Lady Alison: BEATRICE CAMPBELL. Jessie Brown: YVONNE FURNEAUX. Lord Durrisdeer: FELIX AYLMER. With Mervyn Johns, Charles Goldner, Ralph Truman, Francis de Wolff, Jack Berthier, Gillian Lynne, Moultrie Kelsall.

CROSSED SWORDS   Viva Films-United Artists, 1954
Director & Screenplay: Milton Krims. Photography: Jack Cardiff. Art director: Arrigo Equini. Costumes: Nino Novarese. 86 mins.
Renzo: ERROL FLYNN. Francesca: GINA LOLLOBRIGIDA. Raniero: CESARE DANOVA. Fulvia: NADIA GRAY. With Paola Mori, Alberto Rabagliati, Roldano Lupi, Silvio Bagolini, Mimo Billi, Pietro Tordi, Ricardo Rioli.

WILLIAM TELL   Errol Flynn Productions, 1954
Director & Photography: Jack Cardiff. Scriptwriter: Errol Flynn/John Dighton. 29 mins.
Incomplete. William Tell: ERROL FLYNN. With BRUCE CABOT, ANTONELLA LUALDI, ALDO FABRIZI, Massimo Serato, Franco Interlenghi, Vira Silenti, Alberto Rabagliati, Dave Crowly.

LILACS IN THE SPRING (US: **Let's Make Up**)
                                    Everrest–United Artists, 1955
Director: Herbert Wilcox. Screenplay: Harold Purcell. Photography: Max Greene. Music: Harry Parr-Davies. Incidental score: Robert Farnon. Songs & Dances: Philip and Betty Buchel. Wardrobe: Anthony Holland/Maude Churchill. Art director:

William C. Andrews. Based on the play *The Glorious Days*, by Robert Nesbitt. 94 mins.
Carole Beaumont/Lillian Grey/Queen Victoria/Nell Gwynn: ANNA NEAGLE. John Beaumont: ERROL FLYNN. King Charles/Charles King: DAVID FARRAR. Kate: KATHLEEN HARRISON. Albert Gutman, Prince Albert: PETER GRAVES. With Helen Haye, Scott Sanders, Alma Taylor, Hetty King, Alan Gifford, Jennifer Mitchell, Gillian Harrison, George Margo.

THE DARK AVENGER (US: The Warriors)
                              Allied Artists– 20th Century Fox, 1955
Director: Henry Levin. Screenplay: Daniel B. Ullman. Photography: Guy Green. Music: Cedric Thorpe Davie, conducted by Louis Levy. Art director: Terence Verity. Sets: Harry White. Costumes: Elizabeth Haffenden. Technical adviser: Charles R. Beard. Song, 'Bella Marie' by Christopher Hassall. 85 mins.
Edward, Black Prince: ERROL FLYNN. Lady Joan Holland: JOANNE DRU. Count de Ville: PETER FINCH. Marie: YVONNE FURNEAUX. Edward III: MICHAEL HORDERN. With Patrick Holt, Moultrie Kelsall, Robert Urquart, Vincent Winter, Noel Willman, Frances Rowe, Alastair Hunter, Rupert Davies, Ewan Solon, Richard O'Sullivan, Harold Kasket, Jack Lambert, John Welsh, Leslie Linder, John Philips, Robert Brown.

KING'S RHAPSODY   Everest–United Artists, 1955
Director: Herbert Wilcox. Screenplay: Pamela Bower/Christopher Hassall. Based on Ivor Novello's musical play, lyrics by Hassall. Photography: Max Greene. Art director: William C. Andrews. Costumes: Anthony Holland. Choreography: Jon Gregory. 93 mins.
Marta Karillos: ANNA NEAGLE. King Richard: ERROL FLYNN. Princess Cristiane: PATRICE WYMORE. Queen Mother: MARTITA HUNT. With Finlay Currie, Francis de Wolff, Joan Benham, Reginald Tate, Miles Malleson. Singer's voice: Edmund Hockridge.

ISTANBUL   Universal-International, 1956
Director: Joseph Pevney. Screenplay: Seton I. Miller/Barbara Gray/ Richard Alan Simmons. Photography: William Daniels. Art diirectors: Alexander Golitzen/Eric Orbom. Sets: Russell A.

Gausman/Julia Heron. Costumes: William Thomas. Songs performed by Nat King Cole: 'When I Fall In Love' (Young-Heyman), 'I Was A Little Too Lonely' (Evans Livingston). 84 mins.

James Brennan: ERROL FLYNN. Stephanie Bauer: CORNELL BORCHERS. With John Bentley, Torin Thatcher, Leif Erikson, Peggy Knudsen, Martin Benson, Nat King Cole, Werner Klemperer, Vladimir Sokoloff, Jan Arvan, Nico Minardos, Ted Hecht, David Bond, Roland Varno, Hillevi Rombin.

THE BIG BOODLE　　　　　Montefior-United Artists, 1957
Director: Richard Wilson. Screenplay: Jo Eisinger. Photography: Lee Garmes. Music: Raul Lavista. Based on Robert Sylvester's novel. 83 mins.

Ned Sherwood: ERROL FLYNN. Col Mastegui: PEDRO ARMENDARIZ. Fina Ferrer: ROSSANA RORY. Anita Ferrer: GIA SCALA. With Sandro Giglio, Jacques Aubuchon, Carlos Rivas, Charles Todd, Guillerme Alvarez Guedes, Carlos Mas, Rogelio Hernandez, Velia Martinez, Aurora Pita.

THE SUN ALSO RISES　　　　　20th Century Fox, 1957
Director: Henry King. Screenplay: Peter Viertel. Photography: Leo Tover. Music: Hugo Friedhofer, conducted by Lionel Newman. Spanish music: Alexander Courage/Vicente Gomez. Art directors: Lyle R. Wheeler/Mark-Lee Kirk. Sets: Walter M. Scott/Paul S. Fox/Jack Stubbs. Costumes: LeMaire/Fontana Sisters. Bullfight Sequences: Miguel Delgado. Brass band directed by Ramon Hernandez. Based on the novel by Ernest Hemingway. 129 mins.

Jake Barnes: TYRONE POWER. Lady Brett Ashley: AVA GARDNER. Robert Cohn: MEL FERRER. Mike Campbell: ERROL FLYNN. Bill Gorton: EDDIE ALBERT. With Juliette Gréco, Gregory Ratoff, Marcel Dalio, Henry Danilee, Bob Cunningham, Danik Patisson, Robert Evans, Jacqueline Evans, Eduardo Noriega, Carlos Muzquiz, Carlos David Ortigos, Rebecca Iturbi.

TOO MUCH, TOO SOON　　　　　Warner Brothers, 1958
Director: Art Napoleon. Screenplay: Art and Jo Napoleon. Photography: Nick Musuraca/Carl Guthrie. Music: Ernest Gold.

Art director: John Beckman. Sets: George James Hopkins.
Costumes: Orry-Kelly. Based on the book by Diana Barrymore
and Gerold Frank. 121 mins.
John Barrymore: ERROL FLYNN. Diana Barrymore:
DOROTHY MALONE. John Howard: RAY DANTON. Vincent
Bryant: EFREM ZIMBALIST JR. With Neva Patterson, Murray
Hamilton, Martin Milner, John Dennis, Kathleen Freeman,
Edward Kemmer, Robert Ellenstein, John Doucette, Michael
Mark, Francis DeDales, Jay Jostyn, Herb Ellis, Louis Quinn.

THE ROOTS OF HEAVEN   20th Century Fox, 1958
Director: John Huston. Screenplay: Romain Gary/Patrick Leigh -
Fermor. Photography: Oswald Morris/Skeets Kelly/Henri Persin/
Gilles Bonneau. Music: Malcolm Arnold. 'Minna's Theme'
composed by Henri Patterson. Art director: Stephen Grimes. Sets:
Bruno Avesani. Costumes: Rosine Delamare. Special effects: L. B.
Abbott/Fred Etcheverry. Technical adviser: Claude Hettier de
Boislambert. Based on the novel by Romain Gary. 125 mins.
Major Forsythe: ERROL FLYNN. Minna: JULIETTE GRÉCO.
Morel: TREVOR HOWARD. Abe Fields: EDDIE ALBERT. Cy
Sedgewick: ORSON WELLES. Saint Denis: PAUL LUKAS.
Orsini: HERBERT LOM. With Gregoire Aslan, André Luguèt,
Friedrich Ledebur, Edric Connor, Olivier Hussenot, Pierre Dudan,
Marc Doenitz, Dan Jackson, Maurice Cannon, Jacques Marin,
Habib Benlia, Bachir Touré, Alain Saury, Roscoe Stallworth,
Assane Fall, Francis de Wolff.

CUBAN REBEL GIRLS   Exploit Films–Joseph Brenner, 1959
Director: Barry Mahon. Screenplay & Narration: Errol Flynn. 68
mins.
Himself: ERROL FLYNN. Herself: BEVERLY AADLAND.
Johnny: JOHN MacKAY, With Jackie Jackler, Marie Edmund,
Ben Ostrovsky, Esther Oliva, Regnier Sanchez, Todd Brody, Al
Brown, Clelle Mahon.

Appendix III

Errol Flynn: Biopics

MY WICKED, WICKED WAYS: The Legend of Errol Flynn,
1986, 136 mins.
Director: Don Taylor, Teleplay: Doris Keating.
Errol Flynn: DUNCAN REGEHR, Lili Damita: BARBARA
HERSHEY, Jack Warner: HAL LINDEN, Billy Welch: JOHN
DENNIS JOHNSTON, Olivia de Havilland: LEE PURCELL,
Gerrit Koets: DARREN McGAVIN, Raoul Walsh: MICHAEL C.
GWYNNE, John Barrymore: BARRIE INGHAM, Michael
Curtiz: STEFAN GIERASCH.

It is only too easy to be hypercritical of television biopics,
especially when the subects are as universally identifiable as Errol
and those who figured in his great years – this production covers
just eight of his fifty years, from his arrival in America in 1935 –
where he makes his first film, meets Damita, has blues with
Warner and Curtiz, an attack of malaria and a bar-room brawl, *all*
in his first day! – to the rape trial of 1943. Neither is it accurately
based upon the autobiography from which it borrows its title,
though like Errol in his celebrated tome the producers have
changed names, even of persons deceased when the film was
made. It is nevertheless a far more convincing effort than the later
Flynn 'tribute' featuring Australian actor Guy Pearce.

The central story is Errol's rise to superstardom, played out
against the backdrop of his troubled union with Lili Damita. His

other marriages are not referred to – Nora Eddington is seen for a few seconds towards the end of the film, but no hints dropped to non-Flynn devotees as to who she is. Barbara Hershey is superb as the fiery Damita, though Regehr is less effective as Errol – 'popping' his eyes rather a lot and displaying little of Errol's agility in swashbuckling scenes and absolutely none of his charisma. Regehr is also thought to have refused to shave his chest for the love scenes, whereas Errol had been proud of his perfectly smooth torso. As Koets-aka-Erben, established actor Darren McGavin seems unsure whether to employ an Irish or American accent, whereas in truth, Erben's English was virtually incomprehensible. Barrie Ingham's Barrymore, on the other hand, steals every scene he is in and by encouraging the Shakespearean banter they used much of the time brings out a little of the real Errol in Regehr.

Errol's friends William Lundigan and William Meade have been combined as a single character, Billy Welch. There *is* suggestion of a romance with the former, along with one of their forays into Mexico in search of under-age sex. Errol tells him, 'Never, but *never* get married,' to which Billy mischievously responds, 'Not planning on it!' Also, like Meade, Billy dies whilst shooting *The Charge of The Light Brigade*, though not by impalement. Finally, during the rushed-through statutory rape episode only one girl takes Errol to court – she has previously been seen entering his cabin on the *Sirocco*. Worse still is the suggestion that the trial was rigged when Errol honours an earlier promise to give a matronly juror a kiss and his autograph if she gets him off. And at the victory party to which all Hollywood is invited, but only Olivia de Havilland turns up, the story strays even further from reason when, after telling her that *she* is the only woman he has truly loved, he concludes, 'For the rest of my life I'll be known as the guy who showed a girl the moon through a porthole!'

MY WICKED, WICKED WAYS. Channel Four (GB), 1994, 25 minutes.
Director: Rena Rutterwick, Teleplay: Tony Bolbow. Errol: NATHANIEL PARKER, Ed McElroy: IAN McNIECE, David Niven: SEAN PERTWEE, Peggy/Betty: LIZA WALKER, Voice of God: IAN TALBOT, John Barrymore: ROBERT STEPHENS.

Errol would probably have been amused because, like himself, this hugely entertaining little gem never takes itself seriously yet still managed to convey the relevant facts highlighted in his autobiography. The play begins with Beverley Aaland weeping over Errol's corpse whilst an amused, attractive male nurse looks on – in reality an angel waiting to transport him to heaven, though before entering its gates he must first pass a test as a stand-up raconteur, dressed as Robin Hood, at the Paradise Cabaret. This scenario is not as ridiculous as it sounds, not that he is looking forward to spending eternity in a place which reminds him of the Warner Brothers studios, and where there are no 'fags, booze and loose women'. Hell is the place for him because he wants to meet Caligula and 'go muff-diving' with Cleopatra!

In a series of flashbacks Errol reflects on the misery of his childhood, dismissing his mother as 'a sadistic old bitch'. Then he revisits the apartment where he lived with David Niven, who tells him, 'You treated your women like bog-paper.' Returning to New Guinea, he is seen buying Maihiati from her father for five pounds and two pigs. 'Mind you,' he quips, whilst she goes down on him, 'She was worth every rasher in more ways than sixty-nine!' At Mulholland House, John Barrymore is seen urinating through the open window and asked, 'Why don't you piss in the sink the same as everybody else?' And finally there is the rape trial, after which Errol presents his case for the defense, 'I drank, snorted, mainlined, screwed anything that moved. I was bisexual. I was a Nazi spy – believe that, and my dick really *was* fifteen inches long!'... to which the voice of God responds, 'Six, but who's counting?' And ultimately Errol achieves his heartfelt goal – he is dispatched to hell!

ERROL FLYNN: SECRET LIVES. Channel Four (GP), 1996, 50 minutes.
Producer: Michael Ryan, Narrator: Nigel Anthony.

Part of Channel Four's scandal-inspired documentary series which purports to excavate the 'real' stories of a wide range of personalities, mostly deceased, frequently with flimsy evidence and unreliable witnesses. This one begins by reminding us that Errol 'died a victim of his own debauchery' – skimming the surface of his cinematic achievements, it reads very much like a tacky tabloid newspaper. On the plus side there are home movie clips – Errol with Nora Eddington, then with Arlo his dog – rare footage from *William Tell* and a trailer for *Captain Blood*. William Donati also dismisses the suggestion that Errol had worked as a Nazi spy, though he is given insufficient time to explain his theories, which could have formed the basis for a more thorough, less-biased investigation into the Flynn psyche.

Beverly Aadland speaks of Errol's death – *not* in the hospital where it took place, but in their room. Later she speaks of how Errol 'forced himself' upon her the first time they had sex, and she reveals how they were planning to marry in January 1960 – mindless of the fact that Errol was still married to Patrice Wymore and would never have acquired a divorce in time – and that Errol had arranged for a reversal of his (undocumented) vasectomy so that they could have children.

Rose Cox, a former actress with the Northampton Repertory Company whose name strangely does not appear on cast lists between December 1933–June 1934, confesses that, unlike the other girls, she did not find him particularly appealing. Earl Conrad, the ghost-writer of *My Wicked, Wicked Ways*, once more resurrects his fascination regarding the size of Errol's penis.

The worst section of this documentary centres around the rape trial, wherein Errol is accused of lying under oath and therefore of being guilty. Betty Hansen – 'still terrified of showing her face after more than fifty years' – is seen in silhouette and, on the point of hysteria, she recounts a completely different story to the one she told at the time

All in all, a dismal, totally unnecessary exercise in anti-Flynn hogwash which is best consigned to the archives or the trash can!

ERROL FLYNN: PORTRAIT OF A SWASHBUCKLER. History Channel, part of its acclaimed 'Biography' series, introduced by Bob Friend. Producer: Mark Massari, Narrator: Christopher Lee. 1983, 50 mins.

'It wasn't raining when Hollywood said goodbye to Errol Flynn. There was no symbolic outpouring of tears from heaven over the premature death of one of its biggest stars. It was as if Hollywood wasn't ready to say its final farewells to Robin Hood and Don

Juan. And there was no one in the wings waiting to take over for the greatest swashbuckler of them all.'

So says Christopher Lee, standing next to Errol's grave, at the start of this definitive documentary which, though incorporating interviews from the same sources as 'Secret Lives' – Thomas, Niven, Sherman, Aadland – does so sensibly and with compassion. There is footage of Errol's and Patrice Wymore's wedding, clips from his television series and *The Red Skelton Show*, original trailers for *Captain Blood*, *The Charge of the Light Brigade* and *Dawn Patrol*. Even rarer is original black-and-white footage from *The Adventures of Robin Hood*, and extracts from *In The Wake Of The Bounty*, *Deep Sea Fishing* and *Cruise Of The Zaca*.

For once, the rape trial does not take centre-stage. Hal Wallis, who like colleague Jack Warner did not always get along with Errol, nevertheless praises him as 'a charming rogue'. Vincent Sherman and co-star Robert Douglas recall some of Errol's sexual escapades with the emphasis on humour rather than smut – we even get to see photographs of the projection room at Mulholland House. Director John Huston speaks of their famous fist-fight and Rory and Deirdre Flynn remember how their father gave them special treats – chocolate-covered bees and grasshoppers!

On the negative side, there is a superfluous interview with Mickey Rooney, who speaks of his own eight failed marriages and dismisses Errol's alleged fascism with an irate but worthless, 'He was as much a Nazi as I am!' – fortunately, Herman Erben himself has already denied the allegation And Nora Eddington is so dismissive of Errol's bisexuality – 'Seven years married. If he was a homosexual *I'd* be the first one to know!' – that one becomes at once sceptical. One has to remember, of course, that Eddington belonged to that section of society which, in pre-Kinsey America, stereotyped gays as weak, bungling 'nervous-Nellies'. It would therefore be inconceivable for such a person to even *think* that a big, butch, perfect specimen like Errol could actually *enjoy* having sex with other men – that if he did, there must have been something wrong with the woman in his life, which of course is hardly ever the case. One must also point out that, during her marriage to Errol, he spent so much time away from her that like his other wives she cannot possibly have been aware *what* he was getting up to most of the time.

Bibliography:

Primary & Secondary Sources

ANGER, Kenneth: *Hollywood Babylon I & II* (Straight Arrow, San Francisco, 1975; Random Century, GB, 1984)

ARCE, Hector: *The Secret Life Of Tyrone Power* (Morrow, NY, 1979)

CONNELLY, Gerry: *Errol Flynn In Northampton* (Domra, GB, 1995)

CONRAD, Earl: *Errol Flynn, A Memoir* (Robert Hale, GB, 1979)

COTTOM, J V: *Errol Flynn, Espion Où Heros?* (Ciné-Revue, 11/80)

EAMES, John Douglas: *The MGM Story* (Octopus, GB, 1975)

FLYNN, Errol: *What Really Happened To Me In Spain* (*Photoplay*, 7/37)

FLYNN, Errol: *From A Life Of Adventure: The Writings Of Errol Flynn* (Citadel Press, 1980)

FLYNN, Errol: *My Wicked, Wicked Ways* (Putnam, New York, 1959)

FREEDLAND, Michael: *Errol Flynn* (Arthur Parker, GB, 1978)

GREIF, Martin: *The Gay Book Of Days* (W H Allen, GB, 1982)

HIGHAM, Charles: *Errol Flynn, The Untold Story* (Doubleday, 1980)

LEVIN, Martin: *Hollywood & The Great Fan Magazines* (Arbor House, New York, 1970)

MADSEN, Axel: *The Sewing Circle* (Robson, GB, 1996)

MUNN, Michael: *Hollywood Rogues* (Robson, GB, 1991)

NIVEN, David: *Bring On The Empty Horses* (Hamish Hamilton, GB, 1975)

NORMAN, Barry: *The Hollywood Greats* (Hodder & Stoughton, GB, 1979)

QUINLAN, David: *Quinlan's Film Stars* (Batsford, GB, 1996)

ROEN, Paul: *High Camp, A Gay Guide To Camp & Cult Films* Vol I (Leyland, San Francisco, 1994)

THOMAS, Tony: *Errol Flynn: The Spy Who Never Was* (Carol, NY, 1990)

THOMAS, Tony/BEHLMER, Rudy/McCARTY, Clifford: *The Complete Films of Errrol Flynn* (Carol, NY, 1990)

WALLACE, Amy/WALLACE, Irving/WALLACE, Sylvia/ WALLE-CHINSKY, David: *The Secret Sex Lives of Famous People* (Chancellor Press, 1993)

Index

Byington, Spring 50

Cabot, Bruce 73, 80, 81, 82, 83, 88, 89, 96, 100, 107, 111, 112,
   113, 114, 125, 128, 129, 131, 141, 187, 189, 207
Cady, Howard 210, 217, 218
Cagney, James 34, 68, 80
Caldough, George 219, 220
Calhoun, Rory 201
Callahan, Mushy 105
Callas, Maria 183, 211
Campan, Zanie 167
Campbell, Beatrice 182
Cantor, Eddie 115
Capote, Truman 93
Captain Blood 39–42, 43–5, 54, 68, 69, 182
Cardiff, Jack 183, 186, 187
Carrie 3
Carson, Jack 153–4
Castro, Fidel 215–6
Castro, Raul 216
Cathcart Jones, Owen 122
Carson, Jack 115
Cartright, Beatrice 101
Case of the Curious Bride, The 34, 50
Cavens, Fred 70, 91
Chaliapin, Fyodor 57
Chaplin, Charlie 113
Charge of the Light Brigade, The 46–50, 51, 98
Charters, Spencer 124
Chauvel, Charles 14
Chevalier, Maurice 31
Christian, Linda 108
Chronicle and Echo 26–7, 28
Ciné Revue 224
Cinémonde 157
Clarke, Sam 32, 33
Clift, Montgomery 211
Cochrane, Thomas 114, 117, 120, 123
Cohen, Albert J 196